DEVIANT DESIG

DEVIANT DESIGN

The Ad Hoc, the Illicit, the Controversial

Craig Martin

BLOOMSBURY VISUAL ARTS
LONDON • NEW YORK • OXFORD • NEW DELHI • SYDNEY

BLOOMSBURY VISUAL ARTS
Bloomsbury Publishing Plc
50 Bedford Square, London, WC1B 3DP, UK
1385 Broadway, New York, NY 10018, USA
29 Earlsfort Terrace, Dublin 2, Ireland

BLOOMSBURY, BLOOMSBURY VISUAL ARTS and the Diana logo are trademarks of
Bloomsbury Publishing Plc

First published in Great Britain 2022

For legal purposes the Acknowledgements on pp. vii–viii constitute an
extension of this copyright page.

Cover image © Freepik.com

A catalogue record for this book is available from the British Library.

Library of Congress Cataloging-in-Publication Data
Names: Martin, Craig, 1974- author.
Title: Deviant design : the ad hoc, the illicit, the controversial / Craig Martin.
Description: London ; New York : Bloomsbury Visual Arts, 2022. |
Includes bibliographical references and index.
Identifiers: LCCN 2021052917 (print) | LCCN 2021052918 (ebook) |
ISBN 9781350035331 (paperback) | ISBN 9781350035348 (hardback) |
ISBN 9781350035324 (epub) | ISBN 9781350035300 (pdf)
Subjects: LCSH: Design–Moral and ethical aspects.
Classification: LCC NK1520 .M346 2022 (print) | LCC NK1520 (ebook) |
DDC 745.4–dc23/eng/20220106
LC record available at https://lccn.loc.gov/2021052917
LC ebook record available at https://lccn.loc.gov/2021052918

ISBN: HB: 978-1-3500-3534-8
          PB: 978-1-3500-3533-1
          ePDF: 978-1-3500-3530-0
          eBook: 978-1-3500-3532-4

Typeset by Integra Software Services Pvt. Ltd.
Printed and bound in India

To find out more about our authors and books visit www.bloomsbury.com
and sign up for our newsletters.

CONTENTS

FIGURES

ACKNOWLEDGEMENTS

The ideas explored in this book have been gestating over many years, and I would like to thank everyone who has inspired my thinking on the darker side of design. The intellectual stimulus of key authors has been acknowledged throughout the book, but here I offer my gratitude to those whose support has proved invaluable.

Colleagues at the University of Edinburgh have offered generous feedback and discussion of my delineation of the deviant nature of design: in particular, Jamie Cross, Arno Verhoeven and Rachel Harkness, as well as members of the Critical Change research group, students on the MA Design for Change programme at the University of Edinburgh, and numerous PhD students, including Ian Lambert, Neslihan Tepehan, Gordon Hamme and Hadi Mehrpouya, whose insights proved thought-provoking. Audiences at various conferences and symposia have also offered commentary, as have the editors of volumes where ideas contained in *Deviant Design* have been explored, including Mahmoud Keshavarz, Shahram Khosravi, Tim Hall, Tom Scott-Smith and Mark Breeze. In the early stages of drafting the manuscript I was invited to Emily Carr University of Art + Design by Bonne Zabolotney to deliver a talk on deviant design, and I would like to thank Bonne for the opportunity to visit Vancouver, and for the discussions with students and audience members, including Jamer Hunt, whose co-authored book *Design and Violence* has been an important influence on this work. Garnet Hertz at Emily Carr also introduced me to the concept of *shanzhai*.

Others I would like to thank include Adolphe Yemtin, Kim Kullman, Michelle Willets, Dave Beer, Daniel Lie and Giovanni Marmont. Javier Guerrero C has been invaluable in helping me to think through the complexity of the illicit. Likewise, Lorraine Gamman was very generous in discussing the broader contexts of design and crime. Marc Fisher and Brett Bloom from Temporary Services/Half Letter Press kindly allowed me to reproduce the image from another inspirational book, *Prisoners' Inventions*. Three anonymous peer reviewers provided constructive commentary and feedback on the manuscript – I thank them for their attentive and nuanced understanding of this work. The University of Edinburgh has been very generous in providing various forms of funding to support research trips and a research sabbatical at the start of the writing process.

Rebecca Barden from Bloomsbury has been incredibly supportive from the outset when I first mooted the idea of the book. Likewise, Claire Constable and Olivia Davies have always been encouraging and, above all, patient in allowing me that little bit of extra time to deliver the manuscript.

My parents have been generous in their unfailing support, but as with so many things, my partner, Maria Fusco, provides the intellectual and creative stimulus for everything I do.

INTRODUCTION: HETERODOX DESIGN

Diffusing design

Everybody designs. Such a statement might be read in a myriad of ways. It could quite easily be marketing mantra for the almost unlimited choice of combinations consumers have with many contemporary products. It might refer to the selection of domestic décor. To DIY practices. Or those everyday decisions people make, such as repurposing a plastic bottle as a container to clean a paint brush. The phrase, in fact, comes from Ezio Manzini's *Design, When Everybody Designs* (2015), a book that purposefully extends the field of design to encompass a broad range of actors who utilize the practices and tools of design for the purpose of social innovation. In 'diffusing' the field of design to include non-professional designers, Manzini highlights an important facet of contemporary society: everybody should play a role in creating their everyday life-worlds. Such a claim resonates with a range of intellectual, political and techno-material contexts, from anarchist approaches to architecture and design (Wilbert and White, 2011), through to now-historic assertions that new technologies would empower consumers, making them active participants in the creation of their own life-worlds rather than controlled by external forces. Alvin Toffler, in the introduction to his 1970 book *Future Shock* (Toffler, 1970), named these participant consumers 'prosumers', productive consumers. At around the same time in 1972 Charles Jencks and Nathan Silver, in *Adhocism: The Case for Improvisation* (2013:64), also suggested that through technological advancement consumers would have the means to design their own products and have them manufactured. However, Manzini's assertions are rather distinct from the techno-utopianism of the 1970s. His specific idea of 'diffuse design' highlights an important component of the wider culture of design: that individuals have always been active problem-solvers, fixing or repairing artefacts and planning particular approaches to everyday situations. In the context of architecture and dwelling, Lars Lerup (1977) argued that buildings are always unfinished and in constant change through the actions of dwellers who are effectively resisting the impositions of master-designers. Although Manzini continues to see a place for the expert designer, his advancement of the diffuse designer resonates with the core arguments in this book. That is, running parallel to histories and practices of formalized design are the vastly longer trajectories of informal approaches of non-professionals who engage in everyday practices of design to address their specific needs.

Here I take design in its broadest sense as opposed to a narrowly defined field of professional practices. I do so in a heterodox manner that deviates from the established traditions of scholarly engagement with design. I look awry at design. Mindful of the histories of industrial capitalism and the centrality of design to nineteenth- and twentieth-century technical advancement, these canonical readings of design's culture understandably posit the shift from individuated craft-based practices to the division of labour, mass-production and the rise of expert knowledge. However, echoing Richard Buchanan's argument that 'the subject matter of design is not fixed; it is constantly undergoing exploration' (1995:25), this book explores the extremities of design, where familiar debates on its formal conditions are coupled with those that do not fit canonical interpretations. I set out to encompass an expanded repertoire that thinks within design's histories and futures, but also outside what we have traditionally conceived of as 'design' (Dilnot, 2019:xv). Central to this is the interrelationship between formal and informal notions of design, and perhaps even more so the professionalization of design itself. The likes of Manzini and others (Beegan and Atkinson, 2008; Jencks and Silver, 2013) suggest that the binary separation between the professional and non-professional (in design and beyond (Merrifield, 2017)) limits the role that non-professionals play in a range of decision-making processes.[1] So, although designers are actively producing our socio-material worlds, they are not the only ones, a position clearly mapped in the methodologies and ideologies of participatory design, user-centred design or co-design. This has also been a lesson long recognized by anthropologists through their research into how material artefacts are positioned and transfigured in highly complex ways by consumers (Douglas and Isherwood, 1996; Miller, 1987).

Put simply, I argue that design is an everyday social practice that many individuals engage with. We all design. This position is fundamental to the book. It is manifest in countless instances where material, practical, situational, problem-encountering activities are played out. This can, of course, be within the professional context of consumer-centred product or service design, but equally the actions of the individual working out how to best resolve a small-scale, localized and situated problem. Such a claim is far from controversial, an argument dealt with at length in Chapter 4, where I investigate the role of misuse as a form of creative problem-solving under the auspice of 'informal design'. Where the discussions in the book become somewhat more controversial and heterodox is when we consider the nature of *social* practice. Recent discussions of social design (Armstrong et al., 2014) helpfully summarize the growing importance of socially situated design practices that engage with social and political aspects of everyday life. As I consider in Chapter 2, the turn to social design is laudable in wresting design away from perceptions of it as mere surface dressing, aesthetic embellishment or technical skill; however, this nonetheless embraces a rather innocent version of the social and one that is overtly linear (Cf. Design Studio for Social Intervention, 2020). That is, particular actions will have logical effects. In line with Willis (2015:71), I argue that all design is social, so the very notion of social design is something of a misnomer. However, if we are to actively embrace the idea of truly *social* design, then it must be representative of society and all the complexities that social formations entail. This is where the controversies of the social emerge – the tangled, complex, messiness of the social realm (Law, 2004) must form part of how we understand design. So just as I noted above the various ways in which everyone designs, can such an assertion be made for design that is socially complex? I believe so, and I argue for this throughout the book. Critical to the arguments I develop are that various forms of problem-encountering activities permeate different social situations, including those that might be deemed alien to the traditional operative formations of design. Where we may agree that someone redeploying a plastic bottle as a brush-cleaning vessel can be seen as a piece of adhoc design (Jencks and Silver, 2013), would we concur that someone attempting to save money by scanning a cheaper item at a self-scan checkout and then taking a more expensive product is 'designing'? Or a person disguising 1.4 tonnes of cocaine as wooden shipping palettes? These questions are explored throughout the book as a way to consider the growing diffusion of design and its ethics.

Malevolency and the deviant

This book contends that the tactical savviness displayed by the wily customer intent on saving money and the illicit logistical practices of the drug smuggler constitute heterodox forms of design at odds to commonly attributed definitions. Both are forms of social and material practices that deal with particular situations through the use of practical acumen, craftiness, logistical dexterity, contextual awareness and planning know-how – all of which, I suggest, fall under the guise of a particular form of designerly intelligence (Cross, 2011). At the heart of *Deviant Design* then is the contention that design must be fully cognisant of its power, its force: the pleasures it creates; the innovations in material, technological and aesthetic form it has produced; the identities it builds; the functional value of artefacts that make our lives more straightforward. But such familiar readings of design mask the 'dark side' of design (Fisher and Gamman, 2019). The harm it causes, has caused and inevitably will cause in the future must be acknowledged as part of design's place in society. The immanent entanglement of the socially benevolent and malevolent dimensions of design also pervades much of the global crisis seen with the Covid-19 pandemic. Although the book does not explicitly deal with the pandemic, it speaks to many of the themes developed in *Deviant Design*.

Across many countries the combined effects of economic austerity and poor planning have seen stories of medical professionals improvising their own personal protective equipment (PPE). In Spain and the United Kingdom, for example, cases have been reported of medical staff creating gowns out of dustbin liners owing to the lack of PPE provision (Kassam, 2020; Press, 2020). The ingenuity of such cases of informal design is matched by the illicit opportunities afforded by the pandemic. Early reports suggest that although limits on the freedom of movement and the strengthening of international borders are leading to the reduction of organized crime in some areas, the pandemic is creating new opportunities for criminal actors often as a result of police and security forces being deployed elsewhere. These include the actions of organized criminal groups in countries where health systems have been infiltrated (Global Initiative Against Transnational Organized Crime, 2020:2–3; 6–8), as well as the rise of cybercrime in the time of coronavirus (Mahadevan, 2020). Drug traffickers have also identified new tactical opportunities, including the smuggling of cocaine in shipments of face masks from Peru to Hong Kong (Navarette, 2020). Likewise, counterfeiters have sought out entrepreneurial potential, particularly in the production of fake face masks, unsanctioned antiviral medicines and second-rate hand sanitizers (Interpol, 2020). As such, the crisis mirrors many of the social characteristics which are discussed at length throughout the book, particularly the entanglements of licit and illicit activities. Whilst the global pandemic raises many profound new questions about social, economic and political stability, it is also a continuation of these practices. It substantiates one of the book's key assertions: that 'illicit epistemologies' are formations of knowledges and practices that seek illicit opportunities through the complexities of social dynamics. The new 'rules of engagement' that seem to be emerging through Covid-19 are further instances where the heterodox notion of design explored in the book is apparent.

Professional designers have understandably been quick to intercede in these new circumstances in ways that mirror the actions of illicit actors. Just as counterfeiters or smugglers identify potential aporias in the pandemic, design itself addresses opportunities to engage in problem-solving activities. Where William Davies writes that 'a crisis of this scale will never be truly resolved until many of the fundamentals of our social and economic life have been remade' (Davies, 2020), the design professions see themselves playing a central role in this remaking. This has been evident from the outset of the Covid-19 crisis, with organizations such as What Design Can Do featuring articles on design-led approaches to creating social distancing measures labelled 'Design for Distance' (Raviv, 2020); The Index Project listing socio-technical innovations for devices such as fever-detecting helmets and 3D-printed valves for oxygen masks (The Index Project, 2020), or the World Design Organization setting the #COVID19DesignChallenge workshop, which was immediately oversubscribed. Like many professionals, designers understandably wish to mobilize their skills, knowledge or resources, and – as will be seen with discussions in Chapter 1 on the nature of design's engagement with wicked problems – this clearly resonates with the nascent projects emerging to tackle the Covid-19 crisis and post-pandemic times. Designers have mitigated the immediate impact of the virus by working with healthcare professionals on the use of additive manufacturing technologies for the design and manufacture of medical equipment, creating new platforms for digital working practices, redesigning environments in the creation of social distancing norms, or dealing with the effect of social isolation on ageing communities. However, such incremental approaches need to be accompanied by greater understanding of the structural weaknesses and contingencies that have resulted in this global pandemic. As I set out in Chapter 2, design itself is complicit in the creation of structural inequalities, for instance in how cities, office buildings, homes or transport systems are designed in such a manner that makes social distancing an incredibly complex challenge. Likewise, given the centrality of consumer goods to market economies, design is also at the heart of global supply chains which have led to increased transmission of the virus (Moody, 2020).

This book feeds into a growing body of critical design studies literature, examining the ethically fraught territory of design's impact on the socio-political, technological and environmental frontlines of everyday life – to the existential crisis we face (see Fisher and Gamman, 2019; Staszowski and Tassinari, 2021). Tony Fry and Adam Nocek put it in perhaps the most disarmingly frank but necessary terms: design is

> in the crosshairs of the technological, geological, and political economic forces that have produced this dire situation. In other words, modern design is at the ontological root of the universalisms responsible for the asymmetrical forms of violence that human and non-human life are facing today and in the future.
>
> (Fry and Nocek, 2021a:2)

Similar concerns have been addressed by scholars who have argued that whilst we are beginning to understand the increasing power of design in all that we do, with such manifest power comes increased scrutiny of the complicity of design and designers in creating: inequality (Colomina and Wigley, 2016:70), the politics of exclusion through the design of bordering systems (Keshavarz, 2018), gender-based inequity (Criado Perez, 2019) or the visual culture of racialized discrimination (Claver Fine, 2021; Williams, 2019). In addition to this body of literature, exhibitions such as MoMA's 2015 'Design and Violence' (Antonelli and Hunt, 2015) have demonstrated the material manifestations of design's malign potency.

The recognition of design's malevolent social function is difficult for many to hear, particularly those professionals engaged directly with it. For Clive Dilnot there has been a long-held, simplistic assumption that design's purpose was wholly affirmative (2016:xv). Dunne and Raby have spoken of similar conditions in relation to technology, where they state, 'there is no room for doubt or complexity in their [corporate futurologists] techno-utopian visions' (2001:6). Sterilized versions of design or technology's social purpose mask what Dunne and Raby call the 'dark and strange world driven by real human needs' (2001:6). In similar ways *Deviant Design* investigates the social reality of design, where real needs include those that do not adhere to normative ideals or behaviours. Equally, the utopian imaginary that Dunne and Raby again highlight obscures the deeply harmful effects of design. It can, of course, create new possibilities but its centrality in the politics of marginalization and the treatment of the unhoused for example (Rosenberger, 2017; 2020) should not be underestimated. For Rosenberger and others (Lambert, 2013) design is intertwined with law, with the creation of legal-material devices – park benches or bus shelters – designed to enforce marginalized groups to act or behave in prescribed ways. Such technologies are termed 'callous', part of a repertoire of design techniques that form an assemblage of political practices. Understanding the malevolent nature of design (see Micklethwaite, 2009) affords the opportunity to critically address its epistemology, ontology and above all its politics.

This is fundamental to my use of the term *deviant*. Whilst the growing body of studies on design's 'dark' side employ a variety of terms such as *transgressive*, *disobedient*, *subversive*, *hostile*, *malevolent* or *surreptitious*, I believe *deviant* captures the complexity of the social, particularly when used in a two-fold manner: firstly, in relation to a deviation from presuppositions of what constitutes design; secondly, its root as criminalized behaviour which deviates from 'normal' social practices. In doing so, I call for greater understanding of design's politically determined power, and for appreciation of the deeply unsettling place of design in the perpetuation of unjust action. Deviance is also a useful conceptual vehicle for revealing the clandestine dimensions of design's malevolent nature. For just in the same way the sociological study of deviancy is often concerned with invisible social processes (see Downes and Rock, 2011:24), so too the study of design must engage with the deep-rooted deleterious consequences of its manifestations. Related to the criminological dimensions of deviancy is the book's in-depth engagement with notions of legality and illegality, the licit and illicit. Once again, challenging the normative construction of such binary separations, I examine how design can at once play a critical role in the creation of positive futures, whilst simultaneously perpetuating the glaring social inequalities noted above. Damian White identifies this double reading through his suggestion that design 'is of course fundamentally Janus-faced' (White, 2021:202). In addressing the role of the illicit, the book attempts to deconstruct dualistic divisions by arguing that the ingenuity of illegal actions such as the material practices of drug smuggling cannot simply be decried as destructive when so many social practices deemed licit are equally as divisive.

The term *deviant* is controversial. I use it intentionally, just in the manner Bruno Latour (2005) and others (Venturini, 2010; Yaneva and Heaphy, 2012) have adopted the notion of controversies. Typically speaking, controversies are perceived as negative and in need of resolution. However, within the context of Latour's work they are productive, offering a constructive articulation of how social relations function. Rather than attempting to smooth out or tame complexity, the study of controversies affords a richer, more dynamic sense of how the social moves. This is also the case with my rendering of design as deviant, but also the value of the illicit more generally: an attempt to problematize common assumptions of its role in forging social betterment, and to leave open this space to better understand the controversies of design through the illicit.

Ethics of the deviant

The value of the deviant, the illicit or the malevolent lies in acknowledging the complexity of social practices, whilst also maintaining confidence that with such awareness comes the potential for change. In *Deviant Design* I maintain that understanding the manifold ways in which design has been put to use can afford a greater sense of its prospective role in the creation of new social, technological and environmental futures. So, rather than an endorsement of the ingenuity of illicit practices such as drug trafficking or counterfeiting, deviancy is utilized to explore the manifold powers of designerly intelligence and ultimately how this might be transformed. For Tony Fry such an understanding of design is central to the new modes of action that pervade design 'futuring': 'Any practice, not least design, whose actions shape futures has to be brought to the realisation of the crucial importance of this imperative and the enormous challenge this poses' (Fry, 2004:145). This is where the ethos of the book resides. We need to understand the historical complicity of design and designers in creating and perpetuating unsustainable futures, or what Fry calls 'defuturing'. That is to say, the realization that design has been intrinsic to the social structures that have robbed us of a meaningful future, human-induced climate emergency being the starkest example of this. To identify alternatives in the vein that Fry and many other contemporary design-related scholars (Costanza-Chock, 2020; Design Studio for Social Intervention, 2020; Escobar, 2018) argue for, we must understand the structures and practices that have created the current conditions, not least that 'design has had a leading role in neo-liberalism' (Gamman and Fisher, 2019:208). We have to be mindful of the underlying imperatives that drive design, including its ethics. Although this book is not about ethics *per se*, it does, of course, inflect many of the debates. I provide a brief discussion of design ethics that informs the forthcoming chapters.

The ethics of design has often been situated within a professional context of conduct, of subscribing to specified regulations and responsibilities to clients for example. Alongside this are further constraints on action, often social, legal or technical, which determine the material outcomes of the design process. But as Zelenko and Felton (2012:3) suggest, ethics is also formed by culturally and socially inscribed values that extend beyond simple codified professional practices. Indeed, the moral imperatives of design are less measurable, partly because ethics 'is far more pervasively and invisibly inscribed into the design and designed operation of our entire techno-material-symbolic cultures' (Willis, 2004:90). Related to this process of inscription is the dilemma of 'who sets the agendas and evaluates the terms?' (Drucker, 2020:xiii). What position does the designer have in choosing particular ethical perspectives? This raises the intertwined issues of agency and responsibility, and the question of design itself being part of the practice of responsibility (Fry, 2004:146). Whilst the designer might well be working within the constraints of a professional domain, the diffusion and expansion of design discussed throughout the book challenges such narrow ethical confines. Indeed, in many ways the designer is no different to other social actors making moral choices based on what is 'right' and what is thus 'good'. These choices are seemingly driven by moral imperatives which are socially valued or devalued: goodness, fairness, duty, power, sin, evil, etc. Such terms clearly allude to broader modes of social, cultural, political and religious systems. But for Fry,

> What is vital to understand is that while these terms suggest a commonality they do not actually constitute a common language; rather what they mean is plural and contested and frequently a source of misunderstanding and theoretical problems. Certainly one cannot appeal to any ethical category as universal – as soon as content arrives so does relativism.
>
> (Fry, 2004:148–9)

Although it is often easy to criticize the supposedly relativist 'get-out-clause', Fry's argument chimes with the position taken throughout the book, particularly in relation to the social dimension of design. Whilst one may hope that design adheres to a sense of commonality, we, in fact, see that it is an inherent mechanism of division. An obvious context for this claim is consumer culture: the material world of designed goods is marked by distinction and difference, something discussed at length in Chapter 6 in relation to fakes and counterfeits. This position is challenging. To hear that the transformative power of design has resulted in so much unequal development, in the perpetuation of social difference and ultimately the degradation of the earth makes for uneasy listening. This is the deep-rooted ethics of design I try to deal with. Rather than the consensual ethics of right and wrong, I keep to the *contested* ethics described by Fry, but also the 'nomadic ethics' of Rosi Braidotti (2013). Braidotti uses a Deleuzian nomadic ethics to question the universalism of Kantian moral conventions. In this guise ethics is not restrained by the idea of 'rights'; it is set free, becoming a 'discourse about forces, desires and values' (Braidotti, 2013:343). Transcribed into design, Stephen Loo provides a position that I also hold to in the book. We should move away from a predetermined moral code being applied retrospectively and instead encourage 'the testing of the practices at hand in different situations' (Loo, 2012:18).

Alternative innovation

In the same way the book explores the existing ethical parameters of design, it also engages the idea of innovation. I want to say something just momentarily about this. Design has long been associated with ingenuity, technological advancement and ultimately the creation of futures (albeit so often in the guise of defuturing). This is central to the very ontological condition of designing – the construction of the new. As will become apparent in later chapters, design is often associated with novelty and invention. In commercial contexts design is closely related with the potential to drive change. Innovation can be created through design, hence the exponential rise of 'design thinking' (Brown, 2008; Lockwood and Papke, 2018). Just as the book uses deviancy to explore the complexity of social relations, I do not subscribe to such simplistic definitions of design or innovation. I treat them both as controversies. Whilst many of the empirical articulations of the later chapters deal with the radical potential of designerly sensibilities – wresting them away from the instrumentalized logic of 'design thinking' as a neat and easy toolkit for commercial and policy-driven organizations – another vital thread in the book is the originary potential of innovation. Chapter 3 provides a lengthy unpacking of these key debates; however, it is helpful here to summarize these concerns for they are central to my core argument. One of the principal themes of the book is 'change': how design is an instigator of change and thus directly concerned with futuring; but equally how change is a form of becoming, the emergent unfolding of the social that defies a teleological construction of linear development. In the hands of scholars such as Joseph Schumpeter (2003) and Peter Drucker (1985), innovation is now intimately tied up with entrepreneurship and the exploitation of market opportunities through technology. Infamously, Schumpeter described innovation as 'the gale of creative destruction' (Schumpeter, 2003 [1943]:84), where new technologies develop new markets whilst destroying those that fail to innovate. Innovation, then, is also about change: the novelty of new goods, infrastructures, markets, services and organizations. Through the scholarly work of Benoît Godin (2008; 2012; 2015), *Deviant Design* also champions an alternative reading of innovation that imbues it with the spirit of change as radical becoming. Godin (2015) writes how innovation was originally aligned with the *negative* consequences of revolution and changes to the political and religious order. Only in the nineteenth and twentieth centuries does it become an agent of *positive* change through technological development. Just as Godin provides an account of innovation that situates the value of its subversive, transgressive and revolutionary heritage, so too I argue here for an appreciation of innovation as a radical potential for disruption. I treat innovation in a similar manner to the idea of deviancy, where the potential of the illicit allows us to appreciate that innovation is concerned with radical ways of looking at things, processes, practices, systems. And not simply for the pursuit of economic advantage.

Outline of the book

Where the core themes are interleaved throughout the entire book, there are distinct concepts and empirical examples that form the main chapters. The first three chapters deal primarily with the book's contextual, theoretical and intellectual foundations, focusing on both key debates in design studies and related discussions in areas such as criminology. The latter three unpack many of these core ideas and investigate them through a range of different historical, material and geographical settings. By their very nature, these empirically grounded chapters take a small selection of what I term deviant design, the intention being to address three case studies in order to posit a wider appreciation of how prevalent deviant design is. One could equally cite examples such as the design of torture devices (see Antonelli and Hunt, 2015), the design thinking behind scams and viruses (Ogino, 2007) or the now infamous case of the ethics of 3D printed guns (Walther, 2015).

Chapter 1 opens the core thematic debates by considering in greater depth the diffusion of design signalled here in the Introduction. It addresses the expanded field of design, situating it within the broad scope of Victor Papanek's argument that design is fundamentally a human activity (Papanek, 1973:23). Subsumed within everyday practices are distinct attributes that the study of professional design illuminates. The chapter argues that the practical aptitude of planning, inventing, making and doing, as well as the ability to think on one's feet, work with ambiguity and ultimately the importance of synthesis, define design. Keeping with a Papanekian understanding of design as a human condition, Chapter 1 positions these attributes in relation to designerly intelligence's increased prominence in commercial enterprise through the advance of 'design thinking', but more importantly, it holds to Latour's argument that because design is integral to *all* worldmaking projects at different scales (nanotech, through to cities, infrastructures and geo-engineering), the term itself has no longer any limits.

Given the centrality of design to all that we do, its social function becomes ever more critical. Chapter 2 – 'Social Design' is Not Social Enough' – considers this through theories of social complexity by arguing that social relations are emergent rather than bound by normative constructions of social order. Building on the idea of nomadic ethics briefly outlined above, an important discussion in this chapter is the implications for recent practices and scholarship aligned to 'social design'. I argue that in light of the problematic nature of social norms, design must engage with the messiness of society. Employing the heuristic contrivance of 'asocial design', the chapter identifies the social malevolency of design by aligning it with the origins of deviant design. It does so through a reading of design's origins within militaristic technologies and killing machines.

Where I argue in Chapter 2 that social design is not social enough, Chapter 3 expands this beyond design and builds an important theoretical apparatus that considers the value of deviancy and the illicit. These interlinked ideas are considered as productive forms of disturbance. By this I mean they provide important lessons for our understanding of the enmeshing of constructed binaries such as normal/abnormal, licit/illicit. To examine this, the intellectual arenas of criminology and subcultural theory are deployed, including classic studies on labelling theory (Becker, 1991 [1963]). But perhaps the most important context to this chapter is that the seeming benevolence of licit social actors and actions are surreptitious constructions in their own right, masking the inherent inequalities and malevolency of capitalism and neo-liberalism in particular. The chapter extends this by investigating the radical origins of innovation itself, developing in full the thematic contexts discussed above by arguing that there is much to be learnt through the study of innovation as itself illicit. Doing so enables us to develop new ways of looking at the complexity of the social.

The approach taken through the final three chapters is multi-scalar; that is, they build the wider notion of deviant design by considering different levels of controversy. Chapter 4 examines ideas of misuse specifically in relation to deviation from intended purpose. It does so through challenging the functionalist conventions of how things should be used, addressing instead how things are *actually* used. This is, of course, far from controversial in light of illicitness or illegality, but an important rationale for establishing the value of deviation is that it shows how misuse creates novelty and innovation. 'Misusing Things' also considers the parallel discussion of 'who designs?' It does so by returning to important precedents in Jencks and Silver's (2013) work on repurposing and ad hoc material practices. Key to the idea of adhocism is that everybody designs, even when we may not be aware of it. This is considered through my notion of 'informal design', where the characteristics of designerly intelligence are utilized by all. Finally, the materialist aspects of adhocism provide a means to critically investigate ideas of improvisation and potentiality, most notably in relation to the innovations of misusing things.

Potentiality forms a core element of Chapter 5, 'Illicit Design', which addresses the materialities of drug smuggling and crucially how concealment and disguise are designed. Whilst the act of smuggling as a form of deviancy clearly aligns to notions of criminality and illicitness, considering drug trafficking as a form of 'illicit design' differs profoundly from orthodox discourses of design. I set out to challenge this by examining the ways in which drug smugglers employ material and infrastructural knowledge that are akin to traditional design sensibilities. Whilst the chapter considers a range of key aspects of smuggling practices such as knowledge of geography, mobility and infrastructure, it also addresses the importance of logistical planning as a fundamental facet of both design and smuggling. Equally, I argue that practicality, technical know-how and resourcefulness also relate to the two. By drawing together all these different facets, smuggling is essentially about potentiality, the possibility of objects, vehicles and infrastructures to become something else. As such Chapter 5 builds on discussions of dependency between the licit and illicit in Chapter 3, and the material resourcefulness of misusing things in Chapter 4. To examine these debates in greater depth, the chapter focuses on the ingenuity of the concealment and disguise of drugs by traffickers. It does so by arguing that the disguise of narcotics is concerned with the design of perception: consignments of drugs disguised as legitimate material artefacts are designed to be perceived in a certain way, as part of global supply chains for instance. Above all, Chapter 5 investigates how drug smuggling, amongst many other controversies, is constituted by a sophisticated knowledge of organizational, material and visual conventions.

The final substantive chapter moves from the dynamics of production in the two previous chapters to the controversies of consumption by investigating the design cultures of copycats and fake consumer goods. Bringing together discussions of the entanglement of the licit and illicit, as well as marginalized forms of innovation, the key objective of Chapter 6 is to provide a heterodox reading of design's fundamental place in consumer culture, and most importantly that the demand for counterfeit products reflects the logic of capitalism itself. It begins by considering the diverse forms of goods which fall under the wider discussions of copies: from licenced replicas of famous designs through the approximations of copycat goods to illegal counterfeits. Whilst counterfeiting encompasses a broad spectrum of examples such as fake pharmaceuticals (and now fake vaccines (Agence France-Presse, 2021)) or mechanical products, the primary focus of the chapter is consumer goods in the form of clothing, fashion accessories and electronics. There is also an important distinction to be made between consumers who unknowingly purchase such goods and those who deliberately seek them out. I address the latter. Through this focus on intentional consumption of fake or copycat products, the chapter unpacks the rich histories of consumer culture, relating counterfeit goods back to the origins of conspicuous consumption. I make the core assertion that counterfeit products exemplify consumer capitalism: they intensify ideas of status projection, assimilation and conformity. The cheap, throwaway nature of fake or copycat goods also sadly demonstrates the excesses of consumption itself. Running counter to the positioning of originality as emblematic of creativity and innovation, the chapter concludes the book's focus on innovation by contending that imitation itself is innovative. It does so by offering a critique of intellectual property, copyright and patent, establishing this through a reading of them as essentially colonialist forms of market exploitation. The protectionist mindset of contemporary corporations and their attempts to stifle the trade in counterfeits disregard the histories of late-nineteenth-century Western co-option and adaption of non-Western technologies, intellectual and creative labour. *Shanzhai* is offered as a contemporary exemplar of how innovation emerges from copying. The concluding section of the chapter examines the trajectory of technologies associated with *shanzhai* from cheap, illegal copies through to the open development of new market-leading products. This is positioned in relation to a distinctly non-Western reading of originality.

The book's conclusion returns to some of the opening discussions in this Introduction and specifically the prefigurative power of design, its potential of worldmaking as a performing of new futures into being (DiSalvo, 2016) but equally the continued place of design as fundamentally destructive. In doing so I return to a number of the core debates in the book, noting how the importance of designers in creating new social futures through material and infrastructural practices exemplifies the power of design. I also argue that the implementation of change associated with the pandemic cannot simply be incremental; we must understand the need for fundamental structural change whilst recognizing the contested ethics of change itself. As the chapters unfold it will become evident how the heterodox diffusion of design, its seepage into all aspects of life – including the deviancy of illicit practice – demands a reconsideration of design as one of the most vital forces of the social world in all its complexities.

1 EXPANDING DESIGN

Introduction: What is design?

To even pose this question is foolhardy and requires at least an entire book-length study as opposed to the opening section of this wider chapter. Suffice to say I am aware of this. Instead, I pose this question in order to open up a series of challenges: to the very notion of what we potentially mean by design itself, to ingrained assumptions around the status of design as *professional* practice and perhaps an attempt to recalibrate the underpinnings of who can design. What links the various ways of addressing the question is the desire to explore the domain we might consider as 'design'. This opening conceptual chapter sets out to investigate the territorial wrangling over its meaning, purpose, practice and social function. The ultimate aim of the chapter is to make the case that attempts to pin down the definition of design are inherently slippery, in part due to the problem of definitions as such, but equally the fundamentally heterogeneous nature of design as a singular discipline, if it can indeed be called *a* discipline. As discussed below, the foundations to these discipline-defining debates stem from design's identity crisis, so much so that 'professional design expertise needed to find its place as one among other relevant knowledges' (Suchman, 2018:np). Building on a diverse range of debates, the chapter ultimately calls for expanded approaches to design that do not reject the genealogy of design with its roots in the creation of flint tools for instance (Colomina and Wigley, 2016:32) but also recognizes that the diffusion of design across expanded fields – seen with contemporary applications in design thinking and synthetic biology for example – demands new conceptualizations of design's ontological and epistemological identity. Design's place in these new disciplinary domains is encouraging on one level as it exemplifies the centrality of design to all human and increasingly more-than-human action. On another level it raises the stark question, 'who speaks for design?' (see Fry, 2005). This chapter argues that whilst the intellectual canon for traditional notions of design is still to be very much valued (see Mayall, 1979; Pye, 1969) the paradigm shift in the widespread importance of design necessitates divergent discourses and debates that mirror the multiplicities of design today. We need to think design from both the inside and the outside, something the chapter seeks to begin the task of doing.

Establishing the 'essence' of design is no easy feat. Willis (2019) notes that design is instrumental in character, attuned towards serving a purpose. Although there are limitations to such a claim it serves to highlight some of its key characteristics, including technical application. This is also the fundamental premise of Herbert Read's *Art and Industry* (Read, 1966) which stands as a critical benchmark in the study of industrially produced goods. *Art and Industry* is significant because it offers an important framework for a nascent theory of design (see Kinross, 1988). Although Read's approach to the social and cultural value of such mass-produced artefacts is clearly art historical in tone his address of aesthetic characteristics is also situated within the social conditions of technology, notably in reference to William Morris' legacy. To search out an epistemology of design it is important to highlight the core thesis in Read's outline of design: his was a relatively singular application of the abstract artistic process to industrial manufacture. In doing so he established a reading of design which was grounded in the aesthetic, formal characteristics of art applied to industry. The historical context of this approach to design is understandable, in part due to the cross-cutting work of key practitioners in this period, who worked between industrial design, graphic design, furniture and architecture particularly through figures such as Lazlo Moholy-Nagy.

One can also identify a clear link between Read's discussion of the application of artisanal skills to industrial manufacture and Richard Buchanan's (2001) outline of the histories of design's place within the intellectual canon of dominant Western thought. Buchanan notes that between the fourteenth and sixteenth centuries, design was subsumed under architecture and the fine arts, in part due to the fact that the artisanal skills associated with craft-based forms of design did not offer a distinct set of principles as to how designers approached their work. There were no fundamental or underlying principles guiding the production of artefacts – leading to the identification of design as a 'servile activity' (Buchanan, 2001:5), simply the making of things, a reading which still pervades some definitions of design. This schism between intellectual and practical enquiry is rooted in the principles of scientific knowledge and its propagation in universities. Such an outline of the lack of intellectual legacy of design also emanates from the place of design within non-educational contexts. In the early twentieth century design was principally viewed as a trade activity, whereby it dealt specifically with manufacture. Buchanan suggests there are three further categorizations of design: a segmented profession; a field for technical research; and, latterly, a 'new liberal art of technological culture' (1992:5). As suggested later in the chapter, this most recent identity may well have been superseded given nearly thirty years have elapsed since originally posed. But this conception of design as a liberal art framed around technology offers a valuable description as it highlights the way in which design may be seen as an integrative approach to human experience – drawing together 'understanding, communication, and action' (Buchanan, 1992:6). What becomes clear from Buchanan's articulation of the different stages of design is the urgency of attempting to posit the shifting nature of design as a specific domain of knowledge, the tension ultimately based around the particular domains out of which design, as a research endeavour more pointedly, has been framed and might continue to be. This is the desire for design scholars to 'ground design in a body of rigorous domain knowledge' (Margolin, 2002:235) that is, to posit a disciplinary specificity.

The establishment of such a foundation has a number of different casts, but the one I now consider is that of the practice of design as a form of 'designerly intelligence'. What we might term its internal characteristics. The following section considers the writings of a range of design practitioners on the nature of design *practice* itself – what is it to design? To pursue this question the professional contexts under which design activity takes place will be the primary focus, notably in relation to establishing a distinct epistemology of design, a key discussion that pervades many of the arguments in the book. The chapter then proceeds to examine the diffusion of design outside of its traditional domains of practice and application. It does so by considering the rise of 'design thinking' in relation to applications beyond design, particularly in business. I then address the wider implications of design's movement outwards from the confines of both professional design practice and its material settings.

Towards designerly intelligence

Where Buchanan's outline of design's integrative approach or Mayall's (1979:42–55) principle of totality fosters a greater sense of its ontological and epistemological foundations this is admittedly rather abstract. For many design practitioners, such a rendering lacks the groundedness of the design process – the lived realities of grappling with a particular problem. Norman Potter (2002) offers a more everyday examination of a similar problematic. Rather than attempting to identify a set of irreducible principles which designers are said to work to, he provides a descriptive account of the grounded approaches employed: making oneself familiar with a particular situation, accepting instructions from a client, understanding these instructions, considering the possibilities in the situation, discussing the possibilities, making conclusions, offering proposals and modifications to these, communicating through drawings or prototypes to third parties and overseeing elements of the outcome (Potter, 2002:100). However, such descriptions of the design process are also limited in scope, for they do not adequately address the complexities of the working methods of design. To consider the practice of design itself we need to combine wider philosophical foundations with elements of practical and methodological acuity, to which I now turn.

Nigel Cross (1982; 2001; 2011) and others working in this area (see for example Archer, 1979; Dorst, 2003; Lawson, 1980; Lawson and Dorst, 2009; Rowe, 1986) offer an overview of the working processes and methods of design thinking, identifying how the 'discipline' differs from other cognate areas such as art or craft practices, as well as the natural and human sciences.[1] For Archer design is 'the collected experience of the material culture, and the collected body of experience, skill and understanding embodied in the arts of planning, inventing, making and doing' (cited in Cross, 1982:221). As such design stands in contrast to the natural sciences and the humanities through a variety of measures, but ultimately through practical knowledge based upon 'sensibility, invention, validation and implementation' (Archer, 1979:20). The contrasting values between the three domains of the sciences, humanities and design are also instructive. The sciences are seen to be objective, rational and neutral; the humanities subjective, imaginative, committed and just; whilst design is practical, ingenious, empathetic and appropriate (Cross, 1982:222). Above all we can take from this the recognition that the professional practice of design has distinct qualities from the sciences and humanities. As I go on to discuss later in this chapter, such measures of practicality, planning, invention and material implementation are not solely confined to professional design practice and are evident in the growing diffusion of designerly sensibilities. But before addressing this, the specific nature of professional design as a separate domain of knowledge is firstly unpacked.

Cross (2001:49) notes how one of the most significant moments in the expression of design as a distinct practice was the establishment of the 'design methods movement' in the 1960s, notably through the 'Conference on Design Methods' in 1963 (Bayazit, 2004:18). Here the role of design as a rational set of actions and methodologies was foregrounded, particularly in relation to the changing technological conditions in the post–Second World War period, a time of profound social, technological and economic shifts (Parsons, 2016:33). And a time when design's influence was on the rise. Central to the debate on the rationalist and systematic, as opposed to intuitive, approaches to design was the work of Herbert Simon, particularly his 1969 book *The Sciences of the Artificial* (Simon, 1996). Here Simon attempted to establish design as a 'science of the artificial', in that it recognized an approach to design that was grounded in intellectual and methodological rigour: it was seen as attuned to the artificial, human-centred realm in much the same way the hard sciences are to the natural world. He was particularly disdainful of what he saw as the 'intellectually soft, intuitive, informal, and cooky-booky' (Simon, 1996:112) attitude to previous discussions of design epistemology. The basic premise of Simon's work is an increase in the analytic rigour of approach. He was dedicated to 'forms of logic that would lead to efficient methods of problem-solving' (Margolin, 2002:236), the key to which was the context of engineering – in which he was immersed – as opposed to traditions of design emanating out of craft practices.

Simon's now-classic definition of design, 'everyone designs who devises courses of action aimed at changing existing situations into preferred ones' (Simon, 1996:111), clearly assigns design a specific function, that of addressing particular problems or 'situations', and crucially providing new, constructive articulations of better situations. To this end, Simon also offers an important ontology of 'design science': where the natural sciences are framed around the ontological question of 'how things are', design is concerned with 'how things ought to be, with devising artefacts to attain goals' (Simon, 1996:114). This appears agreeable in terms of a clear – if rather abstracted – notion of a material-centred understanding of responses to particular situations. The reason why Simon's work and that of the 'design science' community has been criticized by many (including some of its original protagonists (Cross, 2001:49–50)) is due to this approach. This takes on a particular cadence in terms of language, but also in how this is positioned disciplinarily. Threaded throughout *The Sciences of the Artificial* are specific contexts of how design is to be operationalized, through 'the tools of artificial intelligence and operations research' (Simon, 1996:114), as well as 'management science [and] theories of probability and utility' (Simon, 1996:116). Whilst there is clearly nothing implicitly wrong with such methodologies and methods, for a number of critics the problem resides in the fact that this scientific approach – the model proposed by Simon – cannot adequately account for the complexity of the problems designers encounter (Cross, 2001:50). To a certain degree this is partly bound by the context within which Simon was articulating his argument, that of the teaching of and research in engineering in American universities at this time. Margolin makes a valuable point that this approach was predicated on an awareness that engineers would not understand or engage with human-centred 'judgement or experience' (Margolin, 2002:236) seen in the more phenomenologically grounded context of arts-based approaches to design. The issues of experience and complexity are key to understanding the wider context of the critiques of Simon's work and 'design science', much of which is driven by the uncertainties of real-world problems that designers face.

The issue of 'problem-solving' is often cited as a key determinant of design (if not a fetish (Dilnot, 2019:xi)), and in the narratives surrounding the epistemology of design the question of how problems are conceptualized and addressed are notably evident (Dorst, 2003:15). Parsons addresses design specifically in relation to its problem-focussed nature. His working definition – and one that clearly aligns to a particular philosophical tradition – is as follows: 'Design is the intentional solution of a problem, by the creation of plans for a new sort of thing, where the plans would not be immediately seen, by a reasonable person, as an inadequate solution' (Parsons, 2016:11). Tonkinwise (2011:534) offers a rather more dialogical take on this by identifying the co-evolution of the 'problem-definition/solution-proposition' relationship whilst also recognizing how problems are inherently ill-defined (also see Archer, 1979:17). The work of Rittel and Webber (1973) critiques the notion that problems are inherently understandable and thus transparent in terms of how they can be tackled. Now a well-established text in the study of design and problem-solving, they utilized the term 'wicked' to refer to design problems that were complex and difficult to find a solution to. The context within which they established this notion of 'wickedness' is against the intellectual backdrop of the early industrial period, where they argue a Newtonian metaphysics has persisted in seeing problems as linear, understandable and definable, further grounded by the 'pervasive idea of *efficiency*' (Rittel and Webber, 1973:158 emphasis in original). By contrast, writing in the late 1960s and early 1970s, the problems of modern industrial society were increasingly complex, in part due to the proliferation of open systems in complex societies (see Prigogine and Stengers, 1984). In complex social systems, rather than being bounded, networks interlock and outputs from one network become inputs into another. As a result, it is increasingly difficult to predict tailored solutions, as the nature of the problem itself is ever-more complex. In this situation, how do we define and locate problems? (Rittel and Webber, 1973:159). Their work provides a useful exploration of how problems are dealt with in a range of professional contexts, notably in planning, which has been argued is closest to how the designerly approach to the artificial is conceptualized (Buchanan, 1992). Whereas Rittel and Webber see the natural sciences dealing with problems which are 'tame' or 'benign' in that the solutions are identifiable. Crucially, they suggest that planners are always dealing with '*societal* problems' (Rittel and Webber, 1973:160 my emphasis) given these operate within social, political, economic and governmental powerbases. It is this context of the social that drives them to see planning as a professional activity that deals with wicked problems. Owing to the complexity of societal problems, rather tellingly they write that 'social problems are never solved. At best they are only re-solved – over and over again' (Rittel and Webber, 1973:160).

This pragmatic outline of what the planner (or designer) can achieve stands in marked contrast to the surety of approach the likes of Simon appear to propagate in terms of what design can achieve. Rittel and Webber's conception of wickedness highlights the need for designers to, firstly, understand the *societal* nature of the problems they are asked to consider; and secondly, that the very notion of a solution is inherently problematic in itself. However, whilst I suggest this is a constructive articulation of the modesty those involved in design should bring to their work, Buchanan notes that Rittel and Webber only offer a description of the reality in which designers operate, and fail to adequately provide 'a well-grounded theory of design' (1992:16). His reasoning for this is valuable in relation to the broader consideration of what design is. For Buchanan, design is inherently wicked because it does not have the same disciplinary specialism as other areas such as the hard or natural sciences where laws and structures prevail. Rather, design is much broader in scope because it is applicable to so many areas of human action – something we will return to shortly. But design must come to terms with its potential limitlessness by considering the interrelationship between the *general* and *particular* (Buchanan, 1992:17). Here Buchanan provides a clear-cut outline of design epistemology. Designers, he states, operate at a general level by contextualizing their approaches in relation to the wider framework in which they are working, be that materials, forms, histories or methodologies. Critically, it is at the level of the particular where design fundamentally operates, and Buchanan writes that '*there is no science of the particular*' (1992:17 emphasis in original) because it cannot be generalized.

The centrality of the particular to design is inherently related to Rittel and Webber's notion of wicked problems because designers must deal with the specificity of the individual contexts of each problem. There is not a design problem per se; rather, there must be multiple modes of how to deal with particular, complex, situated and wicked scenarios. Parsons makes an important observation in relation to this issue of how one deals with complexity, insisting that it is not a technical problem as such, rather it is a 'political choice' (Parsons, 2016:41) in that no problems or solutions are devoid of ideological contexts. I agree with this. Where the work Herb Simon appears abstracted from the lived realities of problems and their manifestations, and Rittel and Webber's famous text questioned this by repositioning many of the prevailing assumptions around the nature of problems within design epistemologies, the work of Donald Schön has rightly been identified as one of the most important for design practices. Critical to the widespread reception of his 1983 book *The Reflective Practitioner: How Professionals Think in Action* (Schön, 2008) are its reasoned, well-founded arguments, but above all, a clear sense of the realities of doing design work. Fundamentally, he discards the model of 'Technical Rationality' seen with scientific models of design, adding, 'let us search, instead, for an epistemology of practice implicit in the artistic, intuitive process which some practitioners do bring to situations of uncertainty, instability, uniqueness and value conflict' (Schön, 2008:62). Echoing the wickedness of the problems designers are asked to consider, Schön outlines a designerly approach which is an admixture of intuition, reflexivity, tacit knowledge and, above all, 'reflection-in-action'. It is striking in the way it attempts to deal with the lived experiences of action (albeit through just one case study (Cross, 2011:23)). Rather than a pre-determined set of actions carried out in a linear, rational manner, Schön recognized that designers act like other professional practitioners: they bring pre-existing knowledges and skills to bear on a situation. Crucially, they deal with the problem by attending to the situations created by the problem itself, firstly by naming different facets of the problem before framing 'the context in which we will attend to them' (Schön, 2008:52). Decisively, there is an interactive process at work whereby the problem and the designer are in dialogue, the situation of the problem 'talking back' to the designer (Cross, 2011:23). The value of Schön's epistemology of practice is the reality of the situation – so that when the designer attempts a particular approach to the problem this is not the end point. Instead, there are series of '"what if" conjectures' (Cross, 2011:24) where the designer proposes certain tentative manoeuvres around the problem. Schön sees these as a 'local experiment' (Schön, 2008:145) which feeds into the wider 'global' framework used to deal with the problem. As local conjectures of sorts there are a series of dialogical moves, where the designer reflects upon the contingencies and complexities of the problem ultimately through synthesis

(Cross, 1982:223). Schön's work on reflective practice offers an invaluably 'clear account of a typical, fast-moving, "thinking on your feet", live example of designing' (Cross, 2011:25). Given this, for design practice scholars such as Cross, the idea of design as a series of reflections on action has become an important touchstone for design epistemology. Rather than 'scientific design', 'design science', or 'the science of design' (Cross, 2001:53–4), Schön's approach is closer towards a *disciplinary* specificity for design – not a distinct science as such, but as Buchanan (1992) also suggests, there cannot be a *science* of design. Once again, Cross neatly summarizes these debates, culminating in an indispensable articulation of the practice of design. He calls this 'design intelligence' (Cross, 2011:136; also see Cross, 1982:226), which can be described as follows:

- Designers operate across multiple levels, from larger-scale systemic understanding to smaller-scale, material properties.

- Designers do not treat problems as a given, instead they engage in the wider contexts of the problem, bringing imaginative approaches to the wickedness of problems.

- They approach problems through framing them in such a manner that create patterns from the data.

- Designerly intelligence is reflective, enabling designers to move quickly through abstract concepts to concrete solutions, 'between doing and thinking' (Cross, 2011:136).

- Finally, designers recognize that problems are discursive, not only between the problem and the designer but through collaborative teamwork.

The idea of a distinct designerly intelligence opens up a valuable space in which to locate a nascent epistemology of design practice that recognizes the reality of how designers often tend to work. The operative word being 'tend' to work, given that a discipline of design is inherently more flexible than a science of design. However, whilst admittedly a very useful way to frame the working practices and methods employed by designers across a range of sub-disciplines, there is still something of a gap in how we can answer the overarching question posed in the Introduction to this chapter: *what is design*? For if we seek-out all that encompasses design – rather than solely design as a professionally situated domain – we must consider the multiplicity of means through which we engage with it, be that professional design practitioners, or those individuals and collectives who are active participants in the creation of their own material worlds: people such as the prosumers described by Toffler; the tinkerers identified by Jencks and Silver; or more recently the everyday, 'diffuse' designers noted by Manzini (2015). Although many of the design scholars discussed in this section have provided a series of paradigms, these are very much driven by the practice of design in professional settings. This is not enough. Instead, to fundamentally appreciate the power of designerly intelligence we must also engage with the practices of design in pluriversal terms (Escobar, 2018), namely the myriad forms of material practices that also occur outwith the professional sphere.

In making this case I echo the arguments made by Victor Margolin (2002) in his critique of the legacy of Herbert Simon's influence on design. He is not critical of Simon's work per se (in part because it was bound by historical circumstance and taste), more the way it has led to an overt focus on developing a distinct and bounded conception of design's domain of knowledge, a space that is centred on the professional *process* of design above all. The playful title of Margolin's text, 'The Two Herberts', introduces another Herbert into the mix – Herbert Marcuse. Using Marcuse's work within the Frankfurt School tradition, Margolin makes the case for a 'critical theory of practice' (2002:237). He states his position: 'I prefer a much more open conception of design activity that is not preoccupied with justifying a separate sphere of domain knowledge, as the primary purpose of research' (2002:237). I do too. As an alternative, how one approaches design as an activity in producing social worlds has to be guided by multiple realms of engagement: some that address the processes through which design emanates out of established professional disciplinary practices; and simultaneously an approach to design that purposefully jettisons historically aligned notions of what design is, how, and where it operates, as well as who carries it out. This runs counter to Cross' suggestion that 'design practice does indeed have its own strong and appropriate intellectual culture, and [...] we must avoid swamping our design research with different cultures imported either from the sciences or the arts' (Cross, 2001:55). Clearly these differing accounts of design's domain of knowledge are figured in relation to particular viewpoints, and Margolin's position chimes with the broader cultural and social study of design, as opposed to its practice, but nonetheless his position is much more expansive in its recognition of design's complex social function. To limit design to an internal culture of professional practice is to curtail its potential: this approach simply restricts design to a series of professionally sanctioned techniques and technical know-how (Margolin, 2002:239). Rather we need to harvest the multiplicity of ways design affects the social realm, encompassing the range of techniques and processes alongside their cultural and social energies. The value of doing so is foregrounded by Margolin in his assertion that a critical theory of design more broadly

> provides a basis for embedding design thought within the larger activity of social thought rather than isolating design from its social situation and theorizing independently about its processes of invention. By holding design in our vision as a social practice, we are always obliged to consider and evaluate the situations in which it occurs rather than naturalizing design techniques as Simon does.
>
> (2002:239)

What Margolin's approach acknowledges is the need to situate the practice of design and its social power within the same discursive field, that is, the broader cultural and social study of design. Doing so provides an expanded field of socio-material activity that does not limit the practice of design to professional settings alone. For as Simon again said, '*everyone designs* who devises courses of action aimed at changing existing situations into preferred ones' (Simon, 1996:111 my emphasis). The setting of Simon's assertion requires further discussion. He argued that design as the creation of material artefacts was not fundamentally distinct from 'one that prescribes remedies for a sick patient or the one that devises a new sales plan for a company or a social welfare policy for a state' (Simon, 1996:111). In this guise, then, one could construe that design intelligence operates in a wide range of settings. The essential difference between Simon's argument and my assertion that design operates across a pluriverse of professional and non-professional contexts is, of course, that Simon was referring to distinctly *institutionalized* situations.

Any attempt to reformulate his statement that 'everybody designs' might appear a misapprehension of his intentions. Whilst mindful of this I also hold to Margolin's point concerning the need to continually re-evaluate the 'situations in which it [design] occurs'. Equally, and although somewhat counterintuitively, the value of non-institutionalized and non-professional approaches to design is highlighted by both Bruce Archer (1979) and Nigel Cross (1982) in their early articulations of design intelligence. They situate the importance of design intelligence within the need for a broader approach to the education of design, one that would see it embedded in a fuller understanding of design as a socio-cultural practice. As noted earlier, for them design is distinguished from the sciences with its approach to the natural world and the humanities' engagement with human experience: design is ostensibly about the human world and material culture (Archer, 1979:20; Cross, 1982:221). The domain of concrete, material knowledge through making and doing is one of the principle reasons why Archer and Cross called for a more generalized conception of design education that effectively encompasses aspects of professional design intelligence within *everyday* scenarios. For the ill-defined problems that designers deal with 'are like the problems or issues or decisions that people are more usually faced with in everyday life' (Cross, 1982:225). Indeed, at its root design is an inherently human activity that is centred on the configuration of material and symbolic phenomena, which Archer believes lies at the heart of design itself (1979:17).

Ultimately then, it is evident that designerly intelligence is in many ways a distinct set of professional conceptual, material, social and organizational registers that differ from the traditional concerns of the sciences and humanities. However, as also suggested in this section, such a scope of activity is inherently a human endeavour more generally. Professional designers are not the only ones who deal with the practicalities of planning, inventing and attempting to engage with ill-defined situations. This may include anyone who has encountered scenarios where they have utilized such practical skills to overcome the problem to hand. In relation to this key point Suchman (2012) via Akrich (1992) discusses the importance of the 'distribution of competences' (Akrich, 1992:207) when sociotechnical systems are configured. We see a confrontation between designers and users (an aspect unpacked in Chapter 4 through the idea of misuse) where the operation of the thing itself unfolds. A key point to extract from this discussion is the question of the 'ownership of competences', that is, who holds responsibility for both the materialization of things and their ongoing social relationships. This is where Manzini's (2015) 'diffusion of design' comes into play.

Diffusing the limits of design

As is now apparent, the question posed in the Introduction to this chapter 'What is Design?' is incredibly difficult to answer, and, as we will see in this section, increasingly challenging owing to the growing diffusion of design. Where I argued previously that designerly intelligence seeps into non-professional settings in which everyday forms of design are employed to deal with ill-defined problems, this section investigates this seepage across an even wider range of situations, both institutional and non-institutional, and into domains where design would not typically have been encountered. Just as the practicalities of design intelligence – planning competency, contextual and systemic awareness, material affinities – are attuned to everyday forms of resourcefulness, so too are these skills applicable across evermore diverse and diffuse disciplinary boundaries, from the business community through to advanced biological sciences.

Although the material in the preceding section outlined a variety of approaches to design, this tends to speak to an overarching epistemology of design rather than the distinctiveness of these sub-fields (such as fashion, graphics, product, interaction or designing with data) which have their own traditions, trajectories, genealogies, methodologies and crucially pedagogies, often tied to arts or science-based affinities. The cultural baggage of such legacies weighs less heavy when we look at disciplines outside of design that have recognized its growing significance as a social practice. The 'design turn' has become an important facet of anthropology (Gunn et al., 2013; Murphy, 2016; Rabinow and Marcus, 2008) and sociology (Lupton, 2018; Shove et al., 2007) particularly through shared approaches to material culture, human action and social power. A similar tendency is evident in a range of other disciplinary contexts such as the commercial sector as well as the sciences, particularly in fields such as synthetic biology and biodesign (Myers, 2018). Indeed, the place of design in synthetic biology is telling. Whilst many of the approaches to the engineering of living materials pay homage to the traditions of 'problem-solving' discussed already there are more profound changes in the role of design in such complex processes. Most importantly the ethical dimensions of such practices. As Antonelli argues, 'Design transcends its traditional boundaries and aims straight at the core of the moral sphere, toying with our most deep-seated beliefs' (Antonelli, 2018:7). In relation to the practice of design the future-focused nature of design is critical in imagining and speculating about new scenarios for examining the 'design *of* biology' itself (Ginsberg, 2014:52, emphasis in original). Although these tools of speculation, fiction and scenario building imply a move away from the traditional forms of designerly intelligence outlined by the likes of Cross, there are continued allegiances, most notably in the role of design as a mode of synthesis and the designer as a mediator within collaborative platforms. All these factors further highlight the increasing value of design in a growing range of social, environmental and political contexts.

But nowhere is the seepage of design intelligence into non-traditional contexts more evident than in the pervasive presence of 'design thinking' within the corporate sector and beyond (see Dorst, 2011). By turning to 'design thinking' this section outlines the way in which the variety of methods and processes of design intelligence have been disseminated and applied beyond the professional design community so that the very notion of design 'expertise' is distributed through a range of different non-design actors. In many ways this resonates with the origins of participatory design's approach to design as collaborative effort, and this section will address design thinking's challenge to the 'omnipotent designer' (Bjögvinsson et al., 2012:101) whilst at the same time critique the transformation of design approaches into corporatist paradigms.

Although the origins of 'design thinking' in the corporate context became evident over fifteen years ago (Kimbell, 2011:287), the term itself has been employed at various times to consider the broader conditions of design much in the same way that Cross' account of design intelligence attempted to position specific design methodologies (Buchanan, 1992; Rowe, 1986). Whilst the boom in 'design thinking' as a creative problem-solving methodology in the corporate and policy-oriented spheres has led to a vast array of literature two key organizations have been responsible for its spread across numerous new markets: namely, IDEO and the Hasso Plattner Institute of Design at Stanford University, more popularly known as the d.school. Both have exemplified the term in recent times amongst a wider public of corporate and public-sector audiences. 'Design Thinking' by Tim Brown (CEO of IDEO) (Brown, 2008; 2009), published originally in the Harvard Business Review, has played a significant role in articulating the benefits of design thinking processes in sectors not typically associated with design, including the public and third sectors (see Brett and Bloom, 2014). For Brown, design thinking 'is a methodology that imbues the full spectrum of innovation activities with a human-centered design ethos' (Brown, 2008:86). Aligned with many traditional notions of the design process, design thinking utilizes a three-step, iterative process of:

1   *Inspiration*: what are the parameters for success; what's the problem and what opportunities exist; importance of interdisciplinarity; use spaces to share group insights; tell stories.

2   *Ideation*: brainstorm through sketching and scenario-building; describe the journeys of customers; prototype and test, repeatedly; tell more stories.

3   *Implementation*: 'execute the vision [and] engineer the experience'; develop a marketing strategy. (Brown, 2008:88–9)

Likewise, the d.school version advocates a similar didactic process of empathize, define, ideate, prototype and test (Hasso Plattner Institute of Design, 2010). Subsumed amidst this flurry of design thinking-speak are some interesting and telling attributes. Firstly, it is evident that the design process is recognized as a *systems*-based approach, rather than the creation of discreet artefacts (although some of the examples in Brown's article are object-based outcomes). Secondly, design thinking becomes embedded within the entire business development process as opposed to playing a more typical role at the end of the product/ service cycle. Thirdly – and critically for the diffusion of design intelligence – is the contribution from 'stakeholders' not usually involved in the creation of new ideas, i.e., non-designers playing a role in the utilization and implementation of design processes. The examples cited by Brown show a variety of corporate and non-corporate actors involved in the design thinking process – administrators, policymakers, managers, doctors and nurses. A revealing aspect of Brown's manifesto is the profile of attributes a 'design thinker' should possess: an IDEO employee states, 'my experience is that many people outside professional design have a natural aptitude for design thinking' (cited in Brown, 2008:87). Which in their estimation includes empathy, integrative thinking, optimism, experimentalism and collaboration. Although these traits are purportedly not exclusive to designers Brown's article also makes the case that new types of interdisciplinary designer are key to finding design thinking 'talent', including institutions such as the d.school and, tellingly, from business schools, such as Rotman in Toronto. However, echoing his IDEO colleague, Brown also suggests that 'you may even be able to train nondesigners with the right attributes to excel in design-thinking roles' (Brown, 2008:91).

What this new guise of 'design thinking' suggests then is that the corporate sphere has recognized the potential economic value of design over and above its traditional place at the end of the development cycle. Instead, the values of design thinking – deep understanding through observation, iterative experimentation, role-playing and systems thinking – speak to the changing role of design more generally. It also puts into question the omnipotent centrality of the expert designer within the design process itself, an aspect of 'design thinking' that Kimbell highlights as a point of tension, whereby the specific qualities of designerly knowledge may not be as sacrosanct as they once perceivably were (Kimbell, 2011:298). Amidst an array of other implications (including the further entrenchment of design as a corporatist paradigm), what we ultimately see with design thinking is a de-centring of the role of designer.[2] Not a complete dismissal of their core abilities but rather:

- An appreciation of the collaborative nature of the design process more generally, in both fields such as participatory design, and 'design thinking' where design experts and non-experts are engaged.

- Design itself is now an expanded field of practice and its importance in so many sectors of the social world is increasingly apparent.

So much more is at stake. Design's application in sectors such as social policy (Design Council, 2013), humanitarian design (Brett and Bloom, 2014), healthcare (Aitken and Shackleton, 2014) and in new technological spaces such as synthetic biology (Ginsberg et al., 2014) extends its reach beyond anything envisaged by the likes of Herbert Read. As exclaimed in the book that extolls much of its new-found power, design is now concerned with 'designing organizations, designing organisms, designing programs' (Mau et al., 2004:17), although the ultimate claim is that design is now about 'the design of the world' (Mau et al., 2004:11). Charting the force of design in a more measured manner, Bruno Latour argues that 'design has been extended from the details of daily objects to cities, landscapes, nations, cultures, bodies, genes, and [...] to nature itself' (Latour, 2011:151). For Latour one of the significant shifts in recent years has been design's 'extension' beyond its established parameters. In his keynote speech to the Design History Society Annual Conference in 2008, Latour is the first to admit he is no design historian, but his external observations on the state of design today are perhaps some of the most insightful and thought-provoking in recent times. His ability to cut-through the internal wrangling of the discipline and bring a Science and Technology Studies perspective on design is highly instructive (just as the inverse is).

Whilst the likes of John Christopher Jones highlighted the 'extension of the scale and influence of design processes' (Jones, 1984:26) where products become part of systems, Latour extends this further still. For him design has moved completely beyond the traditional bounds of industrial design in both how it is comprehended and in its material extension (also see Jones, 1984:26). As he notes, if design is central to the re-engineering of eco-systems and cities then the term no longer has any limit (2011). Although Latour appears to switch between design as an adjective and a verb, at the level of comprehension design now includes the entire planning cycle of contemporary society, from logistical planning through meaning making to end of life disposal. This is reflected in the material extension of design beyond discreet products to systems, services and bodies (Colomina and Wigley, 2016:133–4). Although the design of services is not revelatory, Latour's point that such changes affect how 'we deal with objects and action more generally' (Latour, 2011:152) is more telling. A particularly helpful way of understanding the extended parameters of design is to see it fundamentally as a means of 'drawing things together' (2011:3). Akin to Suchman's (2012) notion of configuration, design is an assembly of relations between various actants – this STS reading of design employs Heidegger's notion of things as 'gatherings' where they draw together multifarious collaborators, ones perhaps not typically associated with it in traditional terms. The problem with this reading of design, for Latour, is that designers are often not able to see this, or perhaps more to the point have not been *trained* to appreciate the collaborative nature of design, for 'we are still utterly unable to draw together, to simulate, to materialize, to approximate, to fully model to scale, what a thing in all of its complexity, is' (Latour, 2011:162). 'Collaborative' here moves beyond platitudes around co-design; rather it is concerned with the immanent collaboration of all entities in an assembly of relations, human and more-than-human. Under these changing conditions and scales of design Latour suggests that design is still concerned with *detail*, and as Archer and Cross' earlier discussions outlined, crucially with the act of 'making' (Latour, 2011:153). But it is vital to recognize that making in this guise is radically Other to the craft or skill-based traditions which befall certain design practices to this day. Rather, given the scale and enormity of some of these new challenges, the very notion of making operates at a fundamentally different level, be that the nano or hyperobject scale (Morton, 2013). It is world-making to echo Mau et al., albeit in a slightly different register. What Latour's unpacking of design and its futures leaves us with is difficult to fully determine at this stage. However, a key factor to emerge from his thesis is that design's presence in the world is infinitely more expansive than populist and professional conceptions of 'design thinking' imply. If design itself permeates through the social strata of all that inflects our lives, our bodies, our ecosystems, then a range of fundamental questions begin to emerge: Who is the designer? Where is design?

These questions can be considered in relation to some of the previous points around the ontology and epistemologies of design, notably in terms of the arguments posed by Buchanan (1992) around the shifts in the social position of design. Where his conception of design as the liberal art of technological culture is defined by the common pursuit of purposeful enquiry shared by all, Latour's new rendering of design is such that it permeates even further than our daily lives, percolating instead through the world of the physical exterior and the realm of inner life. These shifting sands of design are, for some, problematic owing to their innate instability. For others (myself included) this fluid situation speaks to a paradigm shift in design, a radical reconceptualization of its place, including the question above regarding the identity of the designer.

Situated in this territory is Manzini's *Design, When Everybody Designs* (Manzini, 2015). It is something of a cross between a manifesto for social change through design, and a how-to-manual for achieving this. Although the projects discussed in the book seem rather unprepossessing compared to the likes of synthetic biology or infrastructural-scale change, it is nonetheless a valuable outline of the perceived transformations in design's place in society. Manzini's core thesis is that we have moved towards a period where the traditional expertise of the designer is now supplemented by the knowledge and skills of the non-designer. The first he terms 'expert design', the latter 'diffuse design'. There is still a place for the 'traditional' notion of the designer, but the expert is no longer the sole repository of design knowledge (also see Buchanan, 1992:8–9); rather, this new ecology of approach is a result of collaborative social structures and new participatory platforms across digital media, including distributed manufacturing and maker spaces. Design knowledge is diffused across a range of networks, although Manzini's moniker of diffuse design is more wide-ranging than that of 'design thinking'. His work also challenges some of the assumptions concerning design's supposedly inherent role in problem-solving (also see Colomina and Wigley, 2016:162). Although he does not deny the importance of problem-solving, he writes there is now an interaction between this and 'sense making' (Manzini, 2015:3). Inherent to design as 'sense making' is the role of the new design protagonist – the diffuse designer. That is, someone who is described as a bricoleur of sorts, using and adapting existing materials, systems, practices, but above all the new design protagonist works through collaboration. Here we see some parallels with Cross' point about the discursiveness of design. This is demonstrated by 'local applications of an idea of well-being based on a new ecology of relationships between people, and between people and their environment' (Manzini, 2015:4). The collaborative nature of the sense-making of diffuse design clearly speaks to the complexity of contemporary social, technical and environmental problems: it is the collaborative approach between expert designers and the new design protagonists that Manzini sees as instigating a new culture of design, one – he claims – which is redolent of industrial design in its social significance. This new diffuse culture is one where design is the epicentre of sociotechnical change: 'It must itself change and become a *widespread activity*, permeating the multiple nodes of unprecedented sociotechnical networks in which we all live and operate.' (Manzini, 2015:29 my emphasis).

Manzini's rationale for considering this new design culture as seismic as the birth of industrial design in the late nineteenth century is strikingly evident. And although these are possibly grandiose claims the collaborative nature of incipient forms of diffuse design demonstrates its ever-increasing spread.

CONCLUSIONS

Victor Papanek famously stated: 'All men [sic] are designers. All that we do, almost all the time, is design, for design is basic to all human activity' (Papanek, 1973:23). Although nearly fifty years old, his remark is incredibly prescient and folds into many contemporary debates on the ontology, epistemology and praxis of design. At its core Papanek's thesis takes a holistic approach to design, partly in keeping with the political discourses of that time, but more importantly as a recognition of design's immanence in all social, cultural and ecological worlds. The importance of contemporary design to an ever-expanding range of contexts such as design's central position within corporate culture may not be all to Papanek's liking but his predictions around the pervasiveness of design more generally have come to pass. We see this in the manifold examples of design at multiple, interlocking scales: from genes, through objects and landscapes to nations, and ultimately to nature itself.

As the title of this opening chapter suggests, we are now in a position where the field of intellectual, creative and critical enquiry that constitutes design has expanded exponentially from its origins in technically focused artisanal skills, and particularly the early twentieth-century application of art to manufacture. Of course, this is still an important factor in the inherent relationship between design and emergent technologies, notably in Manzini's identification of design's centrality to the scope of rampant socio-technical change. We also saw that conceptualizations of design's ontological essence and its epistemological contexts are more widespread than ever. And riven with tension. Not least in establishing the grounds for a rigorous, rationalist approach to the fundamental ways in which professional designers operate, as opposed to an intuitive informality. However, as Manzini and Latour demonstrate, with the profoundly expansive field of design today any attempt to offer an empirically attuned set of irreducible parameters within which design operates is impossible, but equally, problematic. On the one hand, the pervasiveness and ubiquity of 'design thinking' within the corporate sector (and associated public services) shows how designerly intelligence has many valuable attributes, not least in recognizing the place of diffuse designers and collaborative approaches. At the other end of the spectrum is the presence of design within highly sophisticated research into synthetic biology, nanotechnology and robotics. At its core I suggest that design today is constituted by a diffuse discursive community that is not always communicating in the same manner or about the same matters. Although this cacophony of voices might be heard as noise, such is the nature of design that this can be read as one of its strengths (see Serres, 1982). It acts in different ways, is applied in diffuse situations and leads to diverse outcomes. This is why we struggle to assert design's singular essence, for the increasing array of disciplines and approaches that engage it are changing its historical foundations as well as its futures.

Taking the fundamental arguments threaded throughout this opening chapter, it is helpful to draw some conclusions that propel the rest of the book. Although there are broad ranging and divergent concerns there are also commonalities. For example, as Latour (2011:153) asserts, design continues to be concerned with making, albeit of a very different type and scale. Similarly, where advocates such as Archer and Cross identify the disciplinary nature of professional design through its problem-centred approach and methodological basis in planning, inventing, making, doing and above all practical knowledge, such skillsets have become increasingly commonplace in traditionally non-design settings such as policy making. Moreover, the less rigid approaches to design through Donald Schön's work also chime with the wider 'design turn': uncertainty, ambiguity, instability, uniqueness, synthesis, thinking on your feet. The potential of such methodological strengths is clearly evident, and thus understandably valued by 'design thinking' protagonists. Their mantra that empathy, integrative thinking, optimism, experimentation, observation, role-playing, systems-thinking and collaboration are vitally important attributes of the corporate sphere also shows how *design* intelligence more broadly is of fundamental significance to all forms of social action.

Distilling these wide-ranging debates on the nature of design intelligence, I make the case that design is above all concerned with *action*. Referring back to Latour – and specifically the main title of his paper 'A Cautious Prometheus?' – the notion of a Promethean approach to design is such that it has the potential to be *daringly* inventive. In the face of impending ecological crises (see Latour, 2018) the importance of design to social and environmental action through its ability to remake the world becomes more and more crucial. The call to action through design by Latour and others such as Escobar (2018) stems in part from the recognition of the fact that design is essentially a human activity: 'There is no area of contemporary life where design – the plan, project or working hypothesis which constitutes the "intention" in intentional operations – is not a significant factor in shaping human experience' (Buchanan, 1992:8). At its core design is a social practice that is bound up with the human condition, so much so that 'every human being is a designer' (Potter, 2002:10; also see Nelson and Stolterman, 2003:19). Pared back to its core, Heskett argues that design is the capacity to shape the world around us 'in ways without precedent in nature, to serve our needs and give meaning to our lives' (2016:21). Design matters profoundly. This is critical to future action, but also in reflecting on the role design has played in leading us to this very crisis. Design moves beyond the traditions of the plastic arts and associations with discreet objects; instead, it enmeshes every nexus of the artificial and increasingly natural world. In this guise the configurative power of design is clearly evident, and typically one would value this as one of the many reasons why design matters more than ever. However, with such power also comes the deviant potential of design this book deals with. Suchman, in her critique of Mau's book *Massive Change,* provides a useful counter to the assumption that design's ever-increasing presence naturally leads to positive change:

> Design moves from being one among the four primary elements of nature, culture, business, and design (albeit at the core) to being the enveloping, encompassing, and, by implication, directing force, leading to a reiteration of the nineteenth-century declaration of the conquest of nature and the rhetorical query regarding the future: 'Now that we can do anything what will we do?'
>
> (Suchman, 2011:5)

2 'SOCIAL DESIGN' IS NOT SOCIAL ENOUGH

Introduction

In a key paragraph from *Design, When Everybody Designs*, Manzini offers the following:

> Design is a culture and a practice concerning how things ought to be in order to attain desired functions and meanings. It takes place within open-ended co-design processes in which all the involved actors participate in different ways. It is based on a human capability that everyone can cultivate and which for some – the design experts – becomes a profession. The role of design experts is to trigger and support these open-ended co-design processes, using their design knowledge to conceive and enhance clear-cut, focussed design initiatives.
>
> (Manzini, 2015:53–4)

One of the key points to draw from the discussions around the expanded field of design is that its engagement with different social contexts means its importance in the world increases – this reflects the thoughts and ideas of many design scholars, this one included, that design's meaningful presence in everyday life abounds. However, whilst traditionally the place of design in quotidian social practices has been a result of its cross-cutting presence in domestic, workplace or public spaces for example (furniture; spatial layout; information design; infrastructure), the scale of its expansiveness has increased exponentially when we begin to consider the multi-scalar field of design described in the previous chapter. What this means for design as a set of practices and processes is that its social reach moves beyond an aesthetic or formal series of considerations, and as seen with 'design thinking' enters into a much broader range of social contexts: business practices, health, social care, welfare, systems-based policy provision or biodesign.

But as this chapter argues, the infiltration of design into diverse echelons of society also results in evermore complex understandings of what we mean by design, and crucially, it also questions what we mean by the 'social'. So, the key debates in this chapter concern the imbrication of the social realm and design, but fundamentally we need to fully appreciate the social context of design in terms of the different alignments of the social. If – as this book suggests – design is understood as a field of social practice made up of multifarious actors and events, then to fully grapple with this we need to appreciate who these actors and what these events are. For instance, if we return to Richard Buchanan's insightful comments on the definition of design then we begin to appreciate the nuances of its social situation. As a reminder: 'Design is the human power of conceiving, planning and making products that serve human beings in the accomplishment of their individual and collective purposes' (Buchanan, 2001:9). Similarly, as Manzini writes in the above quote, design is concerned with 'how things ought to be in order to attain desired functions and meanings'. With these, and numerous other definitions of design seen in the previous chapter, I want to fully unpack such claims by questioning what is meant by 'how things *ought* to be' and their '*desired* functions and meanings'. Who makes the decision as to the envisioning of how things should be? Can there be a truly collective agreement on this? What type of desire is being discussed: a desire for stable evolution or a desire for something radically different? I wish to pull apart the 'power' in 'human power'; to wrestle with what is meant by claims to 'individual and collective purposes'.

Above all I want to take some of this rhetoric at face value and really challenge the assumptions around the place of design in the social realm by forcing these definitions, propelling them into an understanding of a design ontology and epistemology that sees the 'social' as the radically immanent facet of design. So, where the likes of Manzini holds to a notion of design as an open-ended process engaging human capability, we need to take him at his word and fully engage with a form of radical openness that embraces the human – and the nonhuman – in all their diversity. Not necessarily the human as a centred or centring subject but also as decentred, ineffectual, absent, flawed, criminal. And critically for any discussion of the material realm, a parallel appreciation of the nonhuman as centring, riven with energy, action and potential. But above all the chapter investigates the social as a tangled assemblage of complex interactions, a web of relations where different currents of society come together on a horizontal plane of encounter. The socially 'useful' is challenged to come clean about what is useful in the first place; who is it useful to? Allied to this, where much of the rhetoric around design situates it within a field of betterment (Design Council, 2013), what does it make better? Whose lives are made better?

To consider these points the chapter develops a range of theoretical and contextual approaches to the overarching discussion of design's relationship to the social. Firstly, it deals with normative readings of the link between social value and design by arguing that we need to fully comprehend the ways in which value itself has been positioned in relation to social purpose. I call for a challenge to the normative conception of design, arguing instead for a more realistic understanding of the social: a multiplicitous social realm consisting of classic conceptions of the 'good' society, immanent to an equally social world of the illicit, the illegal, the duplicitous, the destructive. But in doing so I don't mean to position these interrelationships as necessarily binary: rather, in the second section I deal with the way in which the history of design has been pivotal to the non-progressive, potentially destructive, dimensions of the social. Although I term this *asocial* design I do so only as a heuristic device for appreciating the legacy of how the social value of design has been normatively constructed. Instead, this section outlines the origins of a nascent 'deviant design' by considering a range of instances where design has been central to the creation of malevolent social space.

Challenging the normativity of design and social value

In chapter 4 of *Design for the Real World*, entitled 'Do-it-Yourself Murder: The Social and Moral Responsibilities of the Designer', Papanek offers a telling anecdote on the social responsibilities of the designer through his experience as a young designer. Recounting one of his first design jobs in which he was tasked with designing the casing of a desk-top radio, he describes discussions with the client (Papanek, 1973:66). Pointing out that the manufacture of the radio will result in the creation of 600 new jobs in Long Island City, in Queens, New York, the client notes how this will lead to significant social change with production-line employees moving from all over the country, setting up homes with their families. New businesses will emerge to service these new households, with an extended network of subsidiary enterprises. For the client, the social responsibility of the designer is to make the casing of the radio as appealing as possible to consumers otherwise the product will not sell and the workers made redundant. Papanek admits he was initially rather taken with this description of the designer's social responsibility. But with hindsight this is a rather one-dimensional, consumerist reading, perhaps understandable given it was posited by an industrialist.

Instead, the mature Papanek offers a more wide-ranging appeal to the social responsibilities of the designer, insisting that designers must consider their moral position long before products go to market. They should question 'whether the products he [sic] is asked to design or redesign merit his attention at all. In other words, will his design be on the side of the social good or not' (Papanek, 1973:66–7). Such a statement highlights why Papanek's work has become so emblematic for different areas of design practice, most notably within sustainable and ecological design, and more recently with growing awareness of design for social change. Papanek's argument on the need for design as a social good involves a critique of superfluous design which caters for unnecessary products as consumerist lifestyle choices. For example, he contrasts the real needs of impoverished Mexican families who depend on the use of improvised cook-stoves fabricated out of discarded licence/number plates with an American design for a heated footstool which warms feet. The latter is viewed as a facile, pointless artefact. The former is an absolute necessity for survival produced as an anonymous piece of design (of which more will be discussed in Chapter 4) and thus a meaningfully designed object for social good. Papanek offers a diagrammatic outline of the socially purposeless aspects of the majority of design activities at this time in the 1970s (Papanek, 1973:68–72). A triangular representation of the social structure of design in relation to society situates design as a miniscule activity at the tip of the triangle, with the social realm making up the rest of space. Design's intervention in the social world is incredibly limited. For design to have a meaningful engagement with the social good designers must forge a practice that jettisons the superfluity of heated footstools and embrace a range of contexts which speak to the rest of the social world that forms the majority of the triangle. These include projects such as medical devices, teaching aids, safety devices for the home, shelters and walking aids for the visually impaired (Papanek, 1973:73–9). To be sure, such designs now pervade much of the field of social design, particularly healthcare design. But before addressing this, Papanek's triangular depiction of design and the social realm also highlights some important discussions on this relationship. For although the work of Papanek in *Design for the Real World* and his other writings has led to a profound recalibration of design's place in the social world – particularly in design education – I suggest that it fails to address the complexity of the social realm. By this I do not imply that his thesis lacks value, quite the opposite; rather that his rendering of the social does not take into account all that it encompasses, what the majority of the rest of his triangle consists of. He seems to posit a binary version of good versus bad. So, whilst the heated footstool is clearly not *needed* in the way the cook-stove is for survival, it nonetheless speaks to the perceived desires of potential north American consumers. As such it is, in fact, an example of social design in that it encompasses a specific echelon of society, likely a middle-class consumer. Using this as a backdrop to the rest of the chapter I now consider the relationship between design and social value by addressing precisely this notion of social complexity and how design is implicated in the heterogeneity of the social. To do so I deal firstly with the theoretical foundations of social complexity before focusing on how this affects our understanding of a fundamentally *social* practice of design.

The study of the social condition is of course an inherently complex endeavour, and this section can only touch upon the genealogies and theories of 'the social' and society more broadly (Marres et al., 2018). The intention here is to establish the foundations of the social in order to inform the later discussions of design's relationship with the social realm, specifically under the field of 'social design' before making the case for an *asocial* design. As noted above the purpose of doing so is to posit a picture of this relationship that attempts to account for the complexity of this relationship – the messiness that ultimately is the social. All that goes wrong, the systems which breakdown, those that work, the successes and failures of social life, the legal, the illegal, the extra-legal, the actions, activities and processes that fall outwith of the normative. In doing so I do not promote an unstructured, lawless, or anarchic reading of the social. Rather I work with an image of the social that attunes to all the complex relations and interactions between numerous actors. This I suggest offers up a more realistic image that is not perpetuated by traditional conceptions of a structured, ordered milieu. Later in this chapter I argue for a similar understanding of design.

Amongst a wealth of other key resources (see for example Durkheim, 2014; Parsons, 1951), Hannah Arendt's *The Human Condition* (Arendt, 1998) provides an important outline of how the social world has been traditionally understood, notably in terms of 'one-ness'. Prior to the dissolution of the family unit in modern society Arendt suggests that a set of common interests framed around a single opinion constituted the family: a unit conditioned by the head of the household who spoke for the members of the family. She suggests that society continues to be figured around this notion of 'one enormous family which has only one opinion and one interest' (Arendt, 1998:39). Membership of this social family is determined by acceptance of this one opinion, that is, the social norms governing all behaviour. The cohesiveness of the social is then framed around the collective agreement regarding the constitution of the social through this 'one-ness'. For society to function in this guise there is an expectation that its members behave in specific ways through the imposition and acceptance of rules and values. Crucially, Arendt writes that such rules have a tendency to normalize the behaviour of all social actors, restricting their ability to act outwith the codes determined by society (Arendt, 1998:40). Here we see the dominance of conformity as the matrix of social power, where values and 'norms' are determined and codified. Conformity, for Arendt, is one of the key conditions of the rise of economics as a modern science – that is, the statistical basis of modern economics relies upon the conditioning of social beings through specific forms of behaviour that can be managed, accounted for and contained, 'so that those who did not keep the rules could be considered to be asocial or abnormal' (Arendt, 1998:42). In this construction of the social, to be social is to conform to the uniform character of social behaviour, the 'one' version of the social. To be sure, this rendering of society is seen as monolithic, allowing only one type of behaviour that adheres to itself, that is, 'rooted in the one-ness of man-kind' (Arendt, 1998:46). Decisively, for the discussion of the social in relation to the wider interests of this book, Arendt's marking out of the boundaries between the social and asocial, the normal and abnormal is particularly helpful. The establishment of a social sphere predicated on a unitary structure clearly determines the actions and behaviours of social actors – it creates laws, codes and orders of behaviour and belonging, whilst occluding activities and actors that do not adhere to this 'one-ness'. This social formation becomes the defining agent of all that happens within the domain of everyday life. The binary separation between the social and asocial does of course inflect upon our everyday habits and social practices, determining how we act in relation to expectations around what is right and what is wrong; the socially good and the socially bad. Of course, to a certain degree this rendering of the social can produce a shared sense of belonging and community, given that we are supposedly all in the same one social order. The social is conceived as the stable backdrop or foundation upon which all social relations are formed (Latour, 2005:8).

Arendt's critique of the perceived characteristics of the social domain continues to resonate with more contemporary challenges to the purported unitary being of the social. Such critiques emanate from a range of disciplinary and intellectual contexts, but what links nearly all of these discussions is a relentless distrust of the *a priori* nature of the social. For the likes of Latour the social is not a given; it is not 'a stabilized state of affairs' (Latour, 2005:1). Rather, the unitary holism of the social as stable can only ever be a description of what already exists: as a result, it cannot account for change, for the *becoming* of the social. Change is in fact the normal condition of the social (Urry, 2004:32). And as much of the work framed around complexity theory argues, this is not a case of a simplistic reversal of the unitary conditioning of the social into a chaotic free-for-all (Law and Urry, 2004). The complexity of the social is such that it is an amorphous body of heterogeneous associations and relations that are emergent. Complexity theory stresses that the processes of how actors interact in the social realm are *emergent*: actual interactions cannot be predetermined through the individual actors themselves (Urry, 2003:25). Rather, emergent formations come together; they assemble through the ongoing *relational* encounters between different actors. Emergent properties are 'unfolding' as opposed to predetermined causal relations (Byrne, 1998:14; Connolly, 2011). The dynamism of the social is such that traditional conceptions of the social as an unwavering aggregate which lies behind everything else is fantastical. Latour's work in particular on 'associative' relations is notably useful in appreciating the transformational nature of the social, formed of emergent interactions as opposed to stabilized values, norms and laws. The ontological status of relationality demands that the 'in-formation' (Dillon, 2000:9) nature of relations is recognized. With an associative understanding of the social the notion of an orderly underpinning is abrogated. The study of the social is, then, no longer figured upon a monolithic bedrock around and on which all actions are formed. If, as Latour (2005:7) suggests, the social is formed through relations between heterogeneous actors – human and more-than-human alike – then the social is much richer, more textured and accounts for all events, subjects and objects which emerge from the interactions between actors (see Braidotti and Pisters, 2012). Such a social repertoire is limitless, made up of weird juxtapositions, conjoinings and relations between so many different and diverse entities.[1] A many-ness as opposed to a monolithic one-ness.

Following the likes of Latour, and Braidotti and Pisters, the complexity of social relations is such that a unitary identification of the social is no longer valid, if it ever was of course. In terms of what this means for Arendt's point about asocial and abnormal activities we need to take this at face value, particularly in light of how moral, ethical and juridical norms are framed. For if the social is associative, as I suggest it is, then the emergent relations between things problematize the purported ease of establishing what is social, and what is asocial; what is moral and what is amoral. To repeat myself: I do not suggest that the radically emergent relations of Latour's 'sociology of associations' (2005:9) destroys the 'central matrix of power' (Braidotti and Pisters, 2012:1), rather that the norms which supposedly underpin power relations are not stable. In fact, recognizing this leads closer to a non-binary articulation of the social where we cannot simply label something or someone as deviant or abnormal, licit or illicit. Ultimately this is about positing an appreciation of the social in all that it encompasses. Whilst these discussions around 'the social' emanate out of a range of theoretical discourses, my job here is to consider the associative in relation to the broader context of social value in relation to design, to which I now turn.

'Social design' is not social enough

Design's relationship with complexity is not new. As seen in Chapter 1 designers have long dealt with ill-defined, wicked problems that are inherently dynamic and difficult to fully comprehend in a linear fashion. More recently design scholars (Thackara, 2005) have identified shifting parameters of how new forms of design must engage complex formations that are nonlinear. Complex systems are highly diverse, aspects designers are encouraged to address in ways that are mindful of their rich ecologies. For Thackara (2005:215) such an approach can be more sensitive and caring 'to people, contexts, and networks'. Caring and complexity is also a theme addressed in contemporary discourses on the limitations of existing design practices in tackling the challenges of contemporary social, environmental and technological change (The Lancaster Care Charter, 2019). Instead, the 'care of complexity' put forward in this Charter outlines the need for sensitivity and responsiveness across a range of contexts that recognizes diversity. However, whilst such approaches seemingly value the pluriversality of complex systems, they are somewhat understandably bound by the desire to advance design that still values the socially beneficial albeit in a different guise to earlier trajectories that were one-dimensional and invariably colonial.

Just as I highlighted the need for an engagement with the social which values all that manifests it, in this section I look to consider how such complex dynamics have played out in the context of social design in particular. By this I refer to design for social innovation, healthcare, disability, ageing or death. This list of social issues that design today engages with is emblematic of the expanded milieu of design. However, it is not expansive enough. It does not consider the social in its pluriversality: the aliveness of associative relations. Social design is not *social* enough. To really get at the notion of a fundamentally social design, one that echoes the complexity of associative relations, it is necessary to look at how the more widely accepted field of 'social design' engages with the 'social'. Doing so will provide a further context through which we can consider the normative construction of the social in this field. So far, we have seen how the relational complexity of the social provides a much more nuanced appreciation of how different facets of the social coalesce, how they assemble in often strange and unplanned configurations which fall outwith of established norms, values and codes. This will then lead us to consideration of 'deviant design'.

Social design has a long genealogy, initially most commonly aligned with William Morris' socialist material-aesthetic endeavours to improve the everyday lives of people through the design of furniture, wallpapers or textiles, as well as the reformist agendas of the mid-nineteenth century onwards and the legacies of modern design. This thread of social betterment pervaded the work of designers and inventors such as R. Buckminster Fuller (Fuller, 1972) and obviously Victor Papanek. Nigel Whiteley situates social design in a wider framework to include the types of projects on medical design that Papanek advocated, but also feminist design practices and green design (Whiteley, 1993). In doing so he identifies design for society within a continuum of product design and related fields. However, more recent scholarship on social design addresses a change of scale, particularly in the context of the growing awareness of global challenges. The Montréal Design Declaration – issued at the 2017 Montréal World Design Summit – provides a powerful snapshot of the ever-expanding place of design in addressing such global challenges. In a striking opening statement the Declaration claims: 'The Montréal Design Declaration recognizes the potential of design to help better achieve global economic, social, cultural and environmental objectives' (World Design Summit, 2017:3). Such a claim chimes with much of the discussion in Chapter 1 on the increasingly powerful role design has in all aspects of social life. The Declaration continues by providing a 'call-to-arms' for the purposive potential of design and designers in alleviating global problems, notably through identifying a range of collaborative projects: from the ethics of machine learning, the impact of climate change, developing global design standards, to influencing policy at national and international levels. To achieve such aims there is recognition of how design must act and respond, including the importance of greater diversity of contexts in which it operates. Further to this it calls for stronger design advocacy with 'more effective communication of the meaning and value of design and understanding of the design process' (World Design Summit, 2017:6), as well as the need for design to be responsive to a wide range of social, cultural and physical environments. Where the Declaration is at its most enlightening is in terms of two key areas – change and responsibility:

> Design facilitates change. Design enables all aspects of society, public and private, governmental and non-governmental, civil society and individual citizen, to transition through change (i.e. austerity, demographic changes, shifts in services) to deliver a better quality of life for all citizens.
>
> (World Design Summit, 2017:6)

It continues:

> Responsible Design: recognition, by designers, of the impact resulting from their practice, whereby designers must be conscious of their enormous capacity to be constructive, as well as destructive, in the interventions they make. Designers share in the responsibility of refocusing from human consumption to the enhancement of human life.
>
> (World Design Summit, 2017:7)

Under these rubrics the remit of the Declaration is clear – design is concerned with social betterment through improved living standards, along with an ethical underpinning to this whereby the enhancement of the human condition is paramount. Although there is brief acknowledgement of design's potentially destructive potential the overarching message from the World Design Summit is the economically, culturally, environmentally and above all *socially* valuable role design has. The Declaration's underlying message is of course admirable in arguing for design's place in attempting to build better environments, systems, services, and infrastructures. What is perhaps more telling is its broadly familiar tone. Buckminster Fuller's attempts to reshape everyday social habits by reconfiguring the social infrastructure of building or automotive design speak to this very idea that design is a social activity, a practice that has the potential to change behaviour in a profound manner, but without the behaviourist implications of more recent attempts at designing behaviour change (Niederrer et al., 2018). The utopian foundations of the Modern movement are prevalent within the historical analyses of the period, and also within wider contemporary discourses such as the World Design Summit's perspective on the social role of design and its potential to affect meaningful global change.

Much to this end, John Heskett writes: 'if considered seriously and used responsibly design should be the crucial *anvil* on which the human environment, in all its detail, is shaped and constructed for the betterment and delight of all' (Heskett, 2016:19 my emphasis). Instructive points can be drawn from this. Firstly, for design to have a benefit for all it needs to be taken seriously, as opposed to being viewed as a superfluous addendum. Secondly, as with the Montréal Design Declaration, the responsibility of use opens up important debates on the ethical and moral purpose which designers must recognize. And finally, this notion of the responsible use of design's power is clear to see in the metaphor of the anvil. In its material base design can mould different forms of social processes and behaviour. In Heskett's reading it is a 'former' upon which society can be shaped. Akin to Buckminster Fuller's dreams of changing everyday habits, less utopian forms of design can also achieve this – the timer on electric toothbrushes which create new habits; or examples of design that provide improved life experiences, such as Amazon's Echo device which offers 'life-enhancing' improvements for the partially sighted through voice-operated technology (Lanchester, 2017:22).

The ability of Amazon Echo to alter everyday experience more generally is at the root of the radical potential of such new technologies (Greenfield, 2017). This is a profoundly social technology that engages with habits and rituals, the stuff of human behaviour. But as the Montréal Design Declaration states, design needs to go beyond a solely human centred approach to the social condition, embracing environmental challenges and new material infrastructures. This is the challenge for social design today. As a field of practice social design might be seen as something of a paradox, particularly in light of much that has been argued in this and the previous chapter: design is an inherently social practice. It cannot be anything else if it now pervades all that we do, so why the need for a distinct label of 'social design'? It is suggested that social design offers a distinct counter to the more established debates on the nature of design as a technically determined field producing commercially oriented products. As Chen et al. state, social design raises 'questions about the nature of "the social" as an object of design' (2016:4). However, as I argue here, given the points outlined above, the questions raised still pedal a reductive, normative reading of the social – it is not *social* enough. Before addressing this aporia it is important to consider the main debates on social design.

Armstrong et al.'s (2014) report on social design provides an overview of the current discourses and debates on the field, alongside new areas of potential practice. They suggest that social design is a nascent discursive field rather than an established field of practice: herein lies its potential. What marks social design out as distinct from traditional conceptions of design is its drive towards social ends and the public good (Cooper-Hewitt, 2013), with applications across central and local government, healthcare and international development. Crucially, it is argued that social design has the potential to engage with 'large-scale complex challenges' (Armstrong et al., 2014:7), in part due to the withering away of the state (Markussen, 2017:160).[2] Many accounts of social design make precisely this point: it has emerged from a space emptied out by neoliberalism, including the loss of the welfare state as well as various financial crises such as the 2008 crash and the attendant rise of austerity politics. To this end it is clear why social design is engaged in tackling social problems, such as wealth disparity, ill health, migration, climate change, ageing populations or crime – *almost* every area of the social. In tackling such societal challenges social design shares many conceptual and methodological characteristics with participatory design and co-design, including the empowerment of publics to potentially produce transformative outcomes which may reorganize social systems (Gutiérrez and Jurow, 2016). But such broad outlines mask some of the subtle differences in approach taken by a range of social design practitioners, notably within social entrepreneurialism. Armstrong et al. (2014:29) identify three primary areas of approach:

- Design for social innovation with an engagement in new social practices often involving policy-driven and third-sector intersections.

- Socially responsive design, seen as a less programmatic and more specialized version of the former.

- Design activism, where societal issues are addressed through activist methods and approaches.

However, where Chen et al. (2016:4) suggest that social design reframes our understanding of 'the social', this is sadly not the case. What we see is a normative underpinning of the needs of society, principally in relation to the 'public good' (Cooper-Hewitt, 2013:6). Whilst certain approaches to social design recognize the transformative impact of community-driven change (Gutiérrez and Jurow, 2016) the broader suggestion appears to be that design can make the social realm a better place. Notwithstanding the problematic relationship with the parched space of the neoliberal 'state', the key difficulty with such grand claims towards design for the public good (see Design Council, 2013) is the monolithic conception of the social, much in the same vein as Arendt critiqued in 1958. Given these concerns we need to ask who is the 'public good' for? Whilst it might be claimed that it covers the public more broadly, this is patently not the case when we consider access to service provision and other disparities such as the cost factors in the design of medical devices.

Although not directly dealing with my own concerns on the one-dimensional rendering of the social advocated by some writers on social design and the range of empirical examples noted already, there are identifiable pockets of dissension. For example, Janzer and Weinstein (2014) argue in favour of redressing the ethical basis from which social designers engage with social groups. Emanating out of a post-colonial standpoint, they write that designers must 'cultivate a thorough understanding' (Janzer and Weinstein, 2014:329) of the social contexts in which they are expected to operate under the banner of social design, including the cultural, socio-economic and political dynamics of specific geographical settings. To neglect these complex social forces has the potential to lead to a neo-colonialist approach, albeit unwittingly for many social designers. The key point being that to misjudge the complexity of the situations in which social designers are engaged inevitably leads to a top-down agenda whereby the realities of these specific contexts are misunderstood or misrepresented. Janzer and Weinstein believe that such a situation is currently in place: social designers do not deal with the complexity of the social milieu. As they suggest, the primary problem is that 'social change encompasses and affects much more than human interaction with an object' (329). Instead the social must be approached as a dynamic interplay of situated, relational forces. For if social design is supposedly engaged with society it must acknowledge the complexity of the social, including those social dynamics which fall outwith of traditional conception of positive social change.

On the surface, the one area of contemporary design practice which addresses the problematic dimensions of normative readings of design as social 'good' is that of critical design (Malpass, 2017). Known by a range of monikers, including 'critical engineering' (Oliver et al., 2011), 'critical technical practice' (Agre, 1997),[3] 'critical making' (Ratto, 2011), 'disobedient electronics' (Hertz, 2016) as well as 'adversarial design' (DiSalvo, 2012), the primary stance of critical design as a whole is to question the commercial pretexts of design across a range of sub-disciplines including industrial and product design, graphic design and HCI. Instead, it attempts to foster a stronger political dimension to the role of design and designers in society. Alongside some of the material and conceptual innovations that critical design offers, one of the most valuable aspects to emerge from it is the opportunity to reflect in more depth on how its address of the social opens up the need to look again at the social realm in relation to design – to turn our gaze back onto what critical design is critiquing and re-evaluate the social field in which design in its wider sense operates.

Taking critical design as something of a catch-all for these forms of 'design-as-critique' we can see from these examples how designers have to a certain degree reversed some of the approaches noted earlier in this chapter and applied approaches to a critique of design's complicity in capitalist formations. This is particularly marked by Carl DiSalvo's work on adversarial design: this offers one of the most cogent outlines of the debates on critically informed design. Using the work of Ernesto Laclau and Chantal Mouffe on antagonism his core thesis is that adversarial design practice is inherently 'a type of political design' (DiSalvo, 2012:2). To this end it takes on particular tactical formations that often reveal the underpinnings of the structures being critiqued – a key method within the broader context of critical theory. In this way, critical or adversarial design practices do not see themselves as the anvil that Heskett describes. Rather, these approaches imply that the anvil is not design; it is capital itself. And the role of the critical designer is to reveal this structural formation whilst also proffering alternate modes of address.

However, although the projects and discourses on critical design reveal a healthy array of approaches to politically attuned forms of socially immersed design there are a range of issues with this field in relation to the wider concerns of this book. For at the heart of critical design and its attendant practices and debates is a rather niche circle of operation, ultimately formed of predominantly academic practitioners of a particular ideological persuasion. One of the primary criticisms levelled at critical design is that it lacks the pervasiveness of everyday design: one is unlikely to find a graffiti painting robot in our daily lives in the way that other designed products pervade much that we do. Although an intentionally flippant comment it does reveal one of the structural issues with critical design: the alternative forms of design it promotes have limited social reach in that they speak to a small audience. Where my critique of more mainstream social design highlights the narrow reach of access to the tools and services offered by examples of social design, so too with critical design. Central to discussions around social complexity, the principal position of critical design is that the power structures of the neoliberal, capitalist condition need dismantled and replaced with a more robust political discourse and praxis. And whilst I too advocate this within a broader realm of politics, in the context of social complexity it is apparent that this might be seen as another form of design for betterment and the social good, albeit different in tone and persuasion than that promoted by policy bodies such as the World Design Summit.

Counter to this, where I suggest that critical design *does* offer an important tactical approach to the 'social' in the context of design is how it reveals the underlying power dynamics which are central to design. So, whilst it highlights the relations of domination I ultimately question whether the empirical projects developed under this banner achieve anything transformative. Instead we can look to critical design purely as a representational heuristic (Anderson, 2018) that can provide a meaningful vantage point from which to address the complexity of socio-political forces which constitute the social context of design, including the furtherance of neo-liberal agendas (Hardt and Hight, 2006; Holert, 2011; Milestone, 2007). Critical design can unearth some of the social tensions at the heart of social design, and in doing I suggest we need to use this in order to promote a profoundly *social* form of design – a field of discourse and praxis that speaks to the complexity of social life. As such I believe we should promote social practices which challenge the 'one-ness' of the social as a fundamental premise of design. By doing so the immanent relationship between the messiness of social complexity and design becomes evident.

Towards *asocial* design: Controversies and the origins of the deviant in design

To many people – both professionals and interested parties – the designer and architect George Nelson is perhaps best known for products such as the 'Platform Bench' from 1946, the 'Marshmallow Sofa' from 1956, the 'Cube Group' chair designed in 1960, or his gas station plans from the late 1960s. Nelson stands as an important figure in the development of American design and architecture in the mid-twentieth century. Given this, his place in discussions of deviant design and social complexity may seem a little odd. In a sense, his oeuvre is closer to the ideas of social betterment described by Heskett, coupled with the reception of his work as lifestyle products. However, alongside Nelson's work in these areas of design he also dealt with questions of complexity and change in design (Nelson, 1965; 1973), but more bizarrely, in the early 1960s a seemingly strange television show (1960) and later a magazine article transcript (1961) suggest a rather different aspect to his interests. 'How to Kill People: A Problem of Design' is a remarkable title in itself. Taken in isolation these phrases seem quite distinct: the former marked by an almost masochistic tendency; the latter an apparently innocuous, if academic, question discussed earlier in the previous chapter. Juxtapose them – as Nelson does – and the tenor of the television show and magazine article of the same name take on a very different cadence (Harwood, 2008).

The thrust of 'How to Kill People: A Problem of Design' is clear enough from the title. The question of how to kill someone is in itself about solving a particular problem, albeit one that discussions of design thinking and practice obviously shy away from. This is markedly different from the rhetoric of IDEO-promoted 'design thinking'. However, Nelson's measured tone in the CBS *Camera Three* television show and the subsequent magazine transcript – his examination of the fundamental principles of design – is not too distant from the likes of Herbert Simon or Richard Buchanan, as previously discussed. Nelson notes for instance that 'design is the process through which things acquire meaningful form' and 'a designer is a person who gives shape to manmade things', or 'designers create things for people' (Nelson, 1961:46). Such statements, although rather benign in the face of the film/articles title, resonate with established discourses.

Where the film differs from the rather denuded, abstract discussions in Chapter 1 on the nature of designing is through its focus on the development of weaponry. For Nelson the designer is central to this process through the creation of distance and added force. His example is that of a rock, and the transcript from the film offers a clear articulation of his reasoning:

> A wants to kill B. His problem is how to do it. His best chance is to bring the whole thing off as a big surprise. If B knows what's on his mind he tends to react unfavorably.
>
> [PICKING UP ROCK]
> Here is a lethal weapon. It has the great virtue of being harder than the human skull. It is also inexpensive. But it has two serious disadvantages: If A holds it in his hand, it takes him uncomfortably close to B. If he throws it he may miss.
>
> [PICKS UP STONE CLUB]
> When the designer comes into the picture there's a tremendous improvement in the product. It's more interesting to look at. A doesn't have to move quite as close. And the force of the blow is greatly increased. If A has this weapon, with B still relying on rocks, our bets, naturally, are on A. He has the better designer.
> (Nelson, 1961:47)

Embedding the rock in a wooden shaft is an act of design. It facilitates a more efficient use of the rock, providing a neat solution to A's dilemma. Although the description of the 'designer' in this scenario is evidently distinct from traditional conceptions of the expert designer previously discussed, Nelson's depiction of this simple addition of the wooden shaft resonates strikingly with Manzini's notion of diffuse design, albeit many years after the designer of the stone club. The origins of design seen here emanate out of a problem-encountering situation but the act of design itself is carried out by a non-expert. Although Nelson refers to the designer becoming involved in the process of developing the stone club he is more obviously discussing the origins of the design process itself, both the aesthetics of the club and its efficiency.

Similarly, when Nelson injects a little more detail on the social context of design he also speaks something of a truism: 'designers must have society's approval of what they are doing' (Neslon, 1961:46). This is somewhat in keeping with Heskett's point about design being used responsibly, whilst at the same time potentially highlighting the market-driven context of design in terms of consumption. The next sentence in the magazine transcript is jarring: 'Design for killing is interesting because war occupies so much of our attention, receives our unquestioning support. The great advantage for the designer in this area is that nobody cares what anything costs' (Nelson, 1961:46). Although his assertion that war receives unquestioning support may be somewhat of its time, the rest of the commentary is compelling, particularly when read alongside his earlier comment concerning societal approval for design. To this end he makes a further stark assertion regarding the designers' complicity in the military-industrial complex when he states, 'there is a silly myth that generals win wars. What the facts show is that designers do' (Nelson, 1961:47). For what Nelson's reading of design as inherently problem-encountering illustrates is that the nature of the problems themselves are diffuse and subsumed within the complexity and diversity of what constitutes the social. We see from Nelson's curio that design is imbued in all that the social field consists of – relations between power and violence; between complicity and duty; and ultimately morality and responsibility.

Although Nelson's film has been discussed in recent exhibitions such as 'Design and Violence' (Antonelli and Hunt, 2015) its dissemination and reception within the design community and further afield has been limited. As Kjetil Fallan (2015:379) notes, design history as an academic discipline has been rather circumspect in its consideration of design that does not fit particular perspectives of positive social change. For Fallan, one of the reasons for this is the overt focus on the domestic space as the site of design's emancipatory potential. Although Nelson's film and article are not mentioned in Fallan's article the broader discussion of the 'dark side of design' resonates with Nelson's thesis. The context of Fallan's research concerns the arms industry in Norway and Sweden – countries where the perception of design's role in promoting positive social and environmental change is perhaps at its greatest. However, the innovations in the design and engineering of weapons and armaments in these countries are often written out of the public discourses on design (see Fry, 1999:38–47). As with Nelson's unnerving outline of the origins of design in the creation of improvised weapons, so research such as Fallan's offers an important reminder of the entanglement of design in all echelons of society, although this is not always admitted by design scholars: 'The material culture represented by the arms industry has therefore been beyond the pale of both design reform and of design history' (Fallan, 2015:384).

What is striking about Nelson's film in particular, but equally Fallan's article, is that in relation to the military-industrial complex's power the design of weapons – be that prehistorical clubs or sophisticated military hardware and software – is not typically read as 'abnormal' or 'deviant' if compared with Arendt's outline of the normal social order. The struggle to conceptualize such acts of aggression in relation to the normal social order is perhaps one of the reasons why scholars have been reluctant to deal with this field of design. It doesn't fit within the crucible of how design is characteristically packaged in ideological terms. But crucially, this *is* a field of design – weapons or the design of restraining devices (Antonelli and Hunt, 2015), corsets, straitjackets or prisons (Lambert, 2013). These are just some of the many products, devices, technologies and systems which fall under the purview of what I term 'deviant design'. That is, the design culture described in the previous chapter is sprawling and unwieldy – it is a culture where the complexity of the social leaks out across so many different strata of society, both benevolent and malevolent, the good and the bad. Design is an inherent part of this.

Vilém Flusser agrees. Echoing Nelson's thesis, he notes: 'everything that is good for something is pure Evil' (Flusser, 1999:33). The theological underpinnings of this statement are clearly evident, for Flusser argues that the functionality of design, its prowess to enable users to carry out certain tasks inevitably leads to it being used for ill. With efficiency comes threat. As such we cannot simply delimit a separation between good and bad:

> Pure good is pointless, absurd, and, wherever there is a purpose for anything, you will find the Devil lying in wait. From the perspective of pure good, there is only a difference of degree between the elegant and user-friendly designs of a chair and of a rocket: In both cases the Devil is lying in wait.
>
> (Flusser, 1999:33)

To briefly recap: whilst social design's depiction of design for social betterment is an affirmative statement of design's function as a social bedrock, it nonetheless appears to treat the social realm in a one-dimensional capacity, principally engaged in betterment and delight. Where I differ from such definitions is in the complexity of the social milieu and the human condition itself. For as seen in the preceding discussion of social complexity, if the social is considered as an ongoing performance of different associative relations then how does this bear upon design's engagement with the social? To answer this, I believe we need to examine the imbrication of complex social relations with design, including the abnormal and the deviant. Doing so will facilitate a fuller understanding of what is meant by a fundamentally social design, or what I term *asocial* design. I argue that design produces the social, but not through the metaphor of the immutable anvil in Heskett's admittedly alluring rendering. Instead, given the associative relations of the social, design is another set of vitalist relations. Suggesting this is not to limit the power of design overall but to recognize that the social and design are emergent, and as such complex *asocial* design emerges out of heterogeneous relational encounters rather than stabilized social structures. Design is fundamentally a socially complex practice, and as such it also accounts for aspects which fall outwith of need or social betterment. This includes the heated footstool lambasted by Papanek, through to the weapons of pre-history, and illicit design as we will see in examples throughout the book.

The validity of Latour's re-examination of design is plain to see, notably in relation to the way traditional conceptions of design have struggled to deal with the complexity of social relations that design is inherently part of. In the closing comments to his design philosophy paper Latour asks why this is? The answer is relatively straightforward: design and designers are not good at dealing with instability and messy relations – they like linearity.[4] To pursue this, we can return to the discussions around wicked problems discussed in Chapter 1 by trying to fully capture the sense of 'wickedness' developed by Rittel and Webber (1973) – to *really* take them at their word and push the notion of wickedness. A good way to do so is through the addition of Latour's work on controversies and contradictions (2005). By conjoining these two areas we create a hybrid, a 'monster' that produces a greater sense of the social complexity design must be seen against (Law, 1991). We saw in Chapter 1 that wicked problems are inherently complex ones that are societal in nature (Rittel and Webber, 1973:160). These types of problems are in contrast to problems that are simple to address or tame in nature. The issue for Rittel and Webber (also see Churchman, 1967) is that designers and planners have a tendency to address wicked problems by taming them, by refusing to 'recognize the inherent wickedness of social problems' (Rittel and Webber, 1973:161). To do so becomes a moral question: what are designers doing when they reduce the complexity of a problem? When they tame a wicked problem?

A similar question is posed by Latour in both his treatise on design (2011) and his earlier work on social controversies (2005). As briefly noted in the main Introduction to the book, controversies develop when widely held ideas or structures are questioned, thus providing a space for innovation (see Venturini, 2010:262). Critically, the negative portrayal of controversies stems from the assumption that they create a lack of cohesion, of disorder. But for Latour this is far from the case, for their value is precisely concerned with different complex orders. As he puts it:

> To regain some sense of order, the best solution is to trace connections *between* the controversies themselves rather than try to decide how to settle any given controversy. The search for order, rigor, and pattern is by no means abandoned. It is simply relocated one step further into abstraction so that actors are allowed to unfold their own differing cosmos, no matter how counter-intuitive they appear.
>
> (2005:23, emphasis in original)

The tracing of controversies, letting them speak, listening to what they say rather than attempting to eradicate them is, for Latour, necessary if we are to understand how the social realm functions, and 'what allows the social to be established' (Latour, 2005:25). Working *with* controversies and contradictions one can see that the social is not a stable entity. And I suggest that just as controversies are productive, the wickedness of societal problems is the very aspect that design must embrace. Wickedness, controversies, contradictions, messiness, malevolence – these are at the very heart of what *asocial* design is about. The aim then is not to curtail the controversies. Instead I argue that we need to appreciate how the social milieu of design is formed of all the complex relations described by Latour and others. As we saw recently just such a case is evident in Nelson's positioning of the origins of design with weapons development. This is a controversy in itself but one that succinctly highlights the expansiveness of design culture today, and ultimately the overarching definition of deviant design.

For at the root of design's histories and cultures is a form of deviancy. As noted in the book's Introduction, I use this term to emphasize the way in which Nelson's origins of design as well as the more recent histories of weapons design *deviate* from the standardized readings of design's roots within socially progressive ideals. Once again, in suggesting this, I do not deny the value of such progressive desires; rather, I aim to provide a greater sense of the complexity of design's place within the social. To be sure, what is clear from Fallan's statement on the erasure of weapons design from the overwhelmingly domestic settings of much design (historical) research is that the prevailing tendency has been to search out a version of design for social betterment and moral worth. Of course, this reading of design is based on its emancipatory potential, which, in part, I suspect is driven by a desire to promote the importance of design against the historical backdrop of its artisanal and technical heritage, as we saw with Buchanan. Design was and is central to the envisioning of new – and better – social worlds. However, as Nelson's intriguing film and Flusser's theological treatment of design suggest, there are parallel histories and deviant trajectories of design which persist and must be understood.

As is well rehearsed in so many intellectual arenas, the colonialist writing-out of histories and agendas that do not fit prescribed versions of disciplinary canons is commonplace. One might think of the relationship between abstract art and Cold War propaganda (Guilbault, 1985), and within design a similar political power dynamic is evident in the propagation of specific ideologies of national identity, taste and technology advancement. This is notably the case with the promotion of design (product design, industrial design, fashion, architecture) as registers of social freedom and economic growth in the context of twentieth-century Western culture (Crowley and Pavitt, 2008). However, the overtly political dimensions of statist approaches to architecture and design mask the everyday forms of 'deviancy' that pervade the culture of design. Historically, this is perhaps most infamously seen in Vance Packard's critiques (Packard, 1960; 1961) of consumer culture in the United States and specifically the role of design in promoting consumption over all other socio-economic forms. It is tempting to read Packard's work from this period as a recognition of design's complicity within the origins of consumer capitalism, just as the place of design within Cold War geopolitics demonstrates the use of soft power through fashion for example, alongside the hard power of weapon technologies.

Conclusions

Design is always about power relationships (Milestone, 2007). This truism emerges because design is about social action and as a social practice design mirrors the social whilst simultaneously creating it. The social is messy. Design is too. It is not a stable entity that will solve social ills. It has the potential to do so, but designers (professional and diffuse) must appreciate the complexities of the social dimensions of design. We must also be aware of the malevolent underpinnings of design, be that the origins of design through the creation of simple stone weapons through to more recent manifestations of 'cruel design' which are 'purposely conceived to use […] violence in order to assert an absolute power on one or several bodies' (Lambert, 2013:7). Outwith the material practices of power the structural entanglement of design and capitalism is such that 'design routinely constructs radical inequalities. Design is even the design of neglect' (3rd Istanbul Design Biennale, 2016). We see this in how our cities, our infrastructures and our services are designed to exclude marginalized social groups. The power of design to inflict both soft and hard violence is also central to Flusser's argument that the Devil is always lying in wait. In less theological terms, the deviant is immanent to all forms of design, but this has been hidden from the common agendas of design practitioners and wider discourses on design (Dilnot, 2019:xii). This chapter does not make the case for an unethical approach, rather a realistic appreciation of the complicity of design as a fundamentally *social* practice: design that acknowledges the complexity of the social world. Design needs to come to terms with Braidotti's (2013) concept of nomadic ethics as a testing of the forces which constitute design. This is where the 'social complexities of design' must be understood in all their dimensions – for to be responsible we need to challenge certain lazy, rhetorical claims to betterment, value, responsibility and ultimately the 'good'. As this chapter and the last have suggested, instead one must be cognizant of the increasing power of design in so many areas of the social world – from nano-design to global infrastructures. In this situation the designer and all of us who engage with design (i.e. literally all of us) must fully appreciate where design is. It is immanent to all that is social. Plainly everything.

This statement is framed by the discussions in Chapter 1 on the expanded field of design. Its presence in all forms of social practice led me to argue in this chapter that design's enmeshing of the social necessitates deeper consideration of what this relationship is, particularly by appreciating the complexities of the social world. The opening section of this chapter began by positing how design has typically dealt with ideas of social benevolence and social value. Whilst mindful of the importance of changing society for the betterment of all I argued that such objectives have become normalized and we must consider the value judgements of 'good' design for instance. This then led onto similar discussion of how normative ideas of the social world have been constructed. By employing Hannah Arendt's critique of societal 'one-ness' the simplistic codification of behaviour into 'normal' and 'abnormal' is clearly apparent. However, the complexities of social relations are revealed by more recent discussions of the emergent, unstable nature of the social, notably through Latour's work and associated discourses. This theoretical backdrop provided the impetus for my critique of social design. Using ideas of emergence I argued that social design is not social enough. It is too pristine, too ordered. Not messy enough. The awkward composition of the social more generally and social design more specifically is perhaps demonstrated most provocatively through George Nelson's striking film and transcript, 'How to Kill People: A Problem of Design'. Using this I outlined the deviant origins of design and its deep-rooted involvement in the design and manufacture of weapons technology and other devices of control. To paraphrase Nelson, designers win wars (Nelson, 1961:47), a sentiment that resonates with Flusser's equally incendiary statement that the Devil is always lying in wait. It is that which frames the use of the term *asocial* design as a heuristic tool for proposing the deviancy of design.

To summarize the key argument of the chapter: the deviant is at the root of design in its engagement with the social. Whilst I do not promote a *laissez faire* attitude to this by simply advocating a socially divisive design practice, my primary concern has been to recognize the social complexities of design and as a result to consider what we can learn from ideas of deviancy and the illicit in relation to design and the social more broadly. These key ideas on deviant design are further explored in the next chapter through an examination of the wider theoretical contexts of deviancy and the illicit.

3 VALUING THE DEVIANT AND THE ILLICIT

Introduction

The idiot. Such a figure might understandably be thought of in negative terms. Someone who lacks intellectual or emotional authority; an individual devoid of the social character to act responsibly in the world. A fool, a dimwit. Isabelle Stengers sees it differently. She describes the idiot in positive terms (also see Michael, 2012). The idiot 'is turned into a conceptual character, [and] is the one who always slows the other down, who resists the consensual way in which a situation is presented and in which emergencies mobilize thought or action' (Stengers, 2005:994). Thought of in these terms the idiot is a figure who disturbs the smooth operation of the social, someone who delays action because they cannot keep up. But in waiting for the idiot we are compelled to pause, to spend longer addressing the situation to hand. This conceptual character is akin to other quasi-fictional individuals mobilized by philosophers to disturb the consensual ways of thinking about the world; most notably the French philosopher Michel Serres in his use of rats (Serres, 1982; also see Martin, 2009; 2015), harlequins (Serres, 1997) and the Greek god Hermes (Serres, 1983). Serres' characters are sometimes guides in thought; they also rupture it (Martin, 2009).

Although tempting to create my own conceptual characters – perhaps the ad hoc, informal designer, as will be discussed in Chapter 4; the smuggler in chapter 5; or the counterfeiter in Chapter 6 – I am going to resist. Instead in this chapter I want to use the broader ideas of 'deviancy' and the 'illicit' to advance some of the key debates outlined in the earlier chapters. Whilst these chapters considered the evermore complex regimes of design, here I pause slightly – in awe of the idiot – but more readily to locate the social complexity of design in broader discussions of deviancy and the illicit. For the study of both these ideas opens up new conceptual and empirical spaces where the linear, uni-dimensional conception of the social can be problematized even further. As stressed numerous times already, I am not advocating lawlessness, the dissolution of legal parameters, nor the positive aspects of *asocial* design. Quite simply I suggest that the purported binary separation between the deviant and the normal, or the licit and the illicit is too often held up as the inviolability of all 'valid' social action. Deviancy then, like the idiot, is a way to consider the complex relations between actors and actions that slip between the normative construction of the good and the bad. In addressing these allied notions, I position the origins of deviant design in relation to parallel discourses from sociology, criminology and social studies of innovation. Design studies today is equally as attuned to the social sciences as it is to the canonical foundations of the creative arts. So, by broadening the scope of study and moving slightly away from design per se, this chapter attempts to unpack what can be learnt from the study of the deviant and the illicit. Utilizing theories of deviancy the chapter develops the core argument that deviancy is an important tool for understanding the complex constitution of social action: rather than a binary separation between right and wrong, the concept of deviancy is a valuable tool for understanding the moral construction of social norms. It is a way to appreciate the intermingling of the licit and the illicit. Deviancy can be a form of productive disturbance.

The first section deals specifically with the origins of deviancy as a field of sociological study in the early twentieth century through the work of the Chicago School. It then interrogates the importance of deviancy for the study of youth subculture from the 1950s to the present day. By locating deviancy directly within subcultural studies the aim is to build discussions on the role of separation from normative cultures of social action most readily identified with mainstream society, but crucially all youth subcultures are *dependent* on the establishment as a figure of authority. Similarly, I locate deviancy as dependent on the 'normal', and vice versa. The immanent entanglement of the licit and the illicit becomes the focus of the second section where I consider the relations between the two. Juridically there are clear lines of separation but in social terms the dividing lines are often fluid. The distinctions between the two are to a certain degree a matter of context and scale, with grey areas emerging. To draw the chapter to a close the final section builds on these fluid seepages across the boundaries supposedly separating the licit and illicit. It advocates the significance of illicit action in creating innovation through instances of 'illicit innovation'; ultimately making the case that the destructive implications of the illegal can be innovative, including discussion of malevolent creativity (Kaufman and Runco, 2010).

Defining deviancy

What links an elaborately modified Vespa scooter with the addition of numerous extra mirrors; a pair of extra wide, cut-off jeans; or the use of body piercings? They are all material expressions of youth; ways in which youth subcultures display their membership of tribal groups. They are also internalized logics of action often only communicable to members of these groups. To many of us they are perhaps slightly absurdist; markers of a period of maturation that will soon be discarded as these individuals enter the norms of adult life. But above all, what links such examples is that they are taken as signifiers of *deviant* behaviour, a way of acting in the world that stands in violation of what society holds to be normal. These are visual and material manifestations of activities and behaviours purportedly 'abnormal'. This final reading is at the heart of how agglomerations of young people coalescing together under shared forms of taste and expression of identity have been positioned as somehow at odds to what we supposedly hold to be correct ways of behaving. They are 'visible reminders of what we should *not* be' (Cohen, 2011:2, my emphasis). With youth subcultural groups such as Mods, Rockers, Hells Angels, Punks or Soccer Casuals a significant element of their subversive repertoire stems from their visual opposition to mainstream society, whereas for non-subcultural forms of deviancy such as criminal activity there is a desire to remain hidden (Downes and Rock, 2011:23–8). Here then is a core theme of this chapter: how deviancy is positioned; how it is read.

Although the definition of deviancy is incredibly slippery and difficult to pin down – in part due to the competing ways in which criminologists and sociologists have positioned it – a useful starting point is this: 'deviance should be considered as banned or controlled behaviour which is likely to attract punishment or disapproval' (Downes and Rock, 2011:23). Likewise, according to Howard Becker we might think of deviancy in statistical terms as that which 'varies too widely from the average' (1991:4), a simple case of something that falls outwith of the most common; that deviates from the norm. However, whilst these offer initial vantage points they do not adequately account for the 'moral panics' which so often accompany the fear of deviant or delinquent behaviour (Cohen, 2011; Young, 2009). When we revisit some of the histories and genealogies of deviancy and delinquency, particularly those associated with subcultures, the inference is that of a group of people whose behaviour deviates from the codes and rules established by the dominant classes. The study of youth subcultures as deviant has its origins in the work of a group of sociologists at the University of Chicago in the 1920s and 1930s where they developed one of the first coherent, methodical attempts to study criminal activity (Barmaki, 2016; Downes and Rock, 2011:49–73). Although the role of a distinctly subcultural approach to the study of deviancy at Chicago is contested (Blackman, 2014) those working there developed a reading of deviancy in relation to 'codes of conduct' and specifically how deviancy is positioned as deviation from 'the dominant code or the generally prevailing definition in a given culture' (Wirth, 1931:485–6, cited in Barmaki, 2016:798). Immediately, even in these early definitions of deviancy, we see it posited as behaviour which falls outwith the principal values of the dominant echelons of society. This definition has been a commonplace for the study of disenfranchised youth as somehow resistant to dominant value systems, delinquent, dysfunctional in that they do not act according to functionalist measures and ultimately subnormal. The label 'subnormal' is particularly telling for it clearly alludes to the medicalization of behaviour – it is in some way pathological. And as Blackman (2014:498) writes, this approach to deviancy had close ties with the eugenics movement in the United Kingdom in the 1920s. The Chicago School sought an alternative to this by attempting to understand deviancy and delinquency as a result of social context, and it is this legacy which has pervaded the subsequent study of deviancy, particularly within criminology and sociology. That said, there are a range of competing approaches on how deviancy is positioned. For example, 'functionalism' claims that to a certain extent deviancy underpins social order: that is, it provides stability by dint of it being taken as society's Other (Downes and Rock, 2011:3). At the furthest end of the spectrum 'radical criminology' views deviancy as a form of liberation and conformity as collusion with dominant ideologies and worldviews (Downes and Rock, 2011:3). This paradigm is perhaps most closely aligned with subcultural studies and the work of Centre for Contemporary Cultural Studies at the University of Birmingham in the UK (Hebdige, 1979). Counter to this is the work which falls under 'control theory': this speaks to the opposite position of radical criminology where conformity and security are viewed as socially beneficial (Downes and Rock, 2011:3). Although these differing viewpoints may suggest a contested discursive field, this is somewhat inevitable given that the object of study – deviancy – is itself riven with ambiguity, uncertainty and disorder.

For the purposes of this book, the criminological study of deviancy offers a productive meshwork through which to consider how the 'deviant' is manifested in the social realm. The deviant creates new forms of knowledge and practices both within the broader cultures of design and elsewhere. So, in this regard my own positioning of deviancy is perhaps closest to radical criminology where its liberatory potential is part of the complexity of social space. Alongside these radical criminological approaches to deviancy Howard Becker's (1991) work on the 'outsider' offers a particularly fruitful reading. Although the wider idea of 'labelling theory' associated with his work has been contested[1] the value of Becker's writings on deviancy still stands (Grattet, 2011). It also resonates most obviously with the approach I take to the broader rendering of deviancy in this book. In his 1963 book *Outsiders: Studies in the Sociology of Deviance* Becker (1991) dealt with deviancy as a social construction rather than an innate failure or weakness in those labelled as deviant. He suggested that deviance is ascribed to certain individuals and not others. Critical to the designation of deviance is how the rules which define deviancy are created by social groups. Such rules or social codes determine 'correct' or 'incorrect' forms of behaviour. In Becker's reading those who are deviant are the ones who fall outside such rules and do not conform to the enforcement of these codes. The approach taken by Becker and other writers in the 1960s and 1970s falling under 'labelling theory' or a 'societal reaction' perspective (Grattet, 2011) is that the label of deviancy depends on perspective: the outsider may not accept the imposition of these social codes and rules. It may not be in accordance with how they view social behaviour, including their own. This understanding of deviancy leads Becker to offer a particular definition of the outsider: 'the rule breaker may feel his judges are *outsiders*' (1991:2, emphasis in original). So rather than simply assuming that the outsider lies at odds to the social codes of mainstream society the idea of the outsider has a double reading where the imposer of rules is outside the codes and behaviours of the purportedly deviant group. Likewise, the problem with how deviancy is positioned in common-sense parlance is that there is something inherently deviant in actions that somehow break or perceive to break social codes (Becker, 1991:3). In this guise deviancy is taken as a given, an a priori social fact, rather than understood as a constructed and imposed label.

For Becker and others (Cohen, 2011) the traditional sociological models of deviance have a tendency to 'discriminate between those features of society which promote stability (and thus are "functional") and those which disrupt stability (and thus are "dysfunctional")' (Becker, 1991:7). With the functionalist model the definition of stability itself is again dependent on the nature of how this is agreed upon. The more relativist sociological view sees 'deviance as the failure to obey group rules', or as Becker goes on to develop, it could also be 'deviance as the infraction of some agreed-upon rules' (Becker, 1991:8). The addition of the two caveats 'some' and 'agreed-upon' allows for a degree of ambiguity in considering who created the rules and where they come from. But still, we need to understand that deviancy is a social setting created by certain social groups and not others, invariably those who hold power and authority. When viewed in light of domination and power how certain social groups become labelled is more important than attempting to identify particular characteristics: 'deviance [is] the product of a transaction that takes place between some social group and one who is viewed by that group as a rule-breaker' (Becker, 1991:10). Understood in these terms a key distinction becomes evident. The reactions and responses to the deviant act and the outsider are dependent on conditional factors that determine how or whether particular social codes are enforced. For Becker these are conditioned by time; class; race; and gender (1991:12–13). Under the temporal conditioning of social rules the time at which these are enforced can change the level of enforcement. One might think of a particular leniency towards the possession of lower classes of drugs at certain times, as well as changes in values according to particular historical periods, a point developed much more fully in Chapter 5. In terms of class, studies of delinquency cited by Becker (1991:13 n9) point to the imbalance between the convictions of middle-class and working-class boys, the latter inevitably much more likely to be convicted due to the actions of the legislative class. Unsurprisingly, these imbalances are replicated amongst black and minority ethnic communities where social rules and the labelling of deviant are more fully imposed. In the case of gender Becker notes how unmarried mothers were more likely in this period in the 1960s to be punished than fathers (1991:13). The relative approach to the labelling of deviancy and the outsider is particularly clear when the issue of who creates the rules is discussed – as Becker notes, the creation of rules is 'highly differentiated along social class lines, ethnic lines, occupational lines and cultural lines' (1991:15).

The socially inscribed nature of rules is such that the label of deviancy must be understood in relation to particular situations and conditions. Above all, 'deviance is not a quality that lies in behaviour itself, but in the *interaction* between the person who commits an act and those who respond to it' (Becker, 1991:14, my emphasis). As with the earlier outline of how emergent relations create a multiplicitous social realm, the interactional nature of deviance means that it is dependent on the specificities of individual situations and the encounters between those involved. It is about context. It is about scale. For example, where Becker writes that rules are often formed by powerful elites, it is also the case that rules are made by outsiders themselves. One might think of the rule-bound aspects of subcultural groups where often strict rules exist determining particular types of action, argot, behaviour or sartorial codes and thus membership (Hebdige, 1979). Equally, the interactional quality of deviance also raises questions around the scale of deviance (Downes and Rock, 2011:4). This is particularly interesting in relation to the impact of new technologies on social action. For example, recent research (Taylor, 2016) examines how the proliferation of self-checkouts in supermarkets has led to the development of new types of retail theft, but crucially by consumers not typically described as deviant. Shoppers will select a cheaper item from the onscreen menu when in fact they are putting expensive items into their shopping bags. Such actions break social rules but there is a question concerning scale: do these small-scale acts constitute deviancy in the way described above? Indeed, the tactical creativity of these consumers is akin to the methods employed under the guise of workplace ruses where, for example, the under-charging of customers is appreciable in light of the harsh working conditions and poor pay associated with shop work (see Henry and Mars, 1978; Mars, 1983). To a certain extent this is a question of perspective:

> Most important for the study of behavior ordinarily labelled deviant, the perspectives of the people who engage in the behavior are likely to be quite different from those of the people who condemn it. In this latter situation, a person may feel that he is being judged according to rules he has had no hand in making and does not accept, rules forced on him by outsiders.
>
> (Becker, 1991:16)

Although there is a relativist element to rulemaking there is of course a hegemonic jurisdiction over how punishment of rule-breaking is enforced, even if the outsider disagrees with the law and the rules themselves. That said, what Becker's work in particular – and the attendant discourses around labelling theory – highlight is the malleability of how deviancy as a concept and as a set of behavioural practices is understood. For the interactional qualities of deviancy established here show that deviancy is determined by complex sets of relations that often determine the scale of deviancy, as shown recently by Taylor (2016) and through Mars' (1983) research on workplace crime. To be sure, positionality is a fundamental aspect of how we understand the imbrication of the legal and the illegal, the licit and the illicit – to which I now turn.

Enmeshing the licit and the illicit

There is a 'specter haunting globalization': this rather dramatic statement opens discussion of the illicit by Abraham and van Schendel (2005:2). They go on to add that this spectre is the

> international organized crime networks, coterminous with underworld mafias, snakeheads, coyotes, traffickers, and other transnational jetsam. Groups and individuals trafficking in illicit objects and substances [...] have, we are told, taken advantage of the unprecedented ease of communication and movement offered by the new social and technical infrastructures that grid the world today to create an alternative, only partly visible, global system that exists in parallel to legitimate international transactions of corporations, individuals, and states.
> (2005:2)

Much in the same way that Castells (2010) describes the aporias and opportunities created by the Information Society here we have a concise snapshot of the complex enmeshing of the licit and the illicit at the global level (see Sassen, 1998). Organized criminal groups utilize the same means of communication as legitimate social groups; they reach across territorial borders, operating at local, national and transnational scales; they often harness the same socio-material infrastructures of global air networks and shipping routes. These activities run parallel as they note, but they are also often one and the same. The notion of a 'parallel system' implies that even though licit businesses and organizations employ the same infrastructure they are doing so in a markedly different way and for vastly different ends. But as Abraham and van Schendel argue the binary separation between the licit and the illicit is not as clear-cut as state and corporate apparatuses argue (also see Gregson and Crang, 2017:207; Nordstrom 2011). As with the previous discussion of Becker's work on labelling a similar process is evident with the construction of the illicit:

> Many transnational movements of people, commodities, and ideas are illegal because they defy the norms and rules of formal political authority, but they are quite acceptable, 'licit', in the eyes of participants in these transactions and flows.
> (Abraham and van Schendel, 2005:4)

Indeed, the very idea of a concrete separation between the licit and the illicit is impossible to verify for it is built upon a constructed notion of legitimacy that stems from the perspective of the state and colonialist legacies such as the slave trade (Winant, 2014).

As with deviancy, the allied notion of the 'illicit' conjures images of illegal activities such as those described above. To a certain extent the mediated public outcry which surrounds the illegality of organized crime is understandable – for example, the ravage of people smuggling on vulnerable individuals is an almost ever-present feature of contemporary news feeds. To see the plight of boatloads of refugees paying for passage to safer territories one understandably views the practices of people trafficking groups as highly illegal. However, an objective positioning of the illicit in this case is not as clear-cut as one might assume. The illicit is understood as the exploitation of systems, infrastructures and in the case of refugee crises of vulnerable people. But with this example the imbrication of the illicit with the licit is evident: the smuggling of refugees is created by the conditions within the nation-states they are fleeing – conditions which are often the result of civil unrest in the case of Syria, for example. In such circumstances the precise separation of the illicit and the licit is not always evident. But the construction of clear binaries demarcating the pristine positivity of capitalism in contrast to the murky world of organized criminal enterprise is central to the image of the global present. A present marked by the supposed sanctity of global trade. This is a falsehood. For one of the key arguments concerning the development of globalization in the 1970s and beyond has been the entanglement of licit flows of goods and peoples with the illicit. Hudson states that 'there is a chronic interweaving of economic activities and regulatory processes that routinely cross the binary divides of (il)legal and (il)licit' (2019:23). Businesses and organizations deemed licit do operate in a clandestine manner where illicit entrepreneurial practices are clearly in evidence. Further to this, Gargi Bhattacharyya notes how organized crime 'has a necessarily symbiotic relationship with the formal economy and makes its profits from providing an alternative route through the interstices of "legitimate" transnational business' (Bhattacharyya, 2005:63). The scare quotes around legitimate offer a particularly resonant provocation concerning what we mean by the legitimacy of businesses and corporate entities. In the context of global commodity mobilities we see a range of examples where the massive flows of shipping containers circulating the globe have led to illicit business practices which are subsumed under the supposedly legitimate enterprise of logistics and supply chain management, notably with the under-invoicing and misrepresentation of goods shipped in containers (Martin, 2016b). In such cases the declarations identifying the goods being distributed do not adequately state the full quantity, or they identify particular commodities being shipped whereas more valuable ones in fact are (not dissimilar to the example of self-checkouts noted earlier). One of the most highly charged areas where the legitimacy of state-based trade is questionable is that of weapons sales. A report published in March 2018 by the Stockholm International Peace Research Institute (Wezeman et al., 2018) highlighted the steady increase in the sales of major weapons since 2003 including fighter jets and tanks. This includes sales of these items by the United States to Saudi Arabia where the escalation in military engagement in Yemen has claimed many civilian lives whilst causing a refugee crisis (Kamali Dehghan, 2018). In such cases the construction of distinct divisions between the licit and the illicit becomes increasingly problematic given the devastation inflicted by supposedly legitimate commercial practices.

This is not just a contemporary phenomenon. The very history and development of capitalist trade is premised on innovation and an entrepreneurial spirit where new markets are discovered through territorial conquest and the seizure of natural resources and labour.

At the heart of the historical framing of commercial activity imbued with illicit qualities is the creation of profit at the expense of others. For the very notion of capitalism is premised on the defeat of competitors. This can include the creation of market dynamics that lead to illegal activity such as the 'criminogenic market structures' of the US automobile industry in the 1970s (Farberman, 1975).[2] Compared with the activities of transnational criminal actors such as money launderers and people traffickers such forms of illicitness may not seem as morally repugnant, but this is once more clearly premised on the normative assumptions surrounding the actions of recognized transnational corporations.

What are the key arguments to take from these historical and contemporary discussions of the enmeshing of illicit and licit trade in particular? It is clear that the language of the illicit and licit, the legal and the illegal is highly emotive as is any discussion of behaviours and practices which seemingly defy social norms, Arendt's description of 'oneness'. However, what, in fact, emerges from these discourses is that the creation of binary splits between the two is far from an a priori given. Political, economic, legal, social, cultural and moral values change over time and are dependent on the situational power configurations of specific periods. Ultimately the shifting parameters of how the licit and illicit enmesh are such that we need to break the simplistic binary separation between the two, potentially by employing a term such as the '(il)licit' (Abraham and van Schendel, 2005:19), but equally by acknowledging that any discussion of the illicit and the licit must be determined by an in-depth examination of how the empirical examples are situated. The historical lens demands we appreciate the entanglement of nascent mercantile cultures with the illicit practices of 'lawlessness', and likewise how the entrepreneurialism and associated innovations of early capitalism were in part created by the actions that today would be labelled illicit. To that end I now turn to the central premise of this chapter: how innovation and relatedly entrepreneurialism are entwined with the illicit; indeed, how illicit activities have the potential to create innovation, a theme that permeates the rest of the book as well.

Towards illicit innovation

When considering the term 'innovation' the immediate associations that emerge most readily are economic. This is understandable given the plethora of references to innovation management, innovation and entrepreneurship, business strategy and innovation, creativity and innovation or leadership and innovation. Even more so given these combinations are culled from postgraduate degree courses in business schools from across north America and Europe. Under this guise innovation is seen as the engine of economic advancement, growth and competitive success. For Drucker:

> Innovation is the specific function of entrepreneurship, whether in an existing business, a public service institution, or a new venture started by a lone individual in the family kitchen. It is the means by which the entrepreneur either creates new wealth-producing resources or endows existing resources with enhanced potential for creating wealth.
>
> (Drucker, 1985:67)

The commercial context of innovation is patently clear and is also premised on the seeking out of new opportunities for market exploitation (Drucker, 1985:72; Salter and Alexy, 2014:29). A further context for innovation is the 'technological', where innovation is the creation of new technologies and market applications (Marx, 2010:565). Indeed, it is difficult to disentangle the economic and technological basis of the term for it is seen as an economic tradition dealing with technological change: 'innovation [is] technological invention used [...] in the industrial production process' (Godin, 2012:398; also see Drucker, 2015:4–5). Linking both the economic and technological bases of innovation are some key criteria, but especially *change*. Opportunities exist within companies where there are 'unexpected occurrences; incongruities; process needs; industry and market changes', and outwith of company contexts with 'demographic changes; changes in perception; new knowledge' (Drucker, 1985:68). Commercial innovation is marked by the exploitation of opportunities created by these different forms of change, be they technological through the creation of new scientific knowledge, unexpected market dynamics, or new ways of envisioning social dynamics. Critically, though, change in the context of business-led innovation is about controlling the disorderliness of change. Change itself is dynamical; unstable; a form of becoming. But this is distinct from how the typical entrepreneur handles change – they do so by exploiting and above all coordinating the dynamical nature of change for commercial gain. It is the exploitation of change as a positive economic opportunity.

Change, then, is central to the study of innovation. And the term itself has gone through a number of changes since its inception in Ancient Greece through to its current usage. The work of Benoît Godin offers one of the most in-depth examinations of innovation from a range of perspectives, including its conceptual history and crucially for this book its radical heritage (Godin, 2015). His work highlights how contemporary, popular notions of innovation simplify the fraught history of the term in relation to its potential. Whilst it is impossible to do justice to the scope of his research on innovation, his genealogy charts the changes in how the term was understood. One of the common threads linking its emergence in Ancient Greece to its usage today is how the idea of change has been viewed. Prior to the twentieth century 'innovation was a vice, something explicitly forbidden by law and used as a linguistic weapon by the opponents of change' (Godin, 2015:5). Similarly, the economic and technological associations today differ from its origins in Ancient Greece as a political terminology concerned with change in the ruling order. As such its intellectual heritage bears relations with ideas of subversion, transgression and revolution – all registers of change in different ways and terms which clearly reflect the idea of 'outlaw innovation' (Flowers, 2008). In fact, the root of word itself can be traced back to its Greek origins as 'Kainotomia', from the 'Kainos' for new, and 'Tom' for cut or cutting. As in a 'new cutting' or 'making new' (Godin, 2015:8). In similar terms the word 'novation' from the thirteenth-century concerns the legal process of 'redrafting a contract to renew a debtor's obligations' (Mavhunga, 2017:8). In both cases the sense of something already in existence being changed, or an entirely new outcome being created relates to the instigation of something new. Godin goes on to write that the term had relatively few occurrences in ancient texts other than its early Greek usage, but there is also similar usage in fourth-century Latin where the word 'in-novo' meant 'renewing' (2015:8–9).

Decisively, depending on the specific context of use the term itself had both negative and positive connotations. The 'novator' associated with the redrafting of legal contrasts was seen in negative ways (Godin, 2008:24). At the time of the Reformation the valence of the word was also primarily negative, associated with the faddishness of novelty. In the context of the seventeenth and eighteenth centuries the negative cast of innovation was applied to the political transformations of republicans, where the challenge to the orthodoxy of the monarchy was read unfavourably. It was also wedded to the social, specifically in relation to William Sargent's use of the term in his 'Social Innovations and Their Scheme' from 1858, which Godin notes proclaimed 'to overthrow the social order, namely private property' (Godin, 2015:13). How different to today. It is in the nineteenth century when innovation shifts gradually from overtly negative connotations to more positive ones. In part this is due to the realization that the interpretation of the term itself is neutral. There can be good as well as bad innovation or change, depending on whose purpose change serves. It is also concerned with the envisioning of change as 'political, social and material *progress*' (Godin, 2015:14, emphasis in original). Only in the twentieth century does innovation become fully understood as a positive engine of change. As with the development of management science in the post–Second World War period the primary focus of innovation moves from political upheaval to the economy, with '*technological* innovation [...] as commercialized innovation. Technological innovation serves economic *growth*' (Godin, 2015:16, emphasis in original). We move then from a position of change as political or social turmoil to innovation as socio-economic cure-all. At this juncture innovation becomes synonymous with entrepreneurialism and creativity, the latter in particular a catch-all for novelty and invention (Drucker, 2015:229; Godin, 2015:20). At this stage it is worth quoting at length from Godin for he provides a valuable summary of the shift in thinking towards innovation:

- Innovation is no longer seen as subversive to the social order, but simply opposed to traditional ways of doing things.

- The innovator is not a heretic. He is simply different from the masses or from his fellows. He may be deviant, but in a sociological sense: an original, a marginal, a nonconformist, unorthodox.

- The innovator is ingenious and creative. He is an experimenter, an entrepreneur, a leader, he is the agent of change. (Godin, 2015:21)

The key difference then between the origins of innovation and its contemporary usage is how change is regarded: no longer as politically revolutionary but as planned or orderly, *managed* change (Drucker, 1985). Of course, it is fortuitous that Godin also describes the innovator as 'deviant', for he highlights something absolutely critical: innovation as a concept is not simply associated with economic management and technological change. It is imbued with a radical capability for disruption (see Söderberg, 2017:121). Before addressing this in more detail with regard to malevolent creativity and illicit innovation, the potential of creative destruction and disruption through Joseph Schumpeter's work will be briefly considered.

Where the economic and technological aspects of innovation feature in the vast majority of contemporary literature, the economist Schumpeter is perhaps one of the most cited authors. Although many mistakenly suggest Schumpeter was the instigator of innovation as a disciplinary field, he nonetheless is central to its development, particularly through his study of the entrepreneur (Drucker, 2015:15–16), but equally for his now-infamous phrase: 'the gale of creative destruction' (Schumpeter, 2003 [1943]:84). Schumpeter's core argument in his 1942 book *Capitalism, Socialism and Democracy* was that capitalism develops through the incessant development of new products, ideas and services – 'creative destruction' brings these new approaches to the market but it also destroys the old and those that fail to innovate. For Schumpeter,

The fundamental impulse that sets and keeps the capitalist engine in motion comes from the new consumers' goods, the new methods of production and transportation, the new markets, the new forms of industrial organization that capitalist enterprise creates.

(2003:82–3)

In the realm of production this is evident from the move from craft production to the mechanized production line for example (Hounshell, 1984). However, the destructive nature of creative destruction needs to be read alongside one of

Schumpeter's earlier ideas, where he developed the notion of 'new combinations': production processes and practices do not emerge from nowhere, from a *tabula rasa*. They are combinations of pre-existing elements organized in novel ways (something I turn to in Chapter 4 on ad hoc design) (Salter and Alexy, 2014:30). As with the earlier discussion of the legal redrafting of statutes, destruction is in part the mutation of previous practices. The old is destroyed and reconfigured as the new is created through combination. Critical to the importance of Schumpeter's work in this area is the value of disruption. We can see this today with the creative destruction or disruptive innovation (Christensen et al., 2015) of new technologies and forms of wealth production such as digital currencies and blockchain technology (Zuberi and Levin, 2016). But ultimately, the value of Schumpeter's work on creative disruption lies with the notion of *disequilibrium*. Drucker, reflecting on his legacy, states that 'he [Schumpeter] postulated that dynamic disequilibrium brought on by the innovating entrepreneur, rather than equilibrium and optimization, is the "norm" of a healthy economy and the central reality for economic theory and economic practice' (Drucker, 2015:32).

Disequilibrium, incongruities, the gale of creative destruction, the entrepreneur as the figure who 'upsets and disorganizes' (Drucker, 2015:31). Taken at face value, it would be understandable if one read such ideas as a form of social turmoil. But as Godin's account suggests, one of the significant shifts in the development of innovation is how it is now figured as positive. It is also concerned with how these forms of instability are handled: they are channelled into productive forms of governance. This is far from the wholesale plunge into the processuality of becoming (Serres, 1995). The destructive storm of change is contained; it is ordered whilst it simultaneously rips out the old, mutating it into the new. Read in this light the radical potentiality of creative destruction is smoothed out, the incongruities tamed much in the way we saw earlier how the wickedness of social problems are often tamed. However, for all the problems with the tenor of how innovation-as-change has been operationalized under the logic of capital, there are still some ripe aspects to mine. In particular taking Godin's outline of the innovator as deviant, unorthodox and marginal, the radical origins point to some unexplored areas of potential. Developing Schumpeter's work on creative destruction, one particularly fruitful approach is to consider the broader notion of 'creativity' itself. This is an aspect that has remained underdeveloped in studies of his work, for as I now ask: how can we consider the truly disruptive and destructive nature of creativity?

Whilst creativity of course relates directly to the histories of design as an 'industrial art' (Read, 1966) addressing this specifically in terms of the creative act itself, a body of work falling under banner of 'malevolent creativity' (Cropley et al., 2010) offers a fascinating backdrop to the conflation of the deviant and the normal; the licit and illicit. As with the discussions on the imbrication of the two, the notion of malevolent creativity problematizes the lazy assumptions concerning the sanctity of creativity and the 'creative act'. By and large when one considers creativity it comes with a normative message of positivity, for the betterment of the individual and society, in part through the creation of new paradigms and ways of looking at and envisioning the world. Individuated aesthetic creativity is perhaps the most clear-cut in terms of common understandings of creativity as the pursuit of representational and material novelty, invention, innovation and ingenuity. Tied up in this definition is an almost *transcendent* understanding of individuated moral value: those of the human spirit, individual good, moral consideration and solace. A common thread running through these notions of creativity is that of human well-being through aesthetic expression. Indeed, 'discussions along these lines have not infrequently argued that creativity is a principle of nature and that it is, by definition, a universal beneficial force fostering growth and rebuilding in all organic systems' (Cropley, A.J., 2010:2). In many situations creativity is indeed formative in building new systems, practices and ways of being. However, where this becomes even more essentialized is when creativity is promoted beyond the individual and fostered as part of the 'creative economy' (see Mould, 2018). Akin to the co-option of the radical genealogy of innovation, here creativity is determined by the wider socio-economic realm, often in parallel to the rhetoric of design thinking and the 'creative industries', promoting material prosperity, economic growth and strategic prowess as drivers of commercial value through innovation in organizations and socio-technical systems. Like individual creative endeavour, corporatized creativity is also marked by a sense of betterment and well-being in the form of socio-economic advantage. Both are invariably taken as positive. Although there are clearly different contexts in which these two guises of creativity operate there are also commonalities, notably: ideas of 'well-being' in moral, social and economic terms; innovation in aesthetic, material, technological and organizational advancement; envisioning of novelty through formal invention; and individual and collective ingenuity.

Although these various aspects of creativity continue to pervade both common understandings of and academic discourses on creativity, work on 'dark' or 'malevolent' creativity questions such normative assumptions (Cropley, A.J., 2010; Cropley, D.H., 2010; Cropley et al., 2010; McLaren, 1993). As with illicit business practices the economic positioning of creativity with competitive advantage demonstrated through its use in commercial enterprises is similarly 'available to people and organizations with less benevolent motives' (Cropley, D.H., 2010:340). Within these discussions the work of Robert B. McLaren (1993) is seminal in articulating the bond between creativity and malevolent intent. He famously stated: 'In our intoxication with the idea of divine principles, inspiration, and aesthetic characteristics, we tend to ignore the fact that much of human creative effort has been at the service of violent and devious strategems' (McLaren, 1993:137). Similar to previous discussions on the origins of deviant design, where the creative ingenuity of socio-technical innovation has its valuable applications it also has malevolent potential, notably with the example of nuclear energy in McLaren's thesis. Central to this is that the traits of creativity discussed already – material, technological and organizational innovation; the envisioning of novelty through formal invention; and ingenuity – are in some sense applied in contexts that are ill at ease with traditional conceptions of the moral good (or as I develop in the next chapter, they are *misused*). Read in these terms the way in which both creativity and innovation are understood can be rethought, recognizing the 'radical openness of creativity' (De Cock et al., 2013:152). In this context creativity's radical openness is figured on the basis that it is a space of becoming rather than bounded. Much in the way we previously saw how the social is an assemblage of emergent relations, creativity's malevolence is immanent to creativity itself just as deviancy is integral to the non-deviant. However, where much of the discussion in the literature on dark or malevolent creativity addresses it via its counter of being socially purposeful there is a tendency to continue to view the malevolent as wholly negative: by understanding malevolent creativity, it can be marshalled into more benevolent ends. My interest instead lies in understanding the similarities between purportedly good and bad creativity, arguing that innovation can emerge from illicit endeavours and as a result are practices worthy of interrogation.

As noted earlier, according to Peter Drucker one of the foundations of entrepreneurial innovation is seeking out new opportunities and new markets (1985:72). He was clearly referring to perceivably legitimate forms of competitive endeavour. However, as this chapter has set out, the boundaries between legitimate and illegitimate forms of enterprise are rather porous, leaky and fluid. Taking the literature on commercial innovation and entrepreneurialism at its word the seeking out of new opportunities is by no means the remit of licit business practices alone, for as we also saw earlier with Abraham and van Schendel's arguments on the (il)licit, it is in part a question of perception (also see Linstead et al., 2014:168). New market opportunities can just as readily refer to illicit enterprises such as people smuggling or money laundering as it can to licit technological advancement and application. As I argue in this final section, innovation and entrepreneurialism are formed by both licit and illicit enterprise and activities. Although I do not claim a complete mapping of one onto the other, the practices of illicit actors demonstrate clear cases of innovation and entrepreneurialism, much of which will be fleshed out in later chapters. Critically for our broader discussions here, 'illegal entrepreneurs exhibit characteristics, such as strategic awareness, opportunity spotting and networking, shared by licit entrepreneurs' (Smith and McElwee, 2013:48). The creation of new markets and opportunities be they licit or illicit call on similar approaches to entrepreneurialism. Dean et al. (2010:7) provide a useful summary of the key characteristics of illicit entrepreneurial activity in the context of organized crime in particular. Firstly, they suggest that criminal entrepreneurs recognize an opportunity for market exploitation, which does not fundamentally differ from the licit identification of gaps in a market. Secondly, once the commercial opportunity has been identified resources need to be mobilized, that is, money must be raised to facilitate the new venture. The key difference between licit and illicit entrepreneurial activity is how the resources are raised. In the case of licit enterprise, this is through start-up capital (Dean et al., 2010:10), whereas as for illicit entrepreneurs, capital is typically drawn from other criminal activities. What does link both practices is the importance of entrepreneurial creativity, where new resources can be sought. The third area of entrepreneurial activity is that of 'decision-making under uncertainty' where the volatility of the conditions for creating new markets is incredibly dynamic, even more so for illicit enterprise. An important fourth facet of both the licit and illicit is that of 'people cooperation': the creation of an assembly of partners who can facilitate the commercial illicit venture, be they lawyers, bankers, technical experts or government employees, is required. The fundamental difference here is how these individuals are engaged in the illicit enterprise, which as Dean et al. (2010:13) note is often through 'bribery and corruption, combined with violence'. Finally, is the issue of 'profit maximization'. As with legitimate business this is something of a given in terms of the intentions behind commercial enterprise culture, but where licit commerce has time to build market share and profit, criminal entrepreneurs are under 'time pressure' (Dean et al., 2010:14). They need to maximize profit much sooner, partly in order to thwart potential discovery of the criminal enterprise itself. Overall, these five aspects of illicit entrepreneurialism provide an important picture of the similarities with licit enterprise, albeit with significant differences in how these are approached. There are valuable insights from the study of criminal activities for how we understand enterprise culture and organizations more generally (Parker et al., 2014).

To build on these discussions, we also need to be mindful of the entanglement between entrepreneurialism and innovation, but also the differences. As seen above, one of the key determinants of innovation is that of *change*, which I suggest is at the heart of why the illicit and the deviant are useful tools for understanding social complexity. The illicit and the deviant initiate change – *they create new ways of looking at things, systems and processes*. Both are concerned with instability, a form of flux that does not adhere to the codes of behaviour imposed by authorial power. By creating change they simultaneously demand that we consider what type of change is desired. For it is easy to assume that the idea of change advocated by business entrepreneurs is positive: however, as the earlier section on the entanglement of the licit and illicit illustrates it is not always quite so clear-cut as one may assume. The changes instigated by illicit activities, be they through organized crime or small-scale individuated criminal practices, offer a different perspective on what we mean by *change*. It questions the rhetoric of change as positive in much the same way as recent work in political ecologies on degrowth challenges the assumptions around the value of economic growth above all else (Buch-Hansen, 2018). If innovation is fundamentally about change, then illicit innovation invites us to consider what change really is. As such illicit innovation harks back to the originary ideas of innovation as rupture, transgression and subversion. It points to the creative destruction of Schumpeter, but in keeping with the radical openness of creativity identified by De Cock et al. (2013:152). Equally, illicit innovation is concerned with the emergent relations of Schumpeter's 'new combinations'. But again, the socio-technical innovation of the illicit sees different combinatory forms: where the creative disruption of licit commercial enterprise is concerned with disruptive *control*, illicit actions are less about control and more concerned with the ingenuity of exploitation.

This leads to the important question: *what does illicit innovation offer?* To solely focus on the licit is to miss the capacity for change that illicit practices create (see Flowers, 2008; Söderberg, 2010; 2017). Fundamentally I argue that illicit actions create innovation by instigating new ways of looking at the world. Marx, for example, stated that a 'pickpocket becomes a productive worker too, since he indirectly produces books on criminal law (this reasoning at least as correct as calling a judge a productive worker because he protects from theft)' (1993:273). The illicit creates new uses of technologies and systems seen with the sophisticated engineering of narcosubs for example (Guerrero C., 2020); it reveals the hidden infrastructures of globalization through the tactical harnessing of them in the case of transnational drug smuggling; it highlights the asymmetry of the global political system where people smuggling enterprises develop out of civil conflict and the immigration policies of nation states. As we will see in the following chapters, one of the fundamental outcomes of illicit practices is *ingenuity*. That is, how people enact the illicit potential of the material world around them. These are new ways of considering the role that things, systems, processes and infrastructures play in the perpetration of illicit activities. The illicit exploitation of transnational infrastructure such as global shipping or courier networks enables us to further appreciate the strategic as well as tactical dominance and vulnerability of these infrastructures. Putting things to illicit uses – be that a rock repurposed as a weapon or a milk bottle used as a Molotov cocktail – also highlights the sheer 'force of things' (Bennett, 2004) of the seemingly invisible, commonplace things that mediate our everyday social practices. I argue throughout the next three chapters that deviancy and the illicit can be viewed as forms of 'productive disturbance' – similar in some sense to how the rhetoric around disruptive technology has been positioned. Where the market zeal of disruptive tech is marked by a pioneer spirit of change, the productive nature of how deviancy and the illicit disturb the social is through the mirror they hold up to how we are *supposed* to act, or indeed design. To claim that innovation can emerge from illicit practices is not to deny the potentially deleterious effects; rather, it is to read innovation through the lens of radical openness; of the 'new combinations' described by Schumpeter; and ultimately to locate it in the revolutionary histories of creative unorthodoxy, nonconformity and transgression.

Conclusions

Not unlike George Nelson's 'How to Kill People: A Problem of Design', *A Burglar's Guide to the City* is a provocative title. Geoff Manaugh's (2016) book is not so much a 'how-to' guide on burglary, rather a way of looking at the city through the eyes of a burglar: to understand how the urban realm is perceived from an illicit perspective. In a similar way to Isabelle Stenger's use of the 'idiot' as a tactical figure the burglar is also a guide, not one who enables us to pause and look askance at social situations, rather someone who uses space differently, navigating the materialities of the city in ways many of us would not recognize. The figure of the burglar offers a series of fascinating insights into the value of architecture and the city as sites of criminal intent, but also as *generators* of illegality themselves. They call for illicit use; buildings themselves afford the illicit through their design. It also provides an important endpoint to this chapter, for as Manaugh outlines, by following the burglar we begin to see buildings in new ways, we understand the logic of infrastructure differently. In the previous chapter I positioned the study of design cultures in a similar way, suggesting that deviancy and the illicit are critical markers for appreciating the social forces of design. The debates in this chapter open up a further space to consider the complex entanglements of good and bad design, thus challenging many of the normative ethical assumptions about design, an aspect that will form the core of the remaining chapters. But just as importantly the literature surveyed in this chapter further develops this by pointing to the equally murky territory of binary separations between licit and illicit activities more broadly. We saw throughout this chapter that many of the boundaries which have been established as part of the construction of social norms promote a false sense of distance. With deviancy this categorization is arrived at throughout the social codes of dominant groups, many of which change over time according to prevailing sensibilities. Not only this but deviancy also raises questions of scale, particularly in relation to how society positions or sanctions smaller-scale forms of deviant action. Similarly – although there are distinctions between deviancy as an issue of behaviour, and the illicit as more of a structural question – we also saw that the licit is far from an unwavering social bedrock; indeed, in both historical and contemporary contexts the illicit has been and still is intrinsic to enterprise cultures. The origins of capitalism itself are based on the conquest of territories for the exploitation of natural and human resources. The illicit origins of capitalism also resonate with the discussion in the latter sections of the chapter on innovation more generally and the value of illicit innovation specifically. Innovation today is most readily associated with the economic and the technological spheres of enterprise cultures where there is a 'cultural imaginary that posits a world that is always lagging, always in need of being brought up to date through the intercessions of those trained to shape it' (Suchman, 2011:5). But as shown in the latter sections of the chapter this masks its radical heritage, so aptly demonstrated by Benoît Godin's work on its genealogies. It is not only those trained to do so, for we have seen that innovation can emerge from the actions of those deemed illicit. As discussed in the closing comments on the potentialities of malevolent creativity and illicit innovation I hold that we need to return to the origins of innovation and see its radical capability for disruption as an important critical tool for understanding the complexities of objects, practices, systems and infrastructures – of design.

Taking something of a detour from the explicit address of design this chapter has attempted to provide an important contextual and theoretical backdrop to how these concepts have been positioned amidst the literature. Of course, I have selected the discourses and debates that most neatly fit with my own: a reading of the deviant and the illicit that sees them as part of a heterogeneous assemblage of competing accounts of how the social world is constructed. As such this may enable us to question the 'intoxication' – to appropriate an earlier quotation – with social benevolence and appreciate the entanglement of competing social forces. In the following three chapters these social forces and dynamics are unpacked through a range of distinct settings, all speaking to the core delineation of deviant design.

4 MISUSING THINGS

Introduction

Solar cook stoves are a vitally important part of humanitarian efforts to improve the lives of displaced peoples across a vast range of geographical contexts and settings. Alongside other 'humanitarian goods' (Collier et al., 2017) such as water sanitizers, solar cook stoves aim to provide alternative means of cooking in refugee camps such as Goudoubo in the northern territory of Burkina Faso. In this camp and others like it, solar cook stoves are just one of the initiatives of the UNHCR, the UN Refugee Agency, put in place to alleviate the harmful effects of traditional cooking practices in sub-Saharan African countries (see Corbyn and Vianello, 2018). In camps or homes where cooking often takes place in temporary or semi-permanent shelters, more traditional means of heating food such as the use of firewood or charcoal has potential danger to life and health through the inhalation of harmful smoke and fumes. Further to this, in refugee settings such as Goudoubo camp, women are often the ones who gather firewood from outside the perimeters of the refugee camp, with the risk of sexual violence and other forms of harassment. For these reasons and others, the UNHCR has understandably sought alternatives to traditional cooking processes, with solar cook stoves being just one approach, alongside gas and cleaner forms of more traditional practices. In terms of sheer innovation solar cookers are perhaps the most striking in relation to their design. One such example is the Blazing Tube solar cooker (see Figure 1).

Developed originally in 2008 by John Grandinetti, the Blazing Tube solar cooker has gone through prototype testing in Hawai'i as well as field testing in a range of other countries. It is one of the key solar cookers introduced to Goudoubo camp in Burkina Faso by the UNHCR. In terms of design innovation, Blazing Tube makes use of a central glass tube (hence the name) which is placed inside a parabolic reflector – otherwise known as a Compound Parabolic Curve. This is attached to a heat-retaining pot which sits in a cooking box. To function, the heat for cooking is created by the solar heating of vegetable oil which is contained in the glass tube, acting as a heat transfer fluid. So that when the high-heat vegetable oil in the tube is

FIGURE 1 Blazing Tube Solar Cooker, Goudoubo camp, Burkina Faso. Copyright Edoardo Santangelo. With permission of Edoardo Santangelo.

heated it transfers heat to the cooking pot, reaching temperatures up to 150°C. But what makes this important to the study of deviant design and illicit innovation?

Crucially, it doesn't work as planned. The issues are threefold. First, many of the displaced families in Goudobou dislike the smell the vegetable oil leaves on the cooked food. This isn't too much of an issue with highly spiced or flavoured meats, but simple staples such as rice, are tainted by the vegetable oil with an almost petroleum-like smell. Second, cooking is a cultural matter. This is the case in so many diverse cultural contexts, including here in Burkina Faso where solar energy is an unfamiliar technology. As a result, the adoption of this way of cooking has not been widely accepted. Third, Blazing Tube is quite fragile, notably the glass tube itself, which is prone to breaking. However, what is most interesting in relation

FIGURE 2 Repurposed Blazing Tube cooker, with aluminium sheeting used to construct a shelter. Copyright Edoardo Santangelo. With permission of Edoardo Santangelo.

to deviant design is the *afterlife* of these failed solar cookers. For the setting of Goudoubo refugee camp in Burkina Faso was part of a research project in which I was engaged from 2016 to 2018. The project – 'Displaced Energy: Anthropology/ Design Approaches to Artificial Lighting, Heating and Electric Power in Refugee Camps' – set out to investigate how refugees in two camps (Goudoubo, and Kakuma in northern Kenya) utilized different energy technologies in contexts of displacement.[1] The aim of this was to consider situations where top-down energy provision for cooking, lighting and heating had not fulfilled the original remit. One of the key findings to emerge from the fieldwork was the use of improvised practices by refugees in the camps to counter some of the failures of humanitarian energy provision (see Cross et al., 2019; Martin et al., 2020). In the case of the Blazing Tube solar cookers, their failures to meet the cultural needs of Malian refugees alongside weaknesses in the design did not result in the simple rejection and discarding of these objects. Rather, the communities in Goudoubo repurposed the cookers, remaking them into a range of different objects, giving them a new purpose, a new life. Various parts of the solar cookers were used as a wind break for shielding traditional fires; they became parts of a fence for an animal enclosure; they were used for storage shelving; as well as a door. The framework supporting the main glass tube and parabolic curve was used by one family to build a wheelbarrow for transporting jerry cans of water. The framework from another solar cooker had been redeployed by a different family as the arms of a handmade chair which had been fashioned out of other metal tubing, wooden branches as well as the arms from the cooker. Most striking of all however was a shelter constructed out of the sheet metal from broken and discarded Blazing Tube stoves (see Figure 2).

What made the structure initially so arresting was the reflective surface of the aluminium, even more so in the glare of the west African sun. The shelter had been constructed by one of the blacksmiths in Goudoubo camp. Whilst he makes a living out of various blacksmithing jobs for camp residents, this shelter was made for his own domestic needs. In the past he kept food in his main dwelling, a UNHCR shelter, but his goats often ate the food, and at other times the UNCHR shelter leaked, occasionally ruining the food through water ingress. He decided to build a separate shelter in which to store the food, along with tools, gas equipment and firewood. As a blacksmith he had access to some of the materials donated by the UNHCR, but with this second shelter he bought ten aluminium sheets taken from broken Blazing Tube stoves. In addition, he purchased nails, wooden poles and iron to make a lock-holder from the market near to the camp in the town of Dori. The shelter is an assemblage of sorts, fashioned from a range of juxtaposed materials. But the mismatched qualities of materials do not detract from the obvious ingenuity of design, which the blacksmith had created from scratch.[2] Instead, the conjoining of disparate materials speaks to the ingenuity of approach. For the important point about these range of examples from the refugee camp in Burkina Faso is the inventiveness shown through the repurposing of the redundant or broken humanitarian goods. Significantly for this chapter as a whole is that the redeployment of these goods is a form of *misuse*. The various communities of displaced peoples had chosen to ignore the original intended uses of these humanitarian goods. Instead, they could see that the framework of the Blazing Tube stove and other objects could be repurposed into a more useful wheelbarrow, or used to clad a shelter for food and equipment. Crucially for the arguments developed in this chapter is that the ingenuity of approach – what I call 'informal design' – adopted through the needs of Malian refugees highlights the inherent potentiality in the materiality of things themselves coupled with the potentiality of misuse as a way of deploying things.

As a backdrop to the wider debates of this chapter these examples offer a valuable context to this first substantive empirical outline of deviant design. Above all they highlight the way in which the normative conditions under which we encounter the designed world are exactly that – constructions of how things *should* be used, rather than *are* used. Just as Chapter 2 demonstrated the complexity of social relations which pervade the very culture of design, so this chapter begins to consider deviancy as a form of *misuse*. Given the outline of the core theories of deviancy in Chapter 3 it may come as something of a surprise to think of misuse as deviant or abnormal. However, this and the next two chapters begin to build a multi-scalar approach to the question of deviancy and its relationship with design culture. Here I posit the way in which the accidental as well as wilful misuse of objects offers a much richer and fuller appreciation of the way in which people engage with the designed world around them – novelty, ingenuity, inventiveness and, ultimately, innovation can result from things being used *counter* to their intended purpose. Even at this rather domesticated scale we will see that individuals and groups such as those in Goudoubo camp are part of the culture of 'diffuse design' described by Manzini (2015), whereby they are actively producing new forms of design and material culture through putting old things to new uses. As noted in the introduction to the book, I build from Manzini's idea of diffusion and develop misuse as a type of 'informal design' practice that employs many of the traits of professional designerly knowledge but does so outside institutionalized ideas of design.

Emerging from this chapter will be a series of arguments which position misuse and informal design as a critical vehicle for understanding the wider cultures, histories and practices of design. Misuse opens up new spaces for engaging with design, both in its social context and in terms of the implications for understanding the role of the professional designer and the non-professional, the diffuse or more pointedly the *informal* designer. It also elicits important considerations of objects and systems themselves: by misusing things, new usages and potentialities are revealed. As shown earlier in Chapter 2, Geoff Manaugh provides a similar argument about new readings of the built environment through burglary, framing this in the context of Bernard Tschumi's earlier ideas of 'creative misuse' in his 1976-81 architectural project 'The Manhattan Transcripts' (Tschumi, 1981). The project includes one 'event' where a murder in Central Park forces reconsideration of the spatial dynamics of the site, or more specifically how 'an entire city could be transformed by an act of creative misuse' (Tschumi in Manaugh, 2016:198). Linking all these areas together is a vital lesson – how deviation from intended purpose creates novelty and innovation.

The chapter begins by examining the histories of 'use' in design, notably from the perspective of functionality within design practices and principles. I start by exploring the legacy of functionalism, then develop a critique through an in-depth examination of functionalism's plurality. Rather than function being designed *into* an object I explore how function is projected *onto* objects by the user. These debates are framed by a range of disciplinary perspectives, notably Baudrillard's (2005) early work on the functional logic of use value, and the rather different work falling under the name of 'artifact function' (Preston, 2009). Building on this foundational material the substantive focus then turns to the work of Charles Jencks and Nathan Silver in their 1972 book *Adhocism: The Case for Improvisation* (Jencks and Silver, 2013). This book offers an important vantage point from which to examine the relationship between function and misuse, but more specifically the identification of 'informal design': in seeking out a particular function or need people wilfully exploit already existing material artefacts, repurposing or, as I claim, misusing them, in order to suit their own purposes. They do so on their own terms, without the need for an expert designer or other professional. For Jencks and Silver the adhocist sensibility is inherently innovative in its furtherance of the potential of objects and materials. For them this potential comes from the 'openness' of approach adopted by the adhocist, whereby the professional, institutionalized approach to design is jettisoned in favour of the creativity of the consumer, or 'informal designer'. I pursue the idea of openness and informality through a reading of improvisation developed by Peters (2013), whereby the dialectical entanglement of fixity and unfixity offers a platform for thinking about the openness of misuse. The chapter finally draws together the adhocist traditions of informal design with those of contemporary hacker cultures, arguing that the 'open source' ideology of hacking resonates with the innovative potential unlocked through misuse.

From use to misuse: Beyond designed functionality

The vast majority of users of a technology adapt to its limitations. In fact, to use any single thing is implicitly to accept its limitations. But it is in human nature to want to use things *beyond* their intended purpose.

(Petroski, 2006:4, my emphasis)

Henry Petroski, in his book *Success through Failure: The Paradox of Design,* offers a beneficial description of the interactions people have with technology, and by default with designed goods and systems more generally. On a broader level his work exemplifies the complex relationship between technological development and failure as an inherent facet of the design process, noting how designers and engineers learn from the weaknesses and fallibility of existing systems (also see Papanek and Hennessey, 1977). Such examples include the laser pointer, developed as a result of the limitations of the wooden pointer, through to infrastructural-level engineering projects developed through the catastrophic failure of existing infrastructures such as bridges. His primary argument is that new technologies and innovations often emerge through failure. In terms of misuse, the above quote highlights an important point concerning the inherent limitations of technology: nearly all technologies have limitations which users need to adapt to. On the one hand this raises a key concern regarding the lack of effectiveness in human-centred design approaches, but more critically for this chapter, it also shows that the use and functionality of technology and design is inherently limited. Things do not necessarily fulfil their intended purpose, as shown by the opening example of Blazing Tube. Although Petroski does not fully outline why it is human nature to use things beyond their intended purpose he nonetheless raises a further important dimension for the study of misuse: whilst designers set out with an intended purpose in mind, often as a result of a specific client brief, things will invariably be utilized differently. But above all, the quote demands further consideration of the distinction between the *implicit* acknowledgement of technological limitation and an *explicit* will to search out such limitations, perhaps the blatant misuse of things by users or consumers. The implicit understanding that things are limited in their scope may well suggest that designed goods and systems are inherently fallible in their design, raising the question as to the very condition of functionality itself (Akrich, 1992:205). Do things ever function as they are intended to? However, a more pressing question concerns the explicit understanding of limitations as a form of wilful misuse. Crucially we need to ask: what is it to *mis*-use something? To address this question I consider two interrelated perspectives: use and functionality.

To investigate the issue of misuse we can begin by contemplating the allied condition of 'use'. As with the relationship between other dualist constructs such as normal/abnormal; good/bad design, there is a socially constructed entanglement at play here. Just as we previously saw with the creation of deviance as a social categorization, misuse is conditioned into being by its inherent relationship with its purportedly more principled Other. To address the notion of misuse, what is it to actually *use* something?

I pick up the bottle. Its stainless-steel surface marked by greasy fingerprints; scratched by the bottle cage on my bike. The plastic drinking spout is worn from being overly washed in the dishwasher – something I'm not supposed to do according to the manufacturer's instructions. Hand wash only. I pour water into the plant pot to hydrate the new seedlings. I then take a gulp of water myself. Returning to my desk I use the water bottle to hold open the page of a book to allow me to note down a quotation for this book. This is a simple illustration, an example of an everyday interaction with a reusable water bottle. Nothing technologically sophisticated, just a mundane designed artefact. Such an outline of the way in which I use this object speaks to how we all use things: not always as intended by the manufacturer or the designer. This bottle wasn't designed to be used as a prop to hold down a book – this is a side effect of its weight.

How does this relate to the fundamental question of use? I did three things with the bottle: I watered a plant; I drank from it; I used it to hold open a book. Only one of these might be described as the correct use – me drinking from the bottle. But how then do we engage with the two other bifurcations from correct usage? Using the bottle to water a plant is not fundamentally at odds to the *inscribed* function of the bottle (more on this later). Weighting down a page of a book is. However, in average day-to-day interactions with things we likely wouldn't concern ourselves too much with such a circumstance. It is not ethically troublesome, rather a case of using something to hand for a practical purpose. But if I'd used the weight of the bottle to smash a window in order to break into someone's home then the severity and calculability of misuse clearly becomes a graver issue. Here we can begin to see how the simple repurposing of function opens up some important considerations for our interactions with things, including ethical dimensions. There is the point concerning to what degree something is misused and how this ultimately depends on the ethical-moral conditions of accepted behaviour. Alongside this the everyday illustration of use raises further questions this chapter considers: Is there ever a situation where the use of something adheres exactly to intended use?

To build this argument concerning the schism between use and misuse it is vital to consider in more depth the term 'use' and the allied idea of 'function'. For Victor Margolin, the distinction is straightforward: function he sees as a technical capacity, whilst use involves social operationalization (Margolin, 1997:228; also see Baudrillard, 1981:68; Crilly, 2010:312). The former is inscribed into the formal and technical characteristics of products as traditionally defined, the latter reflects how these capacities are engaged and interacted with at a social level. To deal with how things are used it is valuable to see this as an enmeshing of the two, which is precisely how users engage with material goods. We coalesce together in an experiential encounter. The imbrication of technical capacity as function and social application through use provides a valuable space for how we consider the life-worlds of things. In doing so we can see how the act of use itself is dependent on the embodied actions of the user, whilst the notion of usability points to the mattering of an object itself, and thus to the interrelated discussion of function.

Marx's writings on the commodity (see Marx, 1993) provide some of the most authoritative accounts on the complex relations between commodities, production, labour, money, circulation and consumption. Whilst it is not feasible to consider the entirety of these relations, one of the key determinant factors in Marx's consideration of use value is its intimacy with exchange value. Put simply, where we might think of use value as the satisfaction of need it is only through a thing's exchange value that it enters the realm of the commodity, accruing commodity status through its ability to be exchanged. Decisively, the logic of capitalism is such that the satisfaction of needs through a thing's use value is secondary to its circulation as a commodity which is only possible if the thing itself is 'produced as *exchange values*, not as *immediate use values*' (Marx, 1993:196, emphasis in original). The commodity's principal role is to serve as money, as capital. That is, rather than being exchanged or traded 'for the purpose of satisfying a need' (Marx, 1993:165) the commodity is there to circulate as a commodity tradable for another. For Marx, then, exchange value is the dominant force in capital, and understandably he is less forthcoming on the specifics of use value over and above the non-commoditized status of needs.[3] As Baudrillard notes (1981:130) Marx is rather ambiguous about the status of the use value of things more generally, but helpfully Baudrillard provides a more nuanced account of use value. In particular he sees use value as distinct from the commoditized status of exchange value, noting that the idea of utility is a central reality of an object or product. He offers an in-depth examination of the wider logics of signification, including a constructive outline of how they interact. There are four key logics at play:

1 a functional logic of use value;
2 an economic logic of exchange value;
3 a logic of symbolic exchange;
4 a logic of sign value. (Baudrillard, 1981:66)

For my purpose here, key to these logics is the breakdown of each into ascribable traits or capacities. In particular, use value is seen as concerned with practical operation, utility and its status as an instrument. By contrast exchange value is concerned with equivalence, that is in terms of its economic status as a commodity in the market. Symbolic exchange is seen as ambivalent in its commoditized status, primarily active as a gift or symbol of exchange. Finally, Baudrillard's addition of sign value clears a space of difference, where social status is positioned through sign value (Baudrillard, 1981:66). Whilst all four of these logics pervade our interaction with goods it is the functional logic of use value which is key to the discussion of misuse. For if we are to understand how something is misused we must appreciate the operation of things as instruments of utility and practical operation. Key to this are the allied terms of 'practical operation', 'utility' and 'instrument'.

Taking the opening example of the Blazing Tube solar cooker, we can see each of these terms in action. The practical operation of the cooker is seemingly rather straightforward: it is the putting into action of the thing itself (Redström, 2008:411) through the manipulation of the cooker's technical capacities. In the context of the refugee camp in Burkina Faso this would include the placement of the stove to capture the solar energy of the sun; waiting for the vegetable oil in the glass tube to heat up enough to sufficiently cook the food. There is then the familiar understanding of utility as something that is *useful*, akin to the actioning of the stove through putting it into use, above all for the cooking of food. We also might consider utility in terms of the root of the word itself, particularly the adjective utile – where something is advantageous. In this case the solar stove is a utile object, advantageous to cooking. This brings us to Baudrillard's idea of the use value of the technical 'instrument' and the specific role of *functionality*. The solar stove's status as an instrument is determined by its technical usefulness. This resides in its capacity as an instrument, or rather a device for cooking foodstuffs. As a device it offers certain technical capacities such as the ability to heat the vegetable oil to temperatures of 150°C. Here the technical function of the object is clearly apparent and is inscribed in the object itself. In Baudrillard's reading of function he sees this as the initial stage in the logic of the artefact. One of the examples he cites is that of a refrigerator, whose function is the objective 'meaning' of the thing itself. As such the refrigerator is irreplaceable as an object to cool foodstuffs, whereas the other logics are applicable across a range of consumer items (1981:68). Baudrillard quickly moves on to discuss the three other logics, leaving us without an in-depth outline of functionality as such, something that is none too uncommon.

The concept of function itself has a wide range of discourses both within and outwith design (Crilly, 2010:312; Parsons, 2016:85–102), but perhaps one of the most insightful from the design field is this: 'The mode of action by which a design fulfils its purpose is its function' (Papanek, 1973:5, cited in Crilly, 2010:314). Function is the technical fulfilment of an intended purpose that *facilitates action on the part of the user*. The role of the designer in this situation is paramount, for they are the ones who produce artefacts that are inscribed with the necessary attributes that users can identify and employ to action the particular purpose. These discussions on the roots of functionality provide an outline of the fraught debates over the importance of function to our technical artefacts and systems over and above the aesthetic dimensions of design cultures. As noted in Chapter 2, perhaps one of the reasons for the modernists' desire for technical functionality was the combined embrace of new technologies in the early twentieth century along with the potential of design and architecture to solve societal problems. To question function as a central tenet of design is then to question its social value, hence why we also see the negative legacies of styling and consumption-driven planned obsolescence (Packard, 1961). But function is indeed an incredibly fluid, indeterminate idea (Parsons, 2016:85) and one that is debated across a range of cognate disciplines to design.[4]

One in particular that speaks directly to the discussions here on use and misuse is that of 'artifact function' (see Preston, 2009; Scheele, 2005). Although a rather niche subdiscipline of the philosophy of technology, this is described as the 'standard view' approach to questions of function (Vardouli, 2015:142) and does indeed provide a helpful sounding board for the design cultures approaches to function outlined above. At its core the debates in the study of artefact function revolve around the point that if function is an intentional pursuit (i.e., a human agent has created this function within an object or instrument) function itself is uncontroversial. Crucially, these debates offer some telling additions to the material on use and function discussed above, most intriguingly through the notion of 'proper function'. Before discussing this, a little further context to the broader debates on artefact function.

The question of intentional and non-intentional function is one of the most useful ideas from this field. As Preston writes, 'a fairly common view is that artifact functions are directly and *exhaustively determined* by individual and/or collective human intention' (2009:218, emphasis in original). Function is only ascribed to a thing by human action: the technical capability the result of human planning. At the other end of this spectrum human intention plays an indirect part in artefact function – for instance, trial and error is a case in point (Griffiths, 1993:418–19, cited in Preston, 2009:222). Rather than an intentional approach to artefact function this may emerge over time and often unconsciously or non-intentionally. At both ends of the spectrum we find stimulating discussion around 'proper function'. Proper function is concerned with five core ideas (Parsons, 2016:87–8). Firstly, a proper function is what the object is *actually* meant for, that is its intended purpose (Scheele, 2005:26). Secondly – and importantly for the broader discussions of misuse – a proper function is not imposed upon objects, it *is* the intentional function. Thirdly, related to the second point is that proper function is in the object itself. This I take to suggest that the function is designed into the object or inscribed into it. In adopting the term 'inscription' I allude to Latour and Woolgar's (1986:45–53) original use in relation to how texts and other devices play a central role in the production of scientific knowledge, but I also take the notion of inscription more literally in relation to function is *etched* into an object, its purpose determined by the formal, material characteristics of the thing itself. Proper function seemingly inheres in the thing itself.[5] The fourth feature is the provision of function typologies so that proper function facilitates the linguistic labelling of things as one category of object as opposed to another: a solar cook stove rather than a wheelbarrow. Finally, proper function indicates the normativity of function (Preston, 2009:229), whereby we are able to ascertain if something has broken or malfunctioned because its proper function is no longer operative.

Where the material from this admittedly rather dry field of philosophy becomes really interesting is around the issue of *deviation* from proper function, both through this latter point on malfunction and critically non-intentional function. Artefacts can have more than one proper function, seen as a secondary or accidental function (Scheele, 2005:26). Within proper function theory this is viewed as a 'system function' in that this secondary function lies within the scope of the thing itself (Preston, 2009:226). A standard case in point might be that of a screwdriver used for opening a paint tin (Scheele, 2005:26), or an umbrella used as a sunscreen or indeed a weapon (Preston, 2009:215). It is not its proper use, but nonetheless falls under the capacity of the materiality of the thing itself, or what artefact function theorists call the system function. One further way of describing this is that artefacts are 'multiply utilizable' (Preston, 2009:215) – they are not designed to serve just one purpose but multiple roles. Where we might think of the screwdriver as fulfilling a secondary role outside of its proper function, Preston offers the example of uniforms which serve dual purposes of keeping the body dry and protected, whilst signifying status or a particular role. Herein lies a crucial aspect of the debate: the uniform has multiple proper functions, whereas the screwdriver has one proper function, but is utilizable for others such as opening a paint tin or picking a lock.

In addition to the literature on 'artifact function', Madeleine Akrich's work on the de-scription of technical objects (1992) affords an even more nuanced conceptualization of use. As with the networked approach of so much Science and Technology Studies material, Akrich highlights how the supposed end usage of a technical object forms part of a much wider delegation of actors through 'a long chain of people, products, tools, machines, money, and so forth' (1992:205). This clearly attests to the coalition of the technical and the social, both of which are central to discussions of function and use. The social in particular offers us a vantage point for understanding use. For Akrich social dimensions of technical objects correspond to how users 'are able to reshape the object, and the various ways in which the objects may be used' (1992:206). Echoing my comment on how function and proper use is seemingly etched into objects, Akrich delineates the shift from 'script to de-scription'. That is, designers can be seen to *inscribe* particular assumptions about users, including tastes, competences, etc. in such a way that attempts to predetermine the outcomes. Describing this like a film script, Akrich states that 'technical objects define a framework of action together with the actors and the space in which they are supposed to act' (1992:208). To further employ the analogy of the script, there is always a level of improvisation where the actors or users 'may define quite different roles of their own' (1992:208). For Akrich, the space of encounter between the designer and user is one of ceaseless variation, where we see the move between 'the world inscribed in the object' by the designer and 'the world described by its displacement' by the user (Akrich, 1992:209). It is this latter movement or displacement on the part of the user – the change in use – that leads Akrich to talk of de-scription. Where the inscribed function is displaced.

Both 'artifact function' and the de-scription of technical objects address some valuable approaches to the entangled relationship between use and function. Specifically, they raise questions around the intentionality of function, but equally the intentionality of *use*. Where artefact function and proper function in particular is seen to be determined by the person responsible for designing the item, what does this then suggest about intentionality of use? That is, an artefact may be designed for an intended function but the intended use of this same artefact is determined by the will of the user, it becomes displaced. Just as Margolin highlights the social dimension of use we see here how intentionality is open to the needs or desires of the user, coupled with the capacity of the thing itself to be 'multiply utilizable'. Indeed, although I suspect it is aimed at a different argument, Scheele says as much: 'Artefacts have functions, which are related to the goals of the agents using them' (Scheele, 2005:26). As previously noted, Papanek's definition of function also resonates with this: there is a distinction to be made between function as the operation of the thing itself, and use as the putting into action of the thing, no matter what that action is in relation to the intended function. At the same time this can, of course, adhere to the inscribed functional origins of the thing, but equally the actioning of the thing is where it becomes useful which is not dependent upon the intentional function.

By focussing once more on the Blazing Tube solar stove some of these issues are borne out. Where Baudrillard's functional logic of use value ascribes the three aspects 'practical operation', 'utility' and 'instrument' what he doesn't account for is precisely the failures of proper function. As we saw the practical operation of Blazing Tube is not quite so straightforward – the fragility of the glass tube may mean the stove does not always operate to its full capacity; equally the operation of the stove cannot be isolated from the socio-cultural factors surrounding the traditional use of firewood as opposed to solar power. In similar terms a parallel problematic around the utility of the solar cookstove is also evident. The word itself is open to a plurality of readings. In particular we see that the usefulness of the stove is not necessarily true: the cooking oil taints staple foodstuffs such as rice with a petroleum-like smell. It has failed at its proper function, and thus as an instrument to fulfil needs.

Under the rubric of 'misuse', some interesting insights are created when we consider the relationship with the proper function and proper use of the solar cook stove, particularly in light of Parsons' five key categories of artefact function. Firstly, the misuse of the cooker – its repurposing as panelling for a shelter, or a wheelbarrow – imposes a new function on the stove, albeit an improper function. Secondly and thirdly, where proper function is deemed intentional and thus not imposed upon the object, the opposite is the case with misuse: no longer an intentional function designed into the object at the outset, instead the new function is imposed from the outside, and critically, this is carried out by the user, that is by the *non-professional designer*. In this context the empowerment of the user in the form of the non-designer echoes Ivan Illich's critique of professionalism. For Illich the nature of a 'commodity-intensive society' is such that the needs of individuals can only be provided in the form of pre-packaged goods designed and controlled by professionals (Illich, 1980:49). He was deeply sceptical of this and asserted the vital role of individuals in producing collective social worlds.[6] Misuse then is a political act external to the imposition of professional judgement.

Alongside this another important facet of this debate for our broader understanding of design is how misuse creates new typologies of things: we might think of these as hybrid categorizations where a screwdriver's new use as a paint tin opener places it under at least two different typologies. Lastly, where proper function makes it possible to appreciate if something does not work or has malfunctioned the misuse and repurposing of the poor-performing solar cook stove does precisely this: to an extent this can then feed back into the potential redesign of the object. So as with Petroski's belief in the value of failure, misuse may also be seen in a similar positive vein and offer ways in which the proper function of the object may not be as efficient as imagined.

Whilst the discussions around 'proper function' draw us into an admittedly tangled web of intricacies it nonetheless adds valuable flesh to the stark aesthetic bones of utility and function in the canon of designed modernity. More pointedly the enmeshing of function and use as socially determined highlights that use in particular is concerned above all with action. As Margolin puts it: 'Users are social actors who do not come to the product in a vacuum, but instead consider it in relation to their own plans and activities' (1997:232). Where function may be partly inscribed into the technical capacities of the object it is the user who enacts the proper or improper function of the thing. The social dimensions of use means that it must be dealt with in terms of the actions users carry out with artefacts. For just as we saw with previous discussions on social complexity, we must not simplify the social dimension of why people put things to use in ways which deviate from perceived 'proper functions'. Crucially for the broader ontological parameters of this book, the very notion of the social condition is such that the human capacity for action can never be reduced to a simple duality of proper/improper. Indeed, coming to the end of this section, my central argument is that use must be seen as multiple, as pluriversal to use Escobar's term again. For in a somewhat similar vein to Baudrillard's observation that 'the way objects are used in everyday life implies an almost authoritarian set of assumptions about the world' (2005:61), the idea of misuse problematizes our assumptions about how things *should* be used. To adopt such a position is then to question the dualist schism between misuse and use. Seeing misuse as a positive instance of active participation by the user or consumer affords a sense of empowerment where we are not simply subservient to the inscribed will of intentionality (Preston, 2013). We are alive to the potentiality of things. The following section addresses this notion of potentiality through the idea of ad hoc forms of improvisation and ultimately 'informal design' practices.

Ad hoc improvisation: Towards informal design[7]

In comparison with recent examples of the smuggling of drugs into prisons, including by means of drones (BBC, 2017) and drug-soaked letters (BBC, 2018; also see Allison and Hattenstone, 2018), the inventiveness of fashioning a coat hanger from rolled-up newspaper does not seem quite so bold: it appears to lack the ingenuity and cunning of the former examples. But I suggest both approaches display a clear sense of understanding the wider contexts of the situation. In the distribution of drugs into prisons there is an awareness of the security practices in place alongside the mechanisms and methods to overcome these, including the illicit potential of cheap drones. Equally with the creation of domestic furnishings by prisoners a similar appreciation of the systemic limitations of incarceration is evident, as is the ingenuity of 'perpetrator techniques'. These are situations where prisoners have repurposed prison cell furniture, creating new usages such as producing greater privacy (Design Against Crime Research Centre & BA Product Design, 2019).[8] The example of the coat hanger comes from *Prisoners' Inventions*, an intriguing book exploring a diverse range of everyday items created by prisoners (Temporary Services and Angelo, 2003). The author, 'Angelo', offers striking examples of objects designed by prisoners to create a semblance of domestic normality. Alongside the simple coat hanger there are more complex inventions such as 'stingers', otherwise known as immersion heaters for heating water. These are available through the prison at a cost of around USD $6.00, but as Angelo notes, examples abound of versions designed and produced by prisoners themselves. One in particular displays a clear sense of repurposing as ingenuity (also see Eisenman, 2008; Kaufman Singer, 2010). This stinger is created by using parts from a razor, a plastic tumbler, earphones and an eraser. As seen in Figure 3 the plug terminals are fashioned from parts obtained from a safety razor which are then separated with an eraser and held together with melted plastic from a tumbler. The power from the wall socket is then conducted through wire sourced from earphones which is attached to the improvised heating element. The element itself is again constructed out of razor blades insulated with plastic from the same tumbler.

Stinger Variation #1

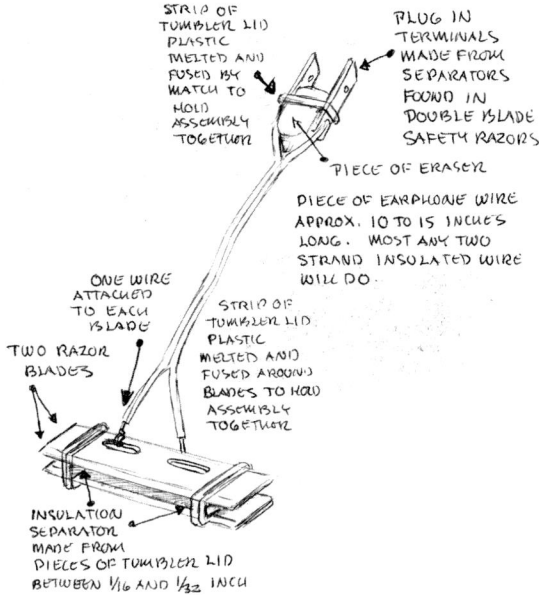

STRIP OF TUMBLER LID PLASTIC MELTED AND FUSED BY MATCH TO HOLD ASSEMBLY TOGETHER

PLUG IN TERMINALS MADE FROM SEPARATORS FOUND IN DOUBLE BLADE SAFETY RAZORS

PIECE OF ERASER

PIECE OF EARPHONE WIRE APPROX. 10 TO 15 INCHES LONG. MOST ANY TWO STRAND INSULATED WIRE WILL DO.

ONE WIRE ATTACHED TO EACH BLADE

TWO RAZOR BLADES

STRIP OF TUMBLER LID PLASTIC MELTED AND FUSED AROUND BLADES TO HOLD ASSEMBLY TOGETHER

INSULATION SEPARATOR MADE FROM PIECES OF TUMBLER LID BETWEEN 1/16 AND 1/32 INCH

This is a design that one of my cellies mass-produced. He could assemble one in about an hour, using parts cannibalized from a couple of double-blade safety razors, a soft tumbler plastic lid, and double insulated wire from an earphone plug.

I'm told that four- to six-blade stingers can be made, though I've never seen any. I'm dubious because of the insulation problems involved.

Warning: Never plug in the stinger unless the blades are in the water, and never remove the stinger from the water while it's plugged in, or it could blow up!

74   PRISONERS' INVENTIONS

FIGURE 3 Angelo's 'Stinger' or Water Heater, from *Prisoners' Inventions* by Angelo, in collaboration with Temporary Services. With permission of Temporary Services/Half Letter Press.

Clashes in the Gaza Strip between peaceful Palestinian protesters and the Israeli military in April 2018 brought widescale condemnation for the actions of the Israeli Defence Force. Although these clashes are sadly all too familiar one of the remarkable images to emerge from this round of conflict was of a young boy – Mazan Al-Najar – wearing an improvised gas mark to protect him from the noxious teargas fumes (Figure 4). This had been devised by cutting a large plastic bottle in half lengthways, leaving the tapered spout intact so that a Coca-Cola can could be attached to the bottle. In the can cotton wool and coal were

FIGURE 4 Palestinian boy with improvised gas mask. © Ibraheem Abu Mustafa/Reuters Pictures. With permission of Reuters Pictures.

then employed to filter out the tear gas. During this conflict other examples of improvised gasmasks were seen: one for another young boy covering his mouth and nose with part of a pomelo fruit; whilst an elderly man was seen with another cut-up plastic bottle held to his face with an onion to protect from the smell of tear gas.

Galliano Island is a small island of around 1000 inhabitants off the west coast of Vancouver nestled to the south-east of Vancouver Island. Famous for its dramatic setting it is understandably a popular destination for tourists, including myself a few years ago. I'd gone here for a vacation after spending time in Vancouver but also as I'd been told of the architectural structures on the Island, a derivation of traditional Canadian log cabins with added aspects of ad hoc, improvised architectural practice. During my time on Galliano I set out to document as many of the buildings that formed the nascent Galliano vernacular style – ultimately, I didn't find quite as many as I'd initially hoped for. However, my time on the Island was not wasted as it sparked my interest in smaller-scale forms of ad hoc practices, or what I call here 'informal design' practices. Driving down into the bay at Montague Harbour I left the car to walk around the harbour. Alongside the typical sailing vessels and small work-a-day dinghies was a slightly more a-typical seaplane, although you do see quite a few around Vancouver itself. What was more striking to my ad hoc-focussed eye was a rubber tyre (Figure 5). Whilst it may seem somewhat churlish to ignore the dramatic scenery it was this tyre that struck me most. A simple, now-treadless, rubber truck tyre. The configuration of the

FIGURE 5 Repurposed tyre as a jetty protector. Photo by author.

wooden jetties was such that to stop them banging into one another and damaging the wooden structures someone had repurposed this car tyre. It had been slashed along the sidewall, the flap then nailed to the side of the jetty with the tyre itself acting as a buffer between the two jetties.

These three examples of adhoc inventiveness speak to a range of social contexts framed by an engagement with the materiality of everyday things: the day-to-day struggles to maintain an impression of normal life under the limitations of incarceration; reacting to the sudden deployment of noxious gases to dispel peaceful protest; through to the everyday practicalities of protecting a jetty in an affluent region of western Canada. Although reluctant to draw patterns of commonality across such broad geographical, social and political situations what is perhaps common is the ingenuity of action. Particularly with the first two examples there are specific limitations and constraints that demand purposeful action. We see a political dimension to the struggle for normality in the face of the penal system; and national identity and statehood in the latter. With all three instances we are once again privy to the creativity of misuse – where the repurposing of a newspaper, a razor blade, drinking vessels and a car tyre deviate from 'proper function' but also display a keen sense of improvised inventiveness and ultimately informal design (also see Brandes et al., 2009; Flood and Grindon, 2014).

In this section I build on the previous discussions of misuse and investigate the ways in which people put things to different uses in a variety of novel ways. More specifically I investigate how things are repurposed and their original functions shifted into new configurations of use. Here, the afterlives of things are just as – if not more – telling as their original purpose. I also deal with how individuals and communities respond to limited resources in particular contexts such as war-torn regions or refugee camps. These discussions are framed under the banner of 'adhocism', a term developed by Charles Jencks and Nathan Silver in their 1972 book *Adhocism: The Case for Improvisation* (2013). Central to the adhocist sensibility is the recognition of the inherent potentialities of materials; the value of already-extant objects; the openness of things to new configurations and trajectories of use; and the creative, improvisational ways in which people engage with things. I also suggest that adhocism as a way of acting with the world speaks to a designerly approach to the materiality of things and as such can be deemed 'informal design', a sensibility that echoes professional design practices in the way problems are addressed, albeit at smaller scales and in more localized settings. Perhaps the clearest analogies between formal or professional design practice and my description of informal design are Cross' notion of design as 'thinking on your feet' and Boguslaw's description of adhoc approaches to design as 'a seat-of-the-pants technique' (1965:22).

Linking together the three examples above and the earlier repurposing of the Blazing Tube solar cook stove is an interest in the ad hoc as a way of acting *with* the world: a way that is attuned to the localized immediacy of need as a form of practical necessity. In all these cases the most expedient way to deal with particular problems or needs was through the resourcefulness of a 'do-it-yourself' approach as opposed to a dependency on formal devices, systems or services. In addition to this all examples show the resourcefulness of reconfiguring artefacts which are already to hand. With the domestic needs of prisoners the nature of incarceration is such that to fashion a water heater yourself is cheaper than purchasing one from the prison authorities. Likewise, the geopolitical situation in Gaza means that it is much more expedient to produce a gas mask out of materials close to hand than to wait for them to be distributed by NGOs for example. In Canada using a discarded tyre is simply easier, quicker, cheaper and ultimately more sustainable than having a special protective buffer manufactured for the jetty. In the setting of Goudobou refugee camp the needs of the displaced community can also be served by the community themselves, rather than solely through the humanitarian sector: as with the other examples it is quicker and easier to produce a shelter or a wheelbarrow out of materials in the camp than to be wholly dependent on the humanitarian community. Equally, the skills and local knowledge of the Malian refugee community here is an invaluable resource in itself. Mindful once more of the diverse settings of all these examples, a series of commonalities still emerge. In particular I suggest there is an adhocist sensibility to these approaches: that is, an awareness of both the economic common sense of these interventions, and crucially the immanent potentiality of 'things' to become something else, to function in ways that diverge from their original functions. Significantly, it also testifies to the inventiveness and ingenuity of those responsible for these designs – in how they recognize the value and potentiality of a tyre, a razor, a broken cook stove or a plastic bottle. Such practices can be seen as enactments of everyday stuff where individuals negotiate with the things to hand and problems to be resolved. Allied to the discussions on the design process in Chapter 1 these problems may not be 'wicked' in the exact sense as described by Rittel and Webber (1973) but as also outlined in Chapter 2 given the social context of all these apparently 'minor' problems they do indeed adhere to dealing with wicked situations. As such these approaches to engaging a diverse array of problems are akin to traditional designerly ways of working, but critically fall outwith the purview of formalized, professional design. Instead we see a more informal idea of design. Informality is notoriously difficult to define, in part as its very nature defies formal explanation. In *The Global Encyclopaedia of Informality* Ledeneva captures the disparate readings of informality, noting that it can refer to a range of contexts such as: relationships that have not been formalized; relaxed attitudes owing to a lack of protocol; local approaches to getting things done; or 'practices that emerge unofficially (such as favelas, slums and other unplanned settlements) or underground, constitute grey areas and form a variety of shadow, second or covert economies' (Ledeneva, 2018:1). For the purposes of this chapter these are enlightening as they encapsulate the ethos of informal design's lack of protocol, the unplanned nature of addressing local problems and, above all, approaches, methods and tools that have not been (or are yet to be) formalized.[9]

Interest in the wider ideas of the ad hoc continues to grow, with recent engagement through the work of designers such as Parsons and Charlesworth (Parsons and Charlesworth, 2011); the 'Design without Designers' exhibition at the XXII Triennale Milano in 2019 (studio d-o-t-s, 2019); and the 'Adhocracy' exhibition at the New Museum in New York (New Museum, 2013). Under the curatorial direction of Joseph Grima 'Adhocracy' set out to investigate how notions of openness and nonlinearity are emerging as key design ideas in comparison with the rigid, standardized practices of modernity. Driven by the collaborative potential offered by open-source technologies, the exhibition press-release notes that 'design is migrating from the rigid domain of bureaucracy towards the rhizomatic realm of adhocracy' (New Museum, 2013). Indeed, central to the exhibition's allusion to the broader contexts of adhocism is the confluence of diffuse design and politics, where the user is central to the emergence of a new design culture. The politics of design is also at the core of Jencks and Silver's book. On its original publication in 1972 the book was part of a wider critique of modernity and the repressive characteristics of bureaucratic planning (see Martin, 2016a:87–91). *Adhocism*, like other architecture and design publications of the period including the *Dome Cookbook* (Baer, 1968) as well as the *Whole Earth Catalogue* and cognate critiques by Jane Jacobs (1962), called for a re-articulation of the consumer. Rather than seeing them simply as passive users of the inscribed (or 'proper') function and meaning of things as outlined in relation to the politics of misuse discussed above, the ideological premise of *Adhocism* and other likeminded resources was framed by the creative empowerment of the user or consumer where design and engagement with the material world more generally was wrested from the grip of hegemonic power structures. *Everybody could be a designer.*

However, whilst the grander contexts of the social critique implied by the book place it within this wider canon of dissent, for the purposes of this chapter the more work-a-day practicalities of adhocism are equally as important. For at its core adhocism is about practicality: this is clear from the outset of the book, where it is described as that which can be

> applied to many human endeavors, denoting a principle of action having *speed* or economy and *purpose* or utility. Basically it involves using an available system or dealing with an existing situation in a new way to solve a problem quickly and efficiently. It is a method of creation relying particularly on resources which are already at hand.
>
> (Jencks and Silver, 2013:9 emphasis in original)

Calling to mind the situation in Gaza, the speed and purpose of making a protective gas mask from objects such as plastic drinks bottles and Coca-Cola cans which are ready to hand is manifestly evident. In this context the practicality of adhocism as a way of dealing with immediate problems chimes with Jencks and Silver's opening definition. Under these conditions the most expedient thing to do is to deal with situation oneself – to rely on the help or assistance of others seems futile. An adhocist approach to problem-solving is very much in keeping with the established legacies of indigenous material practices, most famously described by Claude Lévi-Strauss as *bricolage* (Lévi-Strauss, 1966). Indeed, Jencks and Silver are quick to position their own approach to adhocism in direct relation to the figure of the bricoleur. For Lévi-Strauss the central determinant of bricolage is the primacy of solving a problem as quickly as possible using the tools and material resources one has close to hand. However, although *Adhocism* acknowledges the debt to Lévi-Strauss it passes over this rather quickly, whereas a closer reading of 'The Science of the Concrete' offers some fascinating lines of flight for how ad hoc action might be thought of as informal design.

The idea of bricolage, as set out by Lévi-Strauss, is perhaps most infamously aligned to the difference between the actions and methods of an engineer as compared with the bricoleur. The former – replaceable by the figure of the designer – is said to resolve problems through the use of raw materials and original parts which are then scaled up and applied to larger contexts of mass-production, for instance. By contrast the bricoleur resolves their own problems through the use of materials that are to hand; that are local. Pursuing these ideas in greater depth, a range of important nuances develops. Critically, one of the opening postulations on bricolage is that it is a 'prior' science, an engagement with technology and the material world that stands to a certain degree in contradistinction with modernity. Lévi-Strauss situates the bricoleur as an individual who uses their hands, but interestingly 'uses *devious* means compared to those of a craftsman' (Lévi-Strauss, 1966:16–17, my emphasis). This notion of deviousness relates to the sense of the verb 'bricoler', which he describes as a form of 'extraneous movement', where for example a dog goes astray or a horse swerves to avoid something. It is advantageous to pick up on the use of the word 'devious' in this situation, for it denotes how the bricoleur is a figure at odds with the creative force of the engineer or designer but also the craftsman, all of which are typically reliant on the availability of raw materials. And likewise, for the wider arguments in this chapter and the book, this idea of deviousness offers an important insight into how we think about the use of things, where the misuse and repurposing of something is a movement away or *deviation* from its intended purpose.

In terms of the central postulation of materials being close to hand, Lévi-Strauss' discussion of bricolage offers two dimensions, one mythical, the other technical, both of which he describes as characterized by a 'heterogeneous repertoire' (Lévi-Strauss, 1966:17), an array of materials to hand, albeit limited. The bricoleur begins to tackle problems from this repertoire of materials – it is someone who is able to carry out a broad range of tasks, solving problems through this heterogeneous repertoire of 'things'. Compared with the engineer the tasks of the bricoleur are not fulfilled by raw materials or tools designed specifically for the task. Instead although the bricoleur's repertoire is heterogeneous it is also limited, hence the decisive sense of them making do with 'whatever is at hand'. Crucially for the examination of adhocism and misuse Lévi-Strauss notes that the repertoire is applied across a diverse array of tasks, the same materials potentially applicable to many different problems. I read from this the potential multiplicity of applications of the limited resources the bricoleur has to hand, hence the use of plastic bottles and Coca-Cola cans in Gaza or the broken solar cook stoves in Burkina Faso.

A number of key points can be drawn from the intertwined discussion of adhocism and bricolage in order to focus more fully on the idea of informal design. Here I focus on two central characteristics: firstly, the various examples outlined earlier on are very much *localized* situations; secondly, the spirit of the informal designer sees objects and systems as open and unfixed, where the engagement with the material world is an *improvised* process of ongoing negotiation.

Localized contexts

The local has particular connotations, notably in relation to the perceived progressive identity of its apparent Other, the global. And whilst such claims have now been widely rebuked the relationship between the two is constructive for consideration of informal design. One of the key assertions from Lévi-Strauss concerns the universality of the engineer, whilst the bricoleur 'addresses himself to a collection of oddments left over from human endeavours' (1966:19). The purview of the bricoleur is turned in on itself, to the immediate problem or task to be completed with the materials and tools to hand. It is by definition a localized context. We can extend this further by thinking about the relationship between local context and Jencks and Silver's outline of speed and purpose – this I term the 'localised immediacy of need'. With all the various instances where one can discern an informal design sensibility the specific problems tackled – creating a gas mask, a stinger, a coat hanger or a protective buffer – are all situated. That is, they exist in a very particular geographical context and temporal moment where the problem or the need is close to hand and there is an urgency to resolving the matter. This stands in contrast to the traditional universality of professional design and engineering where the problems themselves are taken as generalized, scalable conditions. For example, designing and manufacturing a gas mask to protect against inhalation of tear gas will, of course, take time with research, user testing, tooling design and production. The investment required for developing this is such that it would, of course, be sold in multiple markets. In rather grander terms Lévi-Strauss puts it like this: 'The engineer is always trying to make his way out of and go beyond the constraints imposed by a particular state of civilization while the "bricoleur" by inclination or necessity always remains with them' (Lévi-Strauss, 1966:19). For formal design to intervene in every situation where an object is deployed would be impossible, hence the universalized approach to how design imposes a uniformity over specific contexts. The messiness and complexity of localized situations is smoothed out (Turnbull, 1993). The inverse is true with informal design – it is always dealing with the situatedness of immediate problems. And this is also one of the reasons why informal design practices remain localized as opposed to being scaled-up in the way that traditional, professional design approaches are.[10]

That said, although the localized problems are distinct, the adhocist methods of dealing with these through informal design have certain commonalities across diverse geographies. Not in the formation of a specific methodology, rather a *sensibility* that recognizes the importance of dealing with problems at a local level alongside the resourcefulness of utilizing and repurposing existing artefacts. Whilst I have already noted the different contexts of US prisons, sub-Saharan settings, Palestine and Canada, examples abound of informal design. In India for instance, Khosla (2017) talks of 'Unconscious Design' in relation to a particular Indian design aesthetic where people put together items of furniture in an ad hoc manner from discarded objects. Akin to Papanek's distinction of 'anonymous design' Khosla terms this 'the Jugaad Aesthetic' in direct reference to the now well-established Indian approach to frugal innovation (Radjou et al., 2012) and other sociocultural practices (Jauregui, 2016).[11] Whilst Khosla acknowledges the interplay between the global and the local he claims there is something distinctly Indian in this aesthetic. However, the examples already discussed here seem to dispel this, as do other cases of informal design carried out by individuals across numerous other geographies. In Brazil a similar practice is called *gambiarra*, which again refers to technical improvisation utilizing materials to hand.[12] The Sámi community in northern regions of Norway, Sweden, Finland and parts of Russia are known for repurposing artefacts for the sake of self-sufficiency (Nango, no date). In the US the idea of *MacGyverism* (from the 1980s TV show *MacGyver*) also speaks to the solution of problems using local resources and materials. Russian culture also has a similar approach to do-it-yourself resourcefulness (Arkhipov, 2006). Whilst in Kenya the term *jua kali* is used to describe practices of 'making do' with limited resources (King, 1996; Swigert-Gacheru, 2011).[13] *Jua kali* and these other geographically dispersed cases of informal design offer particularly rich perspectives on the idea of localized material practices, for they speak to a wider set of debates on the way in which individuals engage with the heterogeneous repertoire of stuff and how this is put to use through improvised practices.

Improvisation

Improvisation would seem to run counter to the 'design science' perspectives of Herbert Simon considered in Chapter 1, where a determinate plan with preconceived ends is advanced. Whilst such rigid standpoints on the design process preclude 'cooky-booky' approaches and the 'intuitive [and] informal' (Simon, 1996:112), the more flexible and nuanced outlooks of Cross and Schön are in some ways closer to the 'making-do' ethos of adhocism and bricolage. In this brief final section I link these earlier conceptions of informal design to improvisation. Although Simon's methodological stance challenges the intuitive, Schön in fact speaks of improvisation in relation to his wider 'reflection-in-action' schema, noting that

> when good jazz musicians improvise together, they also manifest a 'feel for' their material and they make on-the-spot adjustments to the sounds they hear. Listening to one another and to themselves, they feel where the music is going and adjust their playing accordingly.
>
> (Schön, 2008:69)

In the domain of professionalized formal design practice, Schön suggests that a similar choreography of negotiation takes place between designers and their clients, for example. Ideas, forms and materials are adjusted through interplay. So rather than a systematic plan being adhered to Schön recognizes the value and importance of on-the-spot decisions that are of the moment. Crucially, the analogy of musical improvisation raises the importance of 'feeling'; the intuitive hunch when a particular decision works. Given Schön's understanding of the improvisational qualities of formal design how does this differ from the values of adhocism and informal design?

Schön's is, of course, just one reading of the design process, but even his reflexive approach to professional design differs from the informal in a number of ways. Significantly, as we have seen, for many informal design practices associated with adhocism and bricolage the use of materials that are already to hand is key; secondly, informal design's localized perspective does not seek out scalability in the way formal designers do; and finally, improvisation does not become a methodology in itself. To consider these distinctions in a little more detail, the practices of improvisation within informal design can be situated in regard to the wider philosophy of improvisation.

As shown by Schön's usage, music is the creative practice most readily associated with improvisation. Peters (2013:1) describes how improvisation is concerned with 'being in the moment', with the immediacy of the *now*. There is then an important temporal dimension to improvisation that recognizes the ongoing event of playing music in this manner. Rather than the apparent linearity of the formal design process, improvisation is to follow the materials themselves and what they offer in that moment 'as they open up' (Ingold, 2011:216). The eventfulness of improvisation and the potentiality of matter also speaks to the idea of novelty, where new forms emerge through the configuration of existing elements into new ones. Referencing Benjamin's work on the dialectical and Heidegger's notion of co-presence, Peters considers the interplay between preservation and destruction; between that which is fixed in the past and that which emerges from the past being continually rethought (2013:2). To illustrate this, Peters invokes a telling analogy between musical improvisation and an all-but-unnamed version of Jencks and Silver's adhocist sensibility. Referencing popular television shows where contestants have to build new objects out of scrap, the idea of the new is again central to this:

> it is the manner in which such games demand a form of improvisation from the competing teams – within the strictly delimited material universe of the scrap yard – that brings into view the productive interpenetration of origination and re-novation as the new and the old are engaged with simultaneously.
>
> (Peters, 2013:2)

The formation of new assemblages from scrap speaks directly to the idea of change, of scrap becoming utile. New potentialities and possibilities are seen in this supposedly redundant detritus (see Martin, 2016a).[14] However, Peters goes on to describe how many studies of musical improvisation denigrate non-musical versions. Where the philosophical foundations of musical improvisation are concerned with novelty, invention, the now, the new, as he puts it 'improvisation in common parlance [refers to] the makeshift, the cobbled together, the temporary solutions to problems that remain unsolved' (Peters, 2013:9). Although Peters is quick to criticize such claims, it is nonetheless evident that outwith the harmonious nature of improvisation it is often seen in this light. Without a doubt, perceptions of simply 'making-do' and 'muddling through' stand as populist denunciations of everyday improvisation, owing, I suggest, to their lack of formal planning.

Similar debates on the intersection between the formal and informal are present in science, technology and innovation (STI) studies, notably in the context of African innovation. Clapperton Mavhunga (2017) discusses how formal practices of STI relate to more informal means of engagement in a range of African countries. He describes how the typical reading of STI is dominated by an imperialist imposition of technologies and calls such instances 'inbound' forms of knowledge and technology. Critically for my consideration of informal design practices and improvisation, Mavhunga (2017:10) outlines how primarily European technologies are considered formal, whilst anything which falls out with of these technological practices is seen as informal, and by implication somehow inferior. To be sure, the perception of informal material practices and technologies such as those associated with the range of adhocist informal design approaches highlighted already have a particular cadence in discussions of African technologies:

Africans, are portrayed as just tinkering (that horrible word!) and responding without initiative or inventing anything. Tinkering is such a horrible word because it refers to a mender of what is already made, a trial and error person, or, worse yet, a clumsy, unskilled worker.

(Mavhunga, 2017:7–8)

Mavhunga's distaste is framed by how others interpret or perceive it, notably when compared with more formalized practices of design where the typical approach is the creation of something new through rigorous planning and iterative development. By contrast the tinkerer is seen to dabble in the minutiae of a particular object or problem. Tinkering is a material practice by which people adapt objects, deconstructing, refabricating, repairing them. It is defined a 'careful but informal, interdisciplinary, adaptive methodology typically employed by highly skilled "amateurs" undertaking such tasks as inventing or repairing a homemade gadget' (Cabin, 2011:10). Although tinkering scholars (Jacobs, 1977:1163) suggest that tinkerers do not have a particular end goal in sight, others (Nutch, 1996) recognize that tinkering is fundamentally about dealing with practical challenges. Indeed, it is central to problem-driven disciplines such as science, where tinkering is very much part of the improvisational approach to how scientific knowledge is ultimately generated. Outside scientific domains tinkering also has anti-establishment cadences, where people 'reject, mis-use or differently use a device or service' (Jungknickel, 2018:1). This is very much in keeping with the ingenuous cases of adhocist tinkering or informal design examined earlier in the chapter, but also with hacking as we shall shortly see. Whilst referring to the specificities of African STI Mavhunga again puts it succinctly when he states that appreciating the value of informal practice goes beyond typically 'lazy narratives' to argue that people are 'deeply engaged in intellection, firmly anchored in their own philosophies, and alert to the world around and beyond them' (2017:8).[15] Fundamental to these approaches is the potency, vitality and positivity of the way in which ordinary people – non-professionals – work with the material world. Where the traditional conception of the non-professional bricoleur, or *jua kali* mender for example, is formed by the negative connotations of the amateur, tinkerer or dabbler (Cf. Merrifield, 2017), it is clear that these are intensely creative practices in the spirit of Jencks and Silver's empowered consumer.

To be sure, where some see the ad hoc as just an interim solution that is figured around seat-of-the-pants approaches described by Boguslaw (1965:22), I take this as an indication of the inherent potentiality of local, ad-hoc, informal design approaches. For example, tinkering and improvisation are profoundly dialogical practices where the individual is engaged in an in-depth, close and nuanced proximity to material artefacts. Not least it is also the basis for innovation and evolutionary development. As Jacob famously stated: 'Evolution behaves like a tinkerer who, during eons upon eons, would slowly modify his work, unceasingly retouching it, cutting here, lengthening there, seizing the opportunities to adapt it progressively to its new use' (Jacob, 1977:1164).

Conclusions: Hacking innovation

Fundamentally then, the closeness people have with things when they are fabricating a makeshift water heater in a prison or repurposing a solar cook stove to clad a shelter in Burkina Faso demonstrates how the improviser, the tinkerer is invested directly in new forms of creation – in informal design. Addressing such practices through the lens of misuse enables us to see how challenging the inscribed function of things opens up a space where new configurations of use and action emerge. As Akrich asserts, users (or informal designers in my reading) 'are able to reshape the object, and the various ways in which the object may be used' (1992:206; also see Björgvinsson et al., 2012:107). One of the key assertions this chapter has raised is the value of misuse: as both a conceptual paradigm and equally as a practical logic of action. In identifying misuse as informal design and part of the wider repertoire of deviant design, this chapter set out the multi-scalar reading of deviance through the prism of deviation from intended use. In the earlier sections of this chapter we saw that misuse is inherently inscribed into things – however all artefacts, systems, processes are prone to malfunction, to breakages, to poor design, be it at the micro or macro scales (Perrow, 1984). Hence the user is perhaps never able to use things as they were originally intended. Equally, at an ontological level can we ever be sure as to the origin-idea of 'function'? Given the inherent fallibility of all things do they ever function as truly intended? These questions have been critical to my outline of the importance of misuse to the idea of informal design practices. Taking on board the central tenets of Chapter 3 in particular this chapter has made the case for an appreciation of misuse as *deviation* from formal design practices. From the examples cited throughout the chapter it is clear that an ad hoc, improvised approach to localized material circumstances challenges the parameters of professional design whilst at the same time adhering to more recent moves towards the diffusion of design beyond solely professional domains (Manzini, 2015).

Perhaps one of the central conclusions to draw out is the creativity and inventiveness of misuse shown through informal design practices (Manaugh, 2016; Söderberg, 2010). We are provided with new ways of understanding things; seeing the radical potentiality of materials; the ingenuity of how seemingly disparate entities can be configured to create new assemblages of usability. As noted in the discussions of improvisation misuse connotes an openness to change, much in the way the original nature of innovation did.[16] There is an ongoing potentiality to become something else. Whatever that may be. However, this idea of openness should not simply be left in the assumption it will remain so, that is, fully open to constant change. For as with the previous discussions on traditional forms of business innovation change often comes under pressure to be controlled or formalized. And similar tendencies and tensions are evident in discussions of the creativity of misuse, notably in the practices and cultures of hacking.

The Microsoft Kinect was launched in the US on 4th November 2010.[17] As a gaming device the Kinect was innovative in its use of motion sensing devices which did away with the need for a hand-held controller. For many consumers this heightened gaming experience was enough. However, as the *New Scientist* (Giles, 2010) reported, amongst the hacker community the new device was an opportunity to push the technology to its limits. Following its release, Adafruit Industries – an open-source hardware company – announced that it was offering USD $1000 to the first person able to hack the Kinect and enable it to run on MS Windows. This figure was increased to USD $2000 when Microsoft stated that it would pursue those responsible for hacking the Kinect. The story then becomes rather convoluted as the first hacker to control the depth-sensing system and video demanded USD $10,000 from the wider hacker community to release the code. The ultimate winner of the now-USD $3000 prize was a Spanish hacker. What is important about this story is the value created by hacking the Kinect, by wilfully misusing it (Söderberg, 2010). By opening up the technology and releasing its latent potential the Kinect became significantly more important than a gaming device, just as many of the examples throughout this chapter have shown. Cases abound of new applications for the hacked Kinect technology: from robotics research (Giles, 2010), to cheap 3D scanners for archaeological dig sites (Swaminathan, 2011). Crucially, hacking the device and releasing the code as open source has facilitated new avenues of use, pushing the technology beyond the limitations placed on it by Microsoft.

Although the debates on the technical as well as political and ethical dimensions of computer hacking are beyond the remit of the conclusion to this chapter they do clearly relate to the inherent value of misuse. In the case of the Microsoft Kinect the user-driven innovations only came about because the technology was hacked, the original purpose diverted, and the code distributed freely through open-source approaches for others to engage with the device. The relationship between technology and hackers is a complex one (Conti, 2006), but central to many of these debates is the potential of hackers to produce innovative new uses as well as technological improvements (Richardson, 2016). Like many of the subversive practices detailed throughout the book it should not come as a surprise that hacking has, of course, entered mainstream technological culture with the role of 'ethical hackers' (Caldwell, 2011), much in the same way that the informality of Jugaad was co-opted into a business innovation strategy (Radjou, 2012). On a smaller scale the Swedish homeware company IKEA has recently begun to publicize and promote examples of customers hacking their standardized products (Segran, 2019). A desk becomes a coffee table simply by cutting down the metal legs (also see Jaque/Office for Political Innovation, 2018). After serving a 'cease and desist' notice to a website which shared examples of customers' hacks the subsequent validation of these hacks by IKEA is a straightforwardly commercial decision, one that has identified the opportunity to celebrate the 'creativity' of its customers by marketing such approaches back at them. To a certain extent the purpose of 'white hackers' speaks to a similar mindset: the recognition of how illicit activities can be recuperated and transformed into new market opportunities and security protocols. The following two chapters investigate similar instances of the interrelationship between illicit and licit practices, but as these deal with decidedly illegal activities the simple marketization of opportunity is far from evident. Instead these chapters deal with the complexity of such relationships not least the security approaches. But given the fundamental premise of the book such interactions are far from clear-cut.

5 ILLICIT DESIGN

Introduction

Paul Muldoon's poem 'Rita Duffy: *Watchtower II*' is an account of troubled times, of a border politics where identities bestride the imagined and the physical impositions of difference.

> We're in a constant tussle/ with these Seoiníns-come-lately, a constant back-and-forth/ on the business of smuggling fuel. We run it through cat litter or/ fuller's earth/ to absolve it of the dye. By far the biggest hassle/ is trying to get rid of the green sludge/ left over from the process. It infiltrates our clothes. It's impossible/ to budge.
>
> (Muldoon, 2015:31)

It's a reminder of the geopolitical situatedness of so many instances where the illicit smuggling of goods is part of the socio-cultural fabric of people's lives. It's also a measure of the ingenuity, the tactical wherewithal of how to remove the tell-tale traces of the dyes which differentiated the diesel sold in Northern Ireland from that sold in the Republic of Ireland. It's a reminder of commercial and practical acumen; the nous in seeing the opportunities for making money by selling illicit goods. Whilst Muldoon remembers the time of the 'Troubles' in Northern Ireland from the 1960s onwards, he could well have been describing similar instances from throughout history and across geographies. For the evasion of taxes, the knowledge of geography, territorial borders and practical aptitude are common threads which link the actions of smugglers, be they trafficking alcohol, tobacco or drugs. Above all, in addition to being essentially a commercial activity smuggling is about surreptitious movement – here across the Irish border (see Bottos, 2015). The definition of smuggling itself is clear on this: it is 'a clandestine economic practice that we can simply define as bringing in or taking out from one jurisdiction to another without authorization' (Andreas, 2013:x).

Borders play a significant role in the perpetration of illicit mobilities. They create separation on legal, economic, political and identarian grounds. None more so in recent years than the political deadlock over the US-Mexico border wall, deemed by President Trump to rid the United States of illicit drugs and the 'threat' from migrants. The 'war on drugs' won. But as many studies show (Salter, 2012) the creation of borders inevitably leads to their being breached. At the heart of border politics – and by definition the illicit movement of people and goods – is a cat-and-mouse game, where new strategies developed to supposedly secure territory are thwarted by tactical subterfuge. Drug smuggling as we will see in this chapter is just such a game. This is illustrated in stark fashion by the case of Joaquin Guzmán, otherwise known as El Chapo, who, in February 2019, was found guilty of twenty-six drug-related charges and one murder conspiracy. El Chapo was effectively the head of the Sinaloa Cartel, an organized crime syndicate primarily known for narcotics trafficking into the United States, but it also has operations in around a dozen other countries in Africa, Asia and Europe (Loudis, 2019). For the purposes of this chapter the El Chapo case is revealing in how it shows many of the smuggling methods used by the Sinaloa Cartel. As Loudis notes, the trial in New York 'has offered a detailed insight into the way the US-Mexico border has determined the structure of one of the world's most lucrative businesses' (Loudis, 2019:8). Following El Chapo's conviction the US Attorney's Office issued a press release detailing the extent of the cartel's activities, with evidence gained from drug seizures totalling 130,000 kilograms of heroin and cocaine, alongside testimonies from fourteen witnesses, intercepted recordings, text messages, videos and ledgers (Department of Justice, 2019). The systems used by the Sinaloa Cartel saw drugs trafficked from Mexico to wholesale distribution centres in Atlanta, Arizona, Chicago, Los Angeles, Miami and New York, before being shipped to buyers. To smuggle such large quantities of drugs into the United States took ingenious methods, some of which have almost attained folkloric status, particularly the use of a largescale catapult to fire quantities of marijuana into the United States. This incident in 2011 came after a fence had been erected between the border of Mexico and Arizona (Loudis, 2019:8). Other methods used by the Cartel are equally as sophisticated, including the use of semi-submersibles and full submarines, as well as seven tons of cocaine smuggled in cans of jalapenos (Department of Justice, 2019). Another age-old method of concealment was also employed, the use of secret compartments in cars and trains. In their use of cars the Cartel 'would buy as many as 15 cars at a time and install hidden compartments in them that could hold up to thirty kilos of cocaine', and these would then be driven by 'people who lived on one side of the border but worked legally on the other' (Loudis, 2019:8). Hidden compartments were also used for money laundering purposes by smuggling large quantities of money back into Mexico from the United States in trucks, including one seizure in 1989, when El Chapo's brother attempted to smuggle USD1.26 million into Mexico. Their other money laundering activities included the creation of shell companies (juice distributor; fish flour company) as fronts (Department of Justice, 2019). Finally, the US Attorney's Office describes the importance of a sophisticated communications network to the Cartel's operations, particularly the use of encrypted phones and apps which were developed by an IT engineer paid USD 1 million to set up the network. This enabled the Cartel to communicate with operatives in Colombia, Ecuador, the United States and Canada.

Although distinct examples from separate time periods, on different scales, and in distinct geopolitical contexts the smuggling methods used on the island of Ireland and those between Mexico and the United States situate a range of important factors this chapter will consider. These are effectively commercial activities that demand a similar amount of logistical and administrative organization as legal business interests, and they are concerned with the movement of goods across geographical borders. Crucially for the arguments here, the illicit nature of these enterprises is such that the methods of distribution are distinct from the formal economy, but at the same time *dependent* on it. A similar idea of dependency also being present in how artefacts were repurposed in Chapter 4. More specifically, this chapter sets out to investigate the materialities of drug smuggling, and the ways in which artefacts play a central role in the mobilities of illicit drugs across national and international borders. Whilst a wide range of approaches are adopted by traffickers – some of which I briefly outline in the chapter – the primary focus here is on how smugglers conceal illicit narcotics amidst licit goods and more pointedly how they adapt (or again repurpose) existing artefacts in order to disguise their use as conveyors of drugs. I argue later in the chapter that concealment, disguise and invisibility are fundamental to the illicit mobilities of drugs: for I suggest that the harnessing of seemingly legitimate freight (such as the cans of jalapeno peppers) or of mobile infrastructure (motor vehicles crossing the US-Mexico border) are examples of illicit logistical planning coupled with extensive knowledge of infrastructure and the artefactual potential of licit goods.

Needless to say, the question of design is also a key facet of this chapter. I make the case that the distributive practices adopted by smugglers of illegal narcotics (and other contraband) are akin to the power of designerly intelligence and sensibility discussed in Chapter 1. In particular it is the combination of planning, integrative thinking, material understanding, practical skill and collaboration that exemplifies this. As Manzini's work on diffuse design embodies (in licit settings of course) the competences of designerly intelligence are much more widespread than the domain of professional design, for we see a broad range of actors engaged in exploring and adapting existing materials, systems and practices for dealing with specific contexts. In this case smuggling. Likewise, the adaption of licit goods also speaks to the adhocist sensibility of informal design considered in Chapter 4 where the potentialities of everyday artefacts are manifold. They can become almost anything. However, where improvisation plays a critical role in forms of adhocist misuse, by contrast the act of smuggling is often intricately planned. But the fundamental difference of course is that the practical ingenuity of those repurposing everyday artefacts into new configurations and assemblages is legal. The actions of smugglers disguising cocaine as shipping pallets – as we will see later on – are decidedly illegal. But as I consider here the broader *sensibility* of concealment and disguise as a form of design is concerned with an acutely intimate understanding of the materiality of artefacts, their potential beyond their intended purpose, and ultimately an attuned awareness of the configurative power of designerly intelligence.

The chapter sets out to examine these key points, and more explicitly: the relationship between ingenuity as material sensibility and the wider applications of illicit design intelligence whereby infrastructures and networks are harnessed and how distinct types of smuggling address particular forms of innovation, including the use of concealment but more particularly the design of disguise.[1] As with the other chapters in the book threaded throughout this one is the importance of innovation – albeit illicit or 'outlaw' (Flowers, 2008) in nature – and how this emerges from new forms of material practices. I argue that the methods utilized by smugglers point to a distinct form of innovation through the manipulation of particular material, infrastructural and systemic configurations.

Another common facet of smuggling is the direct relationship with the licit: be that economic processes such as tariffs or security measures instituted to disrupt the illicit activities of smugglers. As we saw in Chapter 3 there is an immanent entanglement between the licit and illicit. Smuggling in particular exemplifies this. None more so than Adam Smith, who, in *The Wealth of Nations*, described smuggling in different terms to other moral crimes (Campbell and Ross (1981); also see Deflem and Henry-Turner, 2001:473; Ramsay, 1952). According to Campbell and Ross although Smith did not advocate smuggling on the grounds of the removal of trade barriers, he did suggest that smuggling was of a different moral order than murder for example which is a moral crime, whereas he saw smuggling from an economic perspective. They go on to state that Smith may have seen smuggling 'as a purely artificial misdemeanour based on the flimsy and temporary will of governments' (Campbell and Ross, 1981:89). As such Smith also stresses the bond between entrepreneurialism and illegality, a fact highlighted in contemporary terms by Gargi Bhattacharyya who suggests that organized crime today is reliant on licit economic processes and systems. Discussed previously in Chapter 3, Bhattacharyya's outline of a symbiotic relationship between the two is decisive to my reading of drug smuggling in this chapter, for it underscores both the structural bond between licit and illicit trade but most importantly for these discussions the infrastructural and material dependency on legal distributive networks by drug traffickers. The idea of dependency across a range of different registers will become ever-more important as we proceed through discussions of drug smuggling.

An investigation of smuggling is inevitably accompanied by a range of caveats. In part because it encompasses so many interrelated debates, be that the epidemiological contexts of drug consumption, the geopolitics of land use and drug cultivation or the entanglements of organized crime with other illicit activities. Given this is not a book about the drug trade *per se* the nature of this chapter is such that it inevitably focuses on just one aspect of trafficking – the material culture of smuggling and specifically the ingenuity of the 'designerly' ways in which smuggling is carried out. In such a comparatively short chapter it is not possible to cover these myriad other debates, all of them vitally important to the broader context of the trade in drugs. Most importantly the geopolitical backdrop of the 'war on drugs' are beyond the chapter's scope. Indeed, the debates on the 'war on drugs' and narco-politics attempt to create a binary split between good and bad. Much like the earlier debates in Chapter 3 on the imbrication of the licit and illicit the 'war on drugs' 'rationalize[s] the practices of governance in terms of problems associated with narcotics' (Garriot, 2011:3). Such a simplistic interpretation under the guise of the 'war on drugs' fails to understand the complicity of neoliberal governments in perpetuating geopolitical turmoil. Not only do geopolitical dynamics empower the drugs trade, as Castells highlights the demand for synthetic narcotics is symptomatic of the alienation and despair of many individuals and communities under the lived realities of late capitalism (Castells, 2010:xvii; 179).

Finally, a brief note on methodology, as well as the methods of smuggling themselves. Most presciently, in discussing a variety of smuggling methods I am only considering those that have been intercepted rather than those that have evaded seizure and thus inherently more ingenious. Rather than seeking information from smugglers themselves (see Decker and Townsend Chapman, 2008) the discussion here is framed by methods that have ultimately *failed*. So, in many ways they lack the ultimate ingenuity of eluding capture. Suffice to say that the academic study of criminality is riven with this inherent methodological tension (Natarajan, 2000). Equally, the study of drug trafficking is deeply ethical. Both in relation to the harmful social effects noted already, but also the 'celebration' of ingenuity itself. As I discuss in the chapter there is a fine balance between a considered investigation of the methods utilized by organized criminal groups and the perennial fascination and gratification at such forms of cunning (see Mars, 1983). Although somewhat guilty of the latter my hope is that the former comes to the fore.

Smuggling practices: Shifting perceptions

In straightforward terms illicit activities such as piracy and smuggling might be depicted as entrepreneurial endeavours. Piracy for example has been described as a 'service industry, [and] a business concerned with [...] transport and distribution' (Starkey, 2001:108). Smuggling too can be seen in similar terms, as a business activity focused on 'supply, delivery, finance, and contractual enforcement' (Meyer and Parssinen, 1998:2). It is entangled with the very constitution of trade flows, notwithstanding their illicit qualities. According to Dominguez (1975:92) smuggling is an inherently distributive practice, determined by various types of movement: from small-scale smuggling by individuals, through larger-scale operations such as weapons smuggling, to the 'under-invoicing' of goods declared (Nordstrom, 2007:119–20). As the latter suggests, contraband smuggling directly emerges from the imposition of import duties and taxes (Deflem and Henry-Turner, 2001:473; Karras, 2010:1). Read in this manner the activities of pirates and smugglers differ little from legitimate business ventures, albeit in one decisive manner – their illegality. As discussed at length already the distinct separation between illicit and licit entrepreneurial practices is not quite so clear cut. To be sure, the economic development of the United States is intertwined with 'clandestine commerce', so much so that 'smuggling, it turns out, has been as much about building up the American state as about subverting it' (Andreas, 2013:x–xi). Reading the history of the United States through the lens of illicit practices, and smuggling in particular, provides a counter to the rhetoric of untainted capitalism. For Andreas (2013:3) the histories of smuggling reveal the 'dynamics of borders, foreign relations, government expansion, economic development, and societal transformations'. For earlier historians of smuggling the legacies of foreign trade – this time in the English context – are also intertwined with smuggling: 'It was only the triumph of free trade in the early Victorian age that deprived them [smugglers] of their livelihood' (Ramsay, 1952:131). So, the growing dominance of free trade was the catalyst for the diminution of smuggling as a form of foreign trade. The supposed bifurcation between licit and illicit trade activity is also problematized by the historical roots of many multinationals in illicit trade.

Just such a case is evident in the drug trade. Meyer and Parssinen (1998:2–4) note that in the context of the opium and opiates trade, from the mid-1850s up until 1906 it could be supplied, distributed and sold just as any other legal commodity. Led by China, 1906 saw a change in the international perspective on opiate use. Prior to the Communist revolution in 1949, China was the largest consumer of opiates in the world, with estimates in 1935 identifying 20 per cent of China's 400 million population as addicts (Stilwell, cited in Meyer and Parssinen, 1998:3). The shift in China's outlook towards criminalizing opium and opiates in the early twentieth century marked a significant change in international perception as well. For the USA and Britain were supportive of China's efforts, and by 1921 the 'Opium Advisory Committee' had been set up by the League of Nations. What this illustrates is the de-legitimization of the opium and opiates trade, and the concomitant switch in legal and moral values. Over a relatively short period of time a once licit commodity became illicit, as did the businesses originally set up to manufacture, distribute and sell the drugs.[2] Just such a process of de-legitimization is evident today with local and national-scale changes in the de-criminalization of marijuana, where the boundaries between legality and illegality are 'labile and volatile' (Polese, Russo, and Strazzari, 2019:2)

This is telling on a number of levels. It highlights the market dynamics of the licit trade in opiates in the late nineteenth and early twentieth centuries, with China the main consumer of the drug; it underscores growing international cooperation around the prohibition of certain substances; and for the purposes of this section of the chapter it fundamentally demonstrates how changes in perception are inherent to the discourses and debates on illicit drugs. Once legitimate goods can very quickly become illegal, and vice versa. Where we saw the moral, political and legal mindsets on opium and opiates changing in the early twentieth century the shift in perception of smuggling from the eighteenth and nineteenth centuries is equally as intriguing. In particular the public perception of smuggling practices, including narcotics, that perhaps pervades the historical imaginary is that of the romantic smuggler. The reasons for such a vision of smuggling are culturally complex, but perhaps the clearest basis for this is the collective odiousness at fiscal regulation. Indeed, in a similar vein to the consumer demand for counterfeit goods investigated in Chapter 6 the histories of contraband smuggling are tangled-up in society's dislike of tax and the ultimate desire for cheaper commodities. In an 1846 article entitled 'Smuggling and Smugglers' published in the American periodical *The Albion*, the unnamed author notes that 'it is in human nature to hanker after those things that are prohibited' (No author, 1846:603). There is something alluring about such goods. A slightly later article in *The Washington Post* from 1898 also foregrounds the romantic notion of the smuggler, noting that whist the smuggler has been of peculiar interest for 'time immemorial' it was up until around the mid-nineteenth century that the smuggler's reputation was at its height. For at this time goods could be procured from smugglers at much reduced prices compared with legal traders (No author, 1898:5). In this guise it is clear to see why the smuggler has been viewed as simultaneously criminal and hero, depending on perspective. In the same newspaper column one perceives a further shift in the smuggler's social standing. There is an almost nonchalant tone to the actions of smugglers at this time in the late nineteenth century: 'The capture at port of an affable person whose seeming abundant portliness is found to be the rich padding of highly dutiable lace is not an event of more than mild interest and humorous comment' (No author, 1898:5). But the author goes on to suggest an even more forthright disregard for the smuggler of that period, one that perhaps chimes with contemporary perceptions. It is worth quoting in full:

> The present day smuggler is little if anything better than a sneak thief, and a very selfish one at that. If he is to regain popular favor he must take to the old game of night landings on perilous shores in the teeth of a blinding storm; he must cache his spoil in wonderful surf-bound caves, swear like a pirate, fight like a Turk, and above all, distribute largesse with a liberal hand. Then shall we take him back to our melodrama and give him his old place among the heroes of the yellow covered novel. Meanwhile he must don the stripes.
>
> (No author, 1898:5)

Very much of its time the quote nonetheless illustrates the cliché of the swashbuckling smuggler using their wherewithal to fight the forces of nature and land their goods. But perhaps most tellingly is the perceived redistributive function of the smuggler who provides cheap commodities to the general populace. Smuggling, at least in historical terms, is akin to the classic Robin Hood effect (Parker, 2008; 2009). Such historical accounts do not fully explain the stark shift in perspective from these earlier cases of opium smuggling and the romantic hero-figure of the smuggler to the contemporary moral panic surrounding smuggling today. Clearly the social impact of smuggled lace is vastly limited when compared with drug trafficking and consumption. Perhaps the most obvious distinction between these two historical periods has been the universal rise of the 'war on drugs', the politics of narco-states (Cf. Chouvy, 2016), which pervades much of the representation of the drug trade today, as well as the wider links to global organized crime (Hall and Scalia, 2019). However, even with the climate of moral panic that narco-politics produces there is still a socio-cultural fascination with the drug trade and its attendant lifestyle. One might think of hit TV series such as 'Breaking Bad', 'Narcos' or series two of 'The Wire', through to popular TV documentaries on the security procedures at airports used to intercept illicit narcotics. Rastello puts it succinctly:

> The newspapers like talking about it. It always makes for good copy: stories of gangland shoot-outs in the narrow streets of some Mediterranean city, colourful portraits of dealers great and small, the occasional alarmed – and cliché-ridden – reportage on the increase in consumption, especially the young, in discos and nightclubs.

> (Rastello, 2011:11)

There is then a tension between the political rhetoric surrounding the 'war on drugs' and the 'spectacular' appeal of the drug culture that Rastello describes. Perhaps the common link is the global nature of the drug trade. The language of the 'war on drugs' is permeated by global actors perpetrating transnational crime, whilst at the same time popular fascination surrounds the ingenuity of shipping large quantities of drugs around the globe.

The networked nature of global mobilities is also a key factor in discourses on the contemporary drugs trade. In terms of the shifting parameters of drug production and distribution in the early twentieth century, the starkest difference in contemporary terms is the networked nature of the global scale of distribution in particular. Central to such scalar changes is the *interconnectedness* of the global economy and particularly the cross-border reach of global transportation and infrastructure networks, including small-scale online drug distribution (Martin, J. 2014). Indeed, the increase in networked configuration has also seen important changes in how drug production and distribution – as part of organized criminal groups – operates. Key to this is how, in the last twenty years, previously vertically integrated organized crime groups with a top-down hierarchical structure have changed. Such forms of organization have perhaps most typically been seen with Colombian drug trafficking cartels, notoriously those including Pablo Escobar. However, as with Rastello's comments above, Kenney (2007:234) argues that the infamous hierarchical formation of the cartels stems from a 'cartel myth'. Instead, in interviews with Columbian cocaine traffickers Kenney discovered that family, associates and friends played an independent role in the Columbian drugs trade, rather than solely through hierarchically controlled large-scale groups (also see Naylor, 1997; Williams, 1998). The image typically portrayed of vertical integration within cartel-like structures is that of tightness and control; however, this has now been discredited through the likes of Kenney's work where a richer understanding of loose configurations is evident. Instead, as other criminal activities by organized groups – prostitution, people trafficking, weapons smuggling – demonstrate the structure of drug trafficking in the Colombian context is made up of flexible networks that expand and contract depending on particular commercial opportunities and constraints (Kenney, 2007:235).

This networked configuration has also played a noteworthy role in appreciating the organizational dynamics of global organized criminal activity more broadly (Bouchard and Amirault, 2013). One of the fundamental aspects that networked formations afford, both in illicit and licit enterprise, is *flexibility*. Typically, in vertically integrated configurations the links between individual members are notoriously weak so that If one of the key members of the group is arrested for example a significant gap is left in the structure. With the flexibility of networked structures the link is not as fallible: inherent structural weaknesses are negated through the horizontal nature of the network; that is, there are other members of the network who can take on specific roles, or new ones can be 'plugged in' (Cf. Morselli and Petit, 2007). A critical aspect of the architecture of organized crime networks such as drug trafficking is their 'distributed' nature. Although criminal networks can be localized on a regional as well as national scale, they are not necessarily geographically bounded (Hall, 2012:182). Mirroring the development of licit global infrastructures, a fundamental facet of the structural configuration of global organized crime networks is the infrastructure that facilitates flexibility and distributed reach. These infrastructures of communication and mobility have propelled a range of changes in the constitution of cross-border organized crime, notably increased interaction and integration of activities (see Hall and Scalia, 2019). As we shall shortly see in the next section, of fundamental importance is that for drug smugglers, the various constituent parts that form the network can be situated out with areas of national jurisdiction, this particularly being the case with transportation networks. The distributed quality of crime networks is such that although there are cores and peripheries (Williams, 1998:155–6), there is extensive reach beyond national borders, a key determinant of *global* organized crime including drug trafficking. For my arguments in this chapter one of the most significant factors for both historical but primarily contemporary drug smuggling is how the distributed nature of criminal networks is dependent on the interlinked relationships between a vast array of actors that form these networks. For Williams (1998:155) this is produced by 'individuals, organizations, firms, or even computers'. So rather than individuals forming the entirety of a network it is populated by a wide range of different entities, including the human of course but crucially for discussions in the rest of this chapter – the nonhuman. These might include power networks, or generators; the design of the interfaces; the software; upgrades. But these can move beyond technological infrastructure to smaller scale, seemingly mundane actors such as everyday artefacts. The actors are almost unlimited.

So far, we have seen that perceptions of smuggling have shifted across time. Even within relatively close temporal proximity to the present-day drugs such as opiates – which we now associate with highly detrimental social effects – were legal and part of a burgeoning international trade. Undeniably, medical knowledge of the harmful impact of such drugs has led to changes in classification, but the change of legal status in the early twentieth century highlights how a once-legitimate enterprise can quickly become illegal. Similarly, perceptions of the illegal narcotics industry today are primarily controlled by the US-led 'war on drugs'. By addressing the structure of the contemporary drug trade, particularly in Latin America, it is clear how the networked configuration of much organized crime has spread the activities to a global level, something that is in part dependent on the distributed geographies and mobilities of such spatial formations. In the next section I turn to these final points in more depth and consider how drug smugglers have deployed a range of ingenuous methods and tactics to overcome the increasing securitization of international borders.

Smuggling methods: Illicit ingenuity and the tactics of concealment

A common thread throughout this book has been the interplay between innovation and ingenuity. In Chapter 3 the link between the two was described as the foundation of capitalist entrepreneurialism, particularly through the Schumpeterian idea of technological disruption. But as also discussed in that chapter a key definition of innovation is *change*, notably the radical heritage of innovation as transgressive and revolutionary. Similarly, in Chapter 4 I argued that novelty, ingenuity, inventiveness and innovation emerge from the *misuse* of things. Building on these discussions and the changing perceptions of drug cultures here I broaden the argument by considering a range of examples where smugglers have effectively 'misused' artefacts and infrastructures albeit for fundamentally different purposes than everyday forms of adhocist misuse (as previously noted, the book makes the case for a multi-scalar understanding of deviancy, from everyday repurposing to the illegality of drug trafficking). So, where I termed everyday misuse as a type of 'informal design' such a phrase does not capture the illegality, risk and ultimately the potential harm of the practices discussed here. Instead I employ the notion of 'illicit ingenuity' to capture the relationship between the ingenuity of the creative material methods deployed by smugglers and the illicit nature of these practices.

To examine the diversity of tactical approaches used by smugglers I begin with a discussion of the key methods: these include the difference between the development of new infrastructures of conveyance, as compared with the surreptitious utilization of existing modes of transportation such as commercial airline or shipping routes. These latter methods are essential to this chapter. That is, how smugglers have adopted and adapted the established functions of legitimate artefacts and the material connectivity of physical infrastructures rather than developing new and standalone systems. In doing so it builds on the discussions in the last section by considering how the networked organization of global infrastructures of passenger travel and freight distribution offer or afford particular opportunities for concealing illegal narcotics amongst the diverse array of actors that form these networks.

In the contemporary context the trafficking of illegal narcotics is deeply embedded within the wider sphere of transnational organized crime (Hall and Scalia, 2019). As with the global spatialities of transnational organized crime drug trafficking is imbued with an inherent distributedness. This is clearly so with historical examples but critical to the present-day conveyance of illicit narcotics is the extensive *reach* that organized criminal networks have as a form of subversive mobilities (Cohen et al., 2017). The ability to distribute such goods across international borders is of course central to the constitution of the drugs trade, formed as it is of somewhat traditional patterns of production and consumption: where production of cocaine for example takes place in Latin and South America, whilst the main consumer markets are in North America and Europe (Ameripol, 2013). For Decker and Townsend Chapman (2008:36) the structure of the smuggling enterprises they studied in the United States is to a certain extent akin to licit commercial organizations. They detail how such organizations are formed of various 'offices', the language of which concurs with Caulkins et al's (2009:68) point that their own study-group of incarcerated smugglers believed they were engaged in business activity per se.[3] The offices consist of supply-side operations focused on production; offices of finance and transportation; a distribution office in the United States; as well as independent transporters, brokers and other contacts (also see Ameripol, 2013:66). Although it may seem rather ill-judged to map these illicit enterprises onto legitimate organizational structures their underlying operations are disarmingly similar. They deal with comparable logistical hurdles: both are ultimately concerned with meticulous spatio-temporal planning. As a result, the structural organization of smuggling highlights the centrality of transportation, distribution and mobility to these illicit enterprises. That said, the trafficking of illegal drugs consists of a broad array of approaches that are inherently complex and multifaceted. These depend on the nature of the drug itself, the geopolitical contexts of production and the forms of interdiction. Further to this there are distinctions in approach between the smuggling activities of lower and higher-level distribution (Adler and Adler, 1983). Above all, as Caulkins et al. (2009:69) note there is little evidence to suggest that there are *typical* approaches to smuggling, an argument that is clear in relation to new trafficking methods becoming necessary following interception – the game of cat and mouse noted earlier.

Although a common pattern may not be easily definable, the literature on smuggling methods (see Caulkins et al., 2009; Decker and Townsend Chapman, 2008) does suggest a distinct array of approaches that can potentially be grouped into two core areas. Doing so is not an exercise in reductivism, rather a means to establish distinct approaches to the material-infrastructural ingenuity discussed in this chapter. The earlier discussion of El Chapo's recent incarceration offers instructive means to consider these two areas: the Sinaloa Cartel's use of narco-submarines is a method utilizing transport technologies *separate* to established routes; whereas their use of hidden compartments in automobiles crossing the US-Mexico border at official crossing points demonstrates the covert use of *legitimated* transport infrastructure. These methods are not mutually exclusive, rather they are framed by the needs of specific circumstances and contexts. I identify these two primary programmes of drug trafficking as follows: (1) shadow networks and supply lines; (2) concealing drugs in legitimate transportation routes and supply lines.

Shadow networks and supply lines

Both categories are obviously concerned with the concealment of drugs and their transportation but achieve this in different ways. The technical development of sophisticated smuggling vehicles such as narco-subs is an independent form of distribution where shadow networks and supply lines are created that run parallel to or in the shadow of legitimate mobilities. Although the design and manufacture of narcosubs (Guerrero C., 2020; Ramirez and Bunker, 2015) are perhaps the most 'spectacular' on a range of different levels, rather more mundane examples are prevalent.[4] The use of standard small boats, aircraft and road vehicles to ship quantities of drugs across international borders are common, but crucially these subversive mobilities (Cohen et al., 2017) take place out-with formalized transhipment routes although they could be said to utilize pre-existing natural infrastructure such as sea or airspace. Manuel Castells notes how, in the 1990s, the principal method of transporting drugs to the USA was the use of small private aircraft flown from the Caribbean, including planes which used a landing strip on an islet owned by Carlos Lehder, a dominant trafficker (Castells, 2010:199). But prior to this in the 1970s private light aircraft were also used to smuggle marijuana from Mexico into the United States (No author, 1974). Alongside the use of the drugs cannon employed by the Sinaloa Cartel another example of more sophisticated technologies of shadow trafficking infrastructure is the creation of drug-tunnels crossing the US-Mexico border (Associated Press, 2016). Less logistically or practically complex was the use of 'go-fast' speed boats in the 1980s to ship drugs from the Bahamas or Cuba to Florida (Decker and Chapman, 2008:69). However, following the discovery of their use traffickers resorted to an alternative form of transportation: lobster and shrimp boats. As McMurray notes, smuggler's 'tricks of the trade, their ruses and subterfuges are developed hand-in-hand with the development of the borders meant to control them' (2001:127). In this context the conspicuousness of high-speed boats was inverted by the introduction of fishing vessels which to all intents and purposes were simply engaged in legitimate work. This was furthered by the use of props (fishing equipment, bait, food, beer) to make it *appear* as if the fishing boats had been out in the water all day, whereas they had been involved in transporting drugs (Decker and Chapman, 2008:71). The apparent operation of these vessels as legitimate fishing boats as well as the use of the props leads onto the next substantive approach that deals with methods of concealment, but also to the later discussion of props as a form of disguise.

Concealing drugs in legitimate transportation routes and supply lines

As the move to the use of fishing boats suggests, the two forms of trafficking are not entirely independent, neither is their use by specific groups of traffickers. The example of the fishing boats demonstrates the tactical reversal of the previous smuggling method and the harnessing of legitimate transportation networks and supply lines: in this instance a fishing enterprise. The distinction between the two overall approaches is that with the latter the propulsive force of legal infrastructural mobilities are used illicitly through a range of means, primarily the tactics of concealment that I address now, and disguise which I focus on in more conceptual depth in the final section of this chapter.

Sneak It Through: Smuggling Made Easier is an alluring title in itself, a rallying call to evade border authorities. The book, by Michael Connor (1984), is a libertarian text that provides a vast range of examples for concealing illicit items in everyday artefacts. Whilst the author and publisher provide a caveat in the colophon that they assume no responsibility for the use or misuse of the techniques described in the book, motivation is clear: how to sneak through 'weapons, controlled substances, oranges, you name it' (Connor, 1984: back cover). The techniques of concealment speak to many of the examples already noted, but perhaps more succinctly the ones contained here (including bread rolls; plant pots; handles of tennis rackets; pencils) all highlight the importance of materiality and material knowledge. Awareness of the material potential of these everyday artefacts. Connor also raises another fundamental aspect of smuggling, the importance of cover. The appearance of normality.

As with Rastello's previous assertions about the media's sensationalist approach to certain aspects of drug culture, perhaps the most infamous examples of concealment and the seeming cover of normality are drug mules (Fleetwood, 2014). In the literature 'drug mules' is something of a catch-all term, identifying individuals who intentionally attempt to smuggle illegal drugs using international primarily air travel (but also ships) as their primary means of cross-border transportation. However, there are key differences between the various methods employed: mules include 'body-packers', those who have knowingly secreted drugs about themselves by ingesting them internally in their stomachs or inserting into the rectum or vagina in prepared condoms or the fingers of latex gloves (Ameripol, 2013:37; Fleetwood, 2014:141). The potential dangers of such methods are self-evident (Gill and Graham, 2002). Mules can also refer to individual couriers who strap drugs to their bodies using either adhesive tape or specially designed vests or girdles. The term 'mules' also relates to couriers more generally and those (wittingly and unwittingly) carrying drugs in adapted luggage or other travel goods such as tourist souvenirs or toiletries. In these situations adapted goods also include standard items of clothing with specially sewn-in sections, or drugs hidden in the soles of shoes for example (Ameripol, 2013:84). A relatively recent and perhaps even more ingenious example includes the impregnation of clothing with liquid forms of narcotics (Fleetwood, 2014:75). One case in particular offers an insightful outline of the process. From a forensic science perspective, McDermott and Power (2005) describe a case they were involved with in 2002 where a Brazilian woman was discovered at Dublin airport in Ireland carrying six pairs of jeans in her luggage after having flown from Sao Paolo. Suspicions were raised due to the overly stiff quality of the denim fabric and the use of moth balls in the suitcase, a common tactic to disguise the smell of drugs from drug detection dogs. Upon further examination it was discovered that the denim jeans were impregnated with a liquid form of cocaine: it had been poured onto the denim fabric which soaked up the liquid. Ultimately, when extracted the yield of cocaine from the six pairs of jeans amounted to just under 692 grams (McDermott and Power, 2005:2).

In the context of the UK, Caulkins et al.'s (2009) study of how drugs entered the UK offers a further insightful and practical outline of this approach (also see SOCA, 2009/10:17–19). Through a series of interviews with incarcerated smugglers, the authors describe in detail their trafficking methods. These may seem somewhat mundane in relation to the technological innovation of narco-subs or the logistical bravado of smuggling tunnels, but nonetheless the cases they cite offer a particularly useful angle on the material-infrastructural tactics of using existing transportation networks to smuggle illegal narcotics. In a sample of 222 inmates the most common method was the use of individual passengers or couriers smuggling drugs on scheduled commercial air routes rather than the standalone small aircraft shipments described above. Second to this was the use of couriers employing other forms of transportation such as ferry services or the UK-French Eurotunnel service. Although courier services were the most common method of distribution into the UK, others included corrupt vehicle operators such as lorry drivers hiding drugs amidst freight goods; transportation of commercial flights through corrupt employees; and the use of postal and courier services into the UK (Caulkins et al., 2009:71). As the authors admit, this is only one group of incarcerated smugglers in one geographical context and as such it is impossible to draw wider conclusions from their study. But for the discussion of the materiality of smuggling their findings are insightful particularly in light of the ingenuity of recognizing the potential of specific transportation routes and the material knowledge employed to disguise the drugs themselves within these routes. Before addressing these more fully in relation to a broader geographical coverage of smuggling through concealment, the historical genealogy of these practices is addressed to posit the trans-historical nature of such methods.

Examples from the late nineteenth and early twentieth centuries provide a telling account of the cultures of smuggling – both illegal drugs and bootlegged items like alcohol and tobacco. As with the contemporary examples already described including those in *Sneak It Through: Smuggling Made Easier*, illicit ingenuity is manifest in numerous ways, most notably the intermingling and concealment of illicit goods amidst licit goods, in modes of transportation, or about the body. In his 1906 article 'The Romance of Modern Smuggling' T.C. Bridges describes the changing cultures of smuggling even at this perceivably nascent stage of illicit trafficking. He begins by noting how, in the period from the early 1800s to the time of his writing, the number of articles subject to British import duties had dwindled from around fifteen hundred to roughly three dozen (Bridges, 1906:751). However, the change in importation taxes had not led to the loss of smuggling, for as he notes the cunning practices of smugglers continued. This is particularly evident in the descriptions of the cunning examples where for instance in the early 1900s a passenger was searched at the port of Harwich in England and found to have tobacco about his person, wrapped around his torso in the form of a plaster cast. In addition to this 'he was wearing two pairs of trousers, the inner being stuffed with choice cigarette tobacco' (Bridges, 1906:752). Also at this time Bridges talks of the ingenuity of seamen in smuggling tobacco (1906:752), including one case where customs officials discovered expensive cigars hidden inside dozens of loaves which had had their insides hollowed out. Only when one of the loaves was shaken and its bottom fell out were suspicions raised.

Opium, heroin and hashish were the main drugs of choice in late 1930s Egypt. According to Thomas Russell, the Director of the Central Narcotics Intelligence Bureau (CNIB) of the Egyptian Government, many of the methods used to smuggle these narcotics were ingenious, none more so than an episode from 1938 where pseudo priests and nuns were used to smuggle drugs into the Port of Alexandria (Russell, 1939). This is an intriguing story and one that illustrates the resourcefulness of smugglers, an aspect that will be discussed shortly in terms of illicit design. For now, the story itself is a distillation of many cases of smuggling, with an eye for the contextual detail of a particular situation, an appreciation of how specific individuals and artefacts are culturally inscribed and ultimately the role of informers in thwarting the activities of smugglers. Russell describes how an informant came forward to the CNIB to reveal a plan to smuggle opium and hashish into Egypt by boat, with the drugs brought on shore by two disguised priests and nuns of the Franciscan Order. The CNIB arranged for a female police officer to be used as one of the nuns, assisted in doing so by the informant. Once on board the vessel, the fake priests and nuns were to have the drugs wrapped around their bodies using a thin surgical gauze. Once this had taken place Russell describes what happened next:

> Despite their long flowing robes, complete with girdle and crucifix, giving the impression of being devout members of the Holy Order, the Customs official went up to [the priest], and on feeling his arms discovered that his suspicions were well founded. He immediately arrested him.
>
> (Russell, 1939:346)

The impostors (including the police officer) were found to be carrying thirteen kilograms of opium and eighteen kilograms of hashish.

Russell seemed something of a regular author for *The Police Journal* during this period. In a 1940 article – by which time he was Commandant of Cairo City Police – he offers a telling tale of nonhuman modes of smuggling using camels (Russell, 1940). He notes how Syria and Palestine were the main conduits for illegal drugs to enter Egypt, both of which, alongside Sudan, were also Egypt's main suppliers of camels. As attested to by a number of examples in this chapter large-scale movements of goods, animals or people across territorial borders are common tactical means of smuggling through disguise, just as they were in Egypt. In one brief example the importation of camels was used as a front for smuggling hashish, employing the camels themselves as the 'carriers'. Noting the smugglers' 'ingenuity in disguising their goods if they wish to evade the eagle eyes and keen noses of the patrols', Russell goes on to list a 'recipe' for hashish smuggling:

> Take one camel with a thick woolly coat, shave away an oblong patch of hair on the flank, just below the hump: take a slab of hashish 10 x 5 x 1 inches and glue it on to the bare skin: take the hair previously shaven off and glue it onto the top side of the hashish slab: comb the hair together again. Repeat three times on each side of each camel: do not saddle the camels, and proceed with an innocent look.
>
> (Russell, 1940:300–1)

Whilst it would be interesting if this indeed was an authentic 'recipe' for smuggling, Russell's artistic licence comes across more fully. Nonetheless these actual methods used by the convicted smugglers further underline the points raised above in relation to knowledge of the traditional transit routes for camels into Egypt, as well as creative, or as developed shortly, designerly approaches to understanding the problem-situation. Equally as important for the arguments I pursue below in the following section on designing disguise is the 'potential' offered by the situation itself, particularly the well-established distribution of camels into Egypt.[5] In this same article perhaps a more straightforward notion of 'design' is in evidence – again in relation to the use of camels to smuggle hashish and opium, but this time through the design of material artefacts used in the operation. Russell describes how another informant provided information about a group of Palestinian smugglers who had devised a new method of smuggling narcotics across the border. They had contrived a system of lodging zinc cylinders full of opium and hashish in the stomachs of camels through making the camels swallow them. Twelve camels were discovered with seventy of these cylinders in their stomachs, totalling '38 pounds of hashish and 140 pounds of opium' (Russell, 1940:302). What is particularly revealing about this case is the practical knowledge required for it to be feasible. Firstly, as Russell notes, it calls on veterinary knowledge of camels' stomach physiognomy. For the cylinders to remain in their first stomach and not to pass through to the second and third they had to be of sufficient thickness. The cylinders, some 6 inches long and 1½ inches side, were designed with conical ends so that they could easily pass into the camels' stomachs. Finally, the cylinders were made out of zinc which is less corrosive than tin, required if the cylinders were to remain in the stomachs for any length of time.[6] One final brief example from the early twentieth century is noteworthy for both its ingenuity as well as correspondence with contemporary examples of drug smuggling. At this time saccharin was highly sought after as an alternative to sugar and as a result subject to 'the heaviest duty of any object of import' (Bridges, 1906:752). It was thus a prime candidate for illicit trafficking. Given the material nature of saccharin it has the potential to be mixed with other substances such as sulphate of soda then separated at a later time. This is precisely what happened at the port of Folkestone in England. In this case saccharin was mixed with aniline dyes and sulphate of soda to evade the high import duties, only discovered when a customs official rubbed a little on his hand and detected the sweet taste of the saccharin.

With many of the historic examples outlined above – and these of course are just a tiny sample of the plethora of cases, and obviously those that have been intercepted – I argue that they offer clear evidence of ingenuity. In many ways, as we'll see below the methods and approaches utilized by contemporary smugglers differ very little from historical tactics. There is still application of various knowledge formations: practicality, infrastructural and systemic awareness, technical skills, logistical planning and bribery of security personnel. However, the most straightforward answer to the question is *scale*. This is evident in many of the areas just noted, but principally in the scale of the commercial enterprise itself; and the geographic reach of contemporary smuggling practices. Both these highlight a key distinction – that of the exponential growth of commercial transportation networks (global container shipping channels, commercial airline routes) and communication networks in the late twentieth century and thus the ever-greater opportunity to illicitly harness their infrastructural power. So, where Ramsay – admittedly writing of a different period – notes how the medieval period when compared with the late eighteenth century had 'limited volume of trade, [alongside] dissociated and restricted channels by both sea and land'

(Ramsay, 1952:136), a parallel case could be said of the difference between early twentieth century smuggling practices such as that of saccharin and contemporary cases. Ultimately then whilst the underlying ingenuity of concealment is somewhat constant the unquestionable difference between these two periods is the scalar impact of infrastructural and geographical reach due to networked configurations.

This is most clearly demonstrated through the use of global freight distribution channels where illegal narcotics are concealed amongst legitimate cargo. Examples abound and far too numerous to list in detail here. One includes the seizure in March 2018 of more than USD1.5 million worth of heroin at the Pharr-Reynosa International Bridge on the US-Mexico border where the drugs were concealed amidst a consignment of tomatoes (Sabawi, 2018). An even larger consignment of cocaine was seized at the Port of Baltimore in June 2019 when a shipping container carrying beach chairs was intercepted and loaded with 151 kilograms of cocaine worth USD10 million hidden in black sports bags amongst the chairs (US Customs and Border Protection, 2019). The largest ever haul of narcotics at the port, the shipment had originated in China and travelled to Baltimore through Panama destined for Maryland, highlighting the interconnectedness of cargo mobilities and the resultant infiltration of these networks by smugglers. In Melbourne, Australia a still-larger amount of methamphetamine worth USD840 million (AUS $1.197 billion) was seized by Australian Border Force officials in June 2019. The 1.6 tonnes of the drug were discovered hidden inside a shipment of stereo speakers from Bangkok (Goudreau, 2019a).

Concealment is then one of the most widely adopted methods used by smugglers, and whilst the use of freight transhipments is common other forms of concealment are also seen, in even more seemingly 'innocent' goods. Again in Australia in June 2019 a smaller consignment of methamphetamine, this time weighing three kilograms and worth USD695,000 (AUS $1 million), was discovered hidden inside comic books (Goudreau, 2019b). The leader of the criminal gang had travelled regularly to southern California, where the narcotics were then sent via courier distribution services to Queensland hidden inside the comic books. On a smaller geographical scale concealment of drugs in automobiles is also a well-established tactic, particularly across the Mexico-US border. One case from 2018 is illustrative of the method. A woman was arrested at the Otay Mesa Port of Entry in San Diego, California, after border authorities carried out a scan of her minivan where USD1 million worth of methamphetamine, cocaine and heroin was discovered concealed in the doors, side panels, spare tyre and fuel tank (Associated Press, 2018).

Mindful of the distinct historical, geographical and political contexts there is still much to be learnt from the range of cases outlined above particularly around the illicit ingenuity and planning required for concealing illegal narcotics and other contraband. But as discussed in more depth in the next section, I suggest that these illegal practices exemplify a form of designerly intelligence, that is a sensibility towards the materiality of quotidian artefacts such as denim jeans and automobiles, as well as their embeddedness in global freight and passenger mobilities. In particular, the material infrastructures of global transportation networks offer surreptitious potential to smugglers through their cross-border reach. This highlights how the drugs trade is inherently spatial as well as material. Its histories are formed of territorial evasion, where the control over legitimate spaces such as ports meant that knowledge of clandestine sites to land contraband was part of the smuggling process, and continues to be (Jones, 2019). The deserted beaches and coves of smuggling's romantic period speak to this notion of a 'smuggling landscape', that is, the geographical situation and topography of these spaces afforded specific opportunities for surreptitious practices. Whilst remote locations such as airstrips and coastal regions are still critical to the movement of drugs the spatialities and landscapes of smuggling have extended to include virtual sites as in the case of online distribution on the dark web (Martin, J., 2014). Likewise, the artefacts used for smuggling offer similar potential to the territorial affordances of secluded beaches. Where the seclusion of remote regions limits of the power of surveillance, a similar approach can be seen with concealment. In the next section I consider how the materiality of disguise attempts an even more ingenuous means of evasion.

Illicit designerly intelligence: The design of disguise

The methods of concealment discussed so far appear almost routine when compared with the use of pigeons – or narcopalomas ('drug doves') – to carry drugs. Speaking to the spectacle of fascination described by Rastello (2011) such cases are illustrative of illicit ingenuity, but as I outline here they also demonstrate illicit designerly intelligence. In 2015 prison guards at the La Reforma Penitentiary in San Rafael de Alajuela, Costa Rica, discovered a pigeon in the grounds of the prison with a small cloth bag attached around it (Figure 6). The bag (Figure 7) appeared to be constructed to fit the bird from cotton fabric with fasteners to secure it, and a zipped pouch at the front to store small quantities of drugs (Troup Buchanan, 2015). Inside the bag guards found fourteen grams of cocaine and the same quantity of cannabis. Although a much smaller scale seizure than the multi-million Dollar discoveries outlined above the level of ingenuity is telling in relation to my discussion of illicit designerly intelligence, most readily through the design and manufacture of the cloth bag to fit around the pigeon but crucially through appreciation of the wider opportunities afforded by the situation.

As with nearly all forms of drug smuggling (and other contraband) the key 'problem' is overcoming the securitization of borders, most typically international ones but in this specific case the perimeter walls of the penitentiary. In the move from illicit ingenuity to illicit designerly intelligence I make the suggestion that ingenuity is primarily concerned with the inventiveness of construction and the

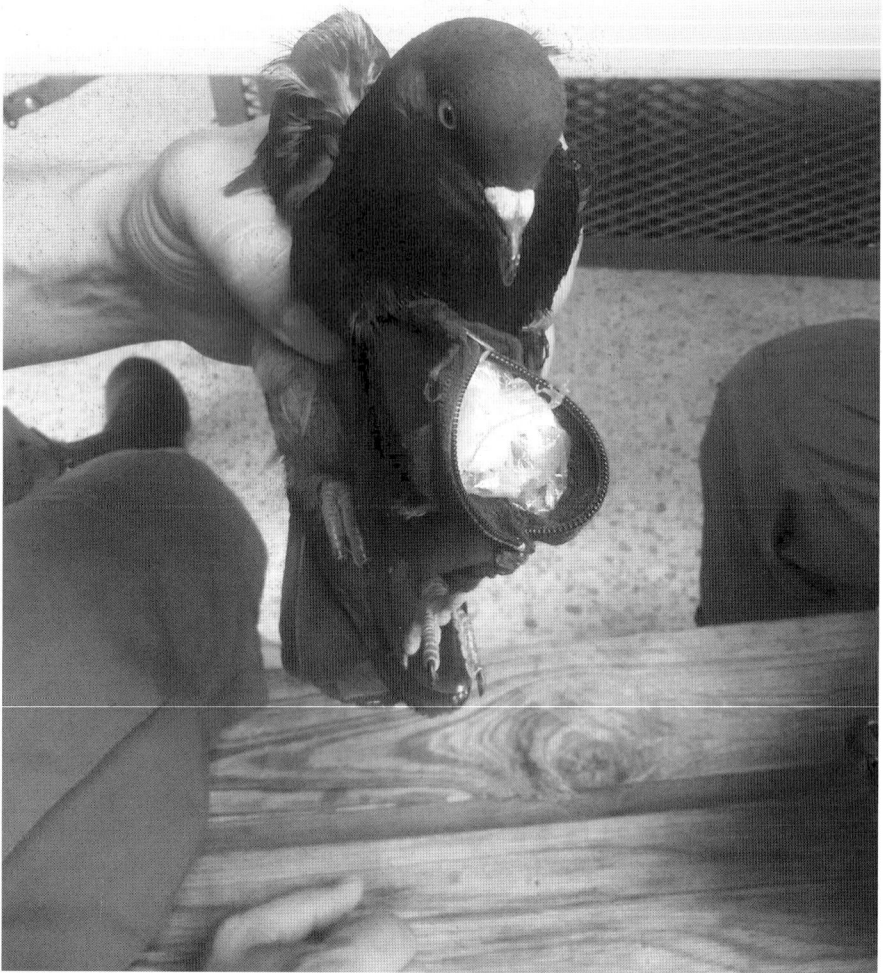

FIGURE 6 Cloth bag attached to pigeon, used to carry drugs. © Reuters Pictures. With permission of Reuters Pictures

contrivance of making something. By contrast, whilst designerly intelligence also engages with material invention it is much more holistic and systemic in approach. In attempting to smuggle the small quantities of cocaine and cannabis into the Costa Rican prison the individuals were clearly not thinking of this as a form of design, rather this was straightforwardly a practical means of overcoming the policing of the perimeter. What I claim here is a *parallel sensibility* between traditional forms of design intelligence and 'design thinking', and the illicit practices of smugglers. Where the practical abilities of creating the pouch for the pigeon are perhaps closest to the material expression of design, more broadly it is apparent that a problem-centred approach is paramount to smuggling the drugs into the prison;

FIGURE 7 Detail of cloth bag. © Reuters Pictures. With permission of Reuters Pictures.

that is, how to overcome the security procedures in place. Further to this there is an appreciation of the broader contexts of the situation such as the policing of the normal entrance points into the prison, whereas the aerial space above the perimeter is perceivably less secured. An opportunity was identified and exploited. Likewise, one of the most important facets of the forms of smuggling outlined in this chapter is an appreciation of *embeddedness*. That is, a recognition of the most common objects, symbols and actors that form specific contexts. So, in this situation the smugglers attempted to capitalize on the familiarity of pigeons in the area and their perceived inviolability. They are taken for granted in their ubiquity. A key basis of the illicit design approach in this situation is the adaptiveness of the smugglers, so that they responded to the opportunities provided by the problem, much in the same way that we previously saw how problems can often 'talk back' to the professional designer (Cross, 2011:23). Appreciating the complexity of how particular situations are configured is paramount to professional design approaches as well as illicit attitudes to problems, as are planning competencies, logistical dexterity and practical aptitude.

In this final section of the chapter I build on the numerous examples outlined so far and focus more specifically on the notion of embeddedness as a central facet of illicit design intelligence both in relation to concealment and even more so with the use of disguise. Doing so will demonstrate how the material practices of trafficking drugs are dependent on sophisticated, tactical understanding of material, systemic and situational opportunities. Embeddedness refers here to both the means smugglers use to conceal consignments of drugs within legitimate freight for example but also more readily to the use of disguise. As I will show, key to the design of disguise is how the artefacts – or the organizations in the case of company fronts – are *designed* to be observed in a particular manner.

In early 2018 a curious story of a banned book emerged. A Spanish court barred Nacho Carretero's book *Fariña* – about drug smuggling in Galicia – after one of the protagonists identified in the book brought legal proceedings against the author and its publisher (Flood, 2018). What marks this case out as worthy of discussion in this chapter is not the book's subject matter itself, although clearly it is related, rather the actions of the Booksellers Guild of Madrid. They decided to challenge the ban by disguising the text of *Fariña* within an online version of Cervantes' *Don Quixote*. *Fariña*'s 80,000 words were highlighted throughout Cervantes' tome so that the book was still readable on a project website 'Finding *Fariña*' (itself now banned). The illicit material was effectively disguised as *Don Quixote*. Although distinct from the subject matter of *Fariña*, there are interesting correspondences between the tactics adopted by the Booksellers Guild of Madrid and the broader practices of drug trafficking. The ingenuity of 'Finding *Fariña*' lies with the recognition of the legitimacy of *Don Quixote*, its ubiquity exploited – becoming a vehicle, or more readily, a *front* for the banned book.

The cases outlined in the earlier sections identify with the familiarity of *Don Quixote* as a culturally inscribed artefact. Clearly the status of an everyday artefact does not match *Don Quixote* but my argument here is that both exhibit a form of familiarity and 'taken-for-grantedness' in their situational contexts. They *fit* in these particular settings.[7] I suggest that these factors play a decisive role in the disguising of illicit practices. Considering the examples already cited in earlier sections of this chapter, in this final one I argue that disguise is utilized as an illicit form of planning and designerly intelligence. In particular I make the case that a designerly approach is adopted by disguising illegal drugs as legitimated material goods and embedding them within infrastructures of transportation routes. Such actions are in part constituted by configuring a wide array of materials, systems and processes so that the 'guilty' artefacts appear to simply be the same as legitimate ones. To examine the idea of 'designing through disguise', I investigate the interlinked themes of organizational and material disguise.

Where *Don Quixote* could be read as a front for the illicit text by disguising it within the legitimacy of the original novel, the notion of a cover or 'front' is also an important method within organized crime. A common approach adopted by traffickers is the use of a shell company that purports to be a legitimate commercial enterprise. We saw this earlier with the Sinaloa Cartel's creation of a juice distributor and fish flour company, and another example further demonstrates how shell companies are used as a form of disguise. Scott Parker, a dual British-South African national, ran a pet relocation business advising clients on transporting cats and dogs abroad. However, Parker's company was a front for drug trafficking, and in June 2014 workers in the Animal Reception Centre at Heathrow Airport in the UK noticed something suspicious about the excess weight of three crates used to transport cats from South Africa to the UK (Evans, 2015). UK National Crime Agency officers discovered that the crates in which the cats were transported had been modified to create a false bottom, in which Parker attempted to smuggle USD1.45 million of high-purity heroin. Rather than a solid bottom to the pet transportation crate a cavity was created to facilitate packets of the heroin to be secreted inside. One of the investigating officers provides a telling statement: 'Parker thought he would avoid our attention' (cited in Evans, 2015). The use of the pet transportation business is intended to obfuscate the illicit activities, to literally avoid the attention of security authorities under the impression this was a legitimate commercial enterprise with the transportation crates simply part of the organizational infrastructure of the company. Masquerading as this business is a form of disguise in itself, an action intended to conceal its actual purposes. But where the pet transportation boxes themselves were adapted to provide false bottoms another example shows the ingenuity of illicit design intelligence in both the use of a company front and an intriguing case of material disguise.

In late 2015 drug traffickers attempted to smuggle 1.5 tonnes of compressed cocaine worth USD310 million into the Port of Valencia in Spain, only to be discovered after Spanish National Police searched a shipping container at the port following intelligence provided by the UK's National Crime Agency. The cocaine was disguised as forty wooden shipping pallets used for transporting bags of charcoal in shipping containers from Columbia, whilst the bags of coal also contained cocaine disguised as the fuel (Harley and Hedgecoe, 2015). As with the Sinaloa Cartel's use of companies as fronts for smuggling, this attempt at smuggling was carried out under the guise of an apparently legitimate charcoal importation business. A forensic expert, Richard Hooker, describes the process through which the smugglers disguised the compressed cocaine powder to make it appear like the pallets as well as the charcoal itself:

> To make the cocaine look like wooden pallets they have dissolved the white cocaine powder with a solvent or glue. It has then been placed into moulds shaped like pallets to set. When the resin dries out it then solidifies. If you mix it with a dye it then gives the wood effect and gives the appearance of dark wood. Once the dealers get it they can then re-dissolve it and reverse the process to extract the cocaine. The same process can also be used to make it look like pieces of charcoal by using charcoal powder.
>
> (Hooker, cited in Harley and Hedgecoe, 2015)

Taken purely in terms of the genealogy of smuggling processes very little appears to have changed from the early nineteenth century when smugglers also disguised illicit cargo, in one case tobacco. Alfred Rive describes examples of 'the use of false bulkheads and linings in ships, hollow stones in the ballast and *tobacco made to look like potatoes or rope*' (Rive, 1929:568 my emphasis). In both the historical and contemporary examples the intermingling of the illicit substance with others is decisive, making the disguised tobacco or in this case the cocaine appear embedded within a legitimate charcoal importation business using familiar 'props' such as wooden pallets and bags of charcoal.

In these various instances the shell company is created to effectively *obscure* the illicit activities which operate behind the apparently legal commercial activities. The visual and spatial characteristics of 'obscuring' and lying 'behind' are illuminating in relation to how different forms of disguise are perceived. We might think of shell companies as a form of *organizational disguise* where the illicit activities are rendered invisible by the foregrounded visible actions of the shell company (see Smith et al., 2018). In the case of the charcoal importation shell company not only was this a form of organizational disguise, the illicit commercial activity afforded the opportunity for *material disguise* through creating the shipping pallets and coal out of compressed cocaine. Just as the company was a front, so with the pallets and coal: in that they drew attention to their physical appearance as pallets and coal rather than their actual materiality as cocaine. The authenticity of the disguise of the pallets is critical to the audacious attempt to smuggle such large quantities of drugs. In particular the coloured dye masks the materiality of the compressed cocaine, making it much closer in appearance to commonplace wooden shipping pallets. But even more so, the use of the screws to apparently fix the pallet together makes the object appear even more ordinary and thus legitimate. With both organizational and material forms of disguise the seemingly licit practices are foregrounded, the illicit backgrounded. Taken in this manner, the notion of disguise is compelling for it highlights the dynamics of how these organizations and artefacts are *designed* to be perceived in such a way that they are fully embedded in seemingly legitimate activities.

Perception is of fundamental importance to the discussion of disguise not least how illicit practices are policed, but also to wider considerations of disguise as a form of design sensibility. Perhaps the most obvious example of this is through the surficial design of camouflage where the mediation of perception is deployed through sophisticated understanding of visual, material and organizational codes (see Forsyth, 2013; Shell, 2012). In similar terms, one of the fundamental traits of illicit design through disguise I wish to put forward is that smuggler understand the material-semiotic conventions of legitimate distribution networks of global trade, passenger transportation or postal/courier deliveries. In a different context James C. Scott highlights this in relation to forms of political resistance: 'the creation of disguise depends on an agile, firm grasp of the codes of meaning being manipulated' (Scott, 1990:139). Such a statement echoes well-rehearsed notions of design as both the creation of material and immaterial phenomena, but crucially the production of meaning (see Archer, 1979:20). The use of disguise in political contexts relies on aspects of anonymity to create forms of resistance that are perceptible to dominant powers but simultaneously without identifiable authors and thus less prone to indictment. They are hiding in plain sight.

The familiar adage of 'hiding in plain sight' offers a constructive means of thinking about how smugglers disguise illicit narcotics in such a way that they are fully in sight but disguised in order to merge into the background. This is in contrast to methods of concealment previously discussed where the smuggled goods are hidden from sight. Such questions are commonplace in a range of intellectual contexts including literature (Poe, 2012) and relatedly in psychoanalysis (Lacan, 1972), but work in cognitive sociology is notably illuminating. In particular how we attend to matter is central to Eviatar Zerubavel's discussion of the 'sociology of attention' (Zerubavel, 2015). For Zerubavel such an enquiry is driven by how we become socialized into concentrating on particular phenomena whilst ignoring others. Drawing on a range of disciplinary traditions from theories of perception to social psychology Zerubavel highlights the importance of distinguishing between figure and background, noting how these represent 'pronouncedly asymmetrical phenomenological distinction[s] between the attended and unattended parts of our phenomenal world' (Zerubavel, 2015:11). The figure is said to always be more pronounced than the background. This is determined by how we tend to focus on the figure standing out against the background, so that the latter recedes from our attention. Zerubavel offers a range of examples from classical antiquity to visual studies, the common factor being the formlessness of the background in contrast to the sharpness of the figure; the contrasting quality between the two determining how we locate the figure against a background. Unsurprisingly the socialization of how we perceive figure from background leads to this becoming habitualized and normalized (Zerubavel, 2015:59).

It is this aspect in particular that I argue relates directly to designing through disguise. In average circumstances, when we seek out specific objects for example we tend to look for those that are more pronounced as figures through their contrastive quality. One might also think of how someone dresses in order to stand out from the crowd, suggests Zerubavel (2015:25). But equally, it is important to stress how the reverse is evident: if we wished to fit into the crowd we would perceivably dress exactly as everyone else, effectively becoming part of the background blur. And here the apparent distinction between figure and background falls away. In part this happens through the sheer mass of a crowd of people where the singularity of individuals is lost (Scott, 1990:150). Zerubavel also argues that we must be mindful not to essentialize the relationship between figure and background as these 'are not inherent qualities' (2015:79). In the case of a crowded environment the mass of people creates a switch in perception where we see the mass as background. This is particularly evident when figures themselves become so ubiquitous that we begin to ignore them.

It is precisely this aspect of shifting modes of perception that I contend highlights an important facet of the design of disguise in the trafficking of drugs. My assertion is that *disguise operates through reversing the habitualized perceptual process*. Put simply, the drugs that have been disguised to look like legitimate artefacts – such as the shipping pallets – become backgrounded. They merge into the sheer mass of other goods being shipped transnationally. They look like every other shipping pallet used to transport goods around the globe. No longer singularized, rather the act of disguise was an attempt by the traffickers (which ultimately failed of course) to create a shapeless background object that blends into the blur of global trade. Such an approach could be described as a 'diversionary tactic' (Zerubavel, 2015:46–7) whereby perception is switched and the focus placed on the background rather than the foreground. In many ways diversionary tactics are employed in a range of settings, such as magic tricks (see Freudenberg and Alario, 2007) and pick-pocketing, where attention is shifted elsewhere. With drug smuggling similar tactics of diversion are employed to distract border forces by focusing their attention on the backgrounded nature of the illicit artefacts, whilst all the time the illicit goods are in front of them – hiding in plain sight. This is clearly evident when they are *designed* to look like legitimate, licit artefacts.[8]

Conclusions

As noted in the Introduction drug use statistics are deeply alarming: the *World Drug Report 2016* states that in 2015, 247 million people used drugs, with 29 million suffering from drug use disorders (UNODC, 2016:x). Although the discussions in this chapter do not focus on the deeply harmful effects of illegal narcotics – neither physically nor socially – such a position does not neglect the consequences of illegal drug production, distribution and consumption. Given the profoundly troubling nature of drug dependency and the social scarification it causes, in some ways focusing on the approaches and creative tools adopted by smugglers might offer an insight for the detection of illicit narcotics. Needless to say, border and security agencies already have a highly developed arsenal of counter measures to combat drug trafficking, hence the fact that all of the examples discussed in the chapter have been seized. Although not an objective of the chapter as such it is clear that understanding the ways in which concealment and disguise operate as a form of illicit design sensibility might provide further awareness of such approaches. To understand the parallel methods of overcoming problems – be they within traditional professional design settings or in illicit situations – could possibly offer strategic tools for interdiction. Whilst aware of the importance of reducing the serious consequences of drug production, distribution and consumption, particularly the impact of the latter on a life of dependency, we also must be cognisant of the complexity of the debate. For as noted in the Introduction cultures of addiction often stem from deeply entrenched forms of social malaise, particularly under the alienation-effect of capitalism (Castells, 2010:xvii; 179). Likewise, as shown in the section on changing attitudes to the drugs trade illicitness is not an a priori fact. Standpoints and legislation alike change over time.

Somewhat counter to this, the chapter has shown that the methods themselves have not changed profoundly over quite broad temporal periods. Given the time-honoured desire to evade taxes and for consumers to pay less for goods the smuggling of contraband has been something of a constant. Concealing cigars in hollowed-out loaves of bread is not entirely distinct from hiding large quantities of cocaine in a shipping container full of beach chairs. Again, mindful of the societal effects of long-term drug abuse and the evasion of taxes in other forms of contraband smuggling, the practices of distributing surreptitious goods have some common ground. The chapter made the case that whilst there are distinct similarities that speak to a genealogy of smuggling the fundamental difference between historical and contemporary forms of trafficking is that of scale and reach. Through the interconnected nature of global transportation and mobilities infrastructure the ability to harness the propulsive force of these networks has afforded innumerable new opportunities for smuggling. The recent examples cited in this chapter prove this. Such infrastructural power is also dependent on objects, be they ubiquitous freight shipment containers, the commodities contained within them or motor vehicles.

The primary intention of this chapter has been to highlight the *material cultures* of smuggling practices. The artefactual potential offered by everyday things: artefacts matter in these situations just as they do everywhere else. In arguing this one of the aims has also been to foreground the profoundly creative way in which smugglers utilize, co-opt and adapt artefacts as clandestine conduits. I suggested that smugglers exhibit a decidedly sophisticated understanding of the potentiality of artefacts and their materiality, be that in modifying automobiles and creating compartments for concealing drugs, or to an even greater degree disguising compressed cocaine as wooden pallets. Such intimate appreciation of the materiality of automobiles, artefacts like wooden pallets as well as the chemical processes required to compress cocaine shows ingenuity in material contrivance. Smugglers misuse artefacts and systems in ways that are akin to the adhocist sensibility of making do with what is to hand; however, as we have seen, when it works the act of smuggling is an intricately planned logistical endeavour. In many ways the practical wherewithal in envisioning the potential of the underside of an automobile or a truck is even more insightful than the average professional design problem which is often comparatively mundane in its remit. But although I argue the ingenuity of smugglers is evident in such approaches to the materiality of artefacts, the combined power of this coupled with systemic and infrastructural knowledge and planning moves beyond the level of ingenuity. One of the most important points raised in the chapter is that the combinatorial sensibility of smugglers in understanding the complexity of transportation routes, supply chains, security constraints and border practices as well as the geographical specificity of different territories is more than just ingenuity: it is akin to the sensibilities of professional design in its utilization of planning competencies, systemic awareness and material affinity. Indeed, returning to Buchanan's argument that design is ultimately concerned with integration (1992:5), this is particularly evident when we consider the ways in which smugglers draw together and configure a wide range of actors. Likewise, parallel to Manzini's manifesto for diffuse design a similar approach can be identified with smuggling, whereby existing materials, systems and practices are adapted. Designers and smugglers alike are agile: they deal with problem-situations by thinking on their feet, adapting to the singularities of particular issues and settings. I attempted to exemplify these parallel sensibilities through the discussion of concealment but principally through the latter focus on designing through disguise. Through a number of key assertions I ultimately come to the conclusion that one of the primary mechanisms employed by smugglers is designing assemblages of artefacts and organizational structures (such as fake companies) to be *perceived* in a specific or fixed way – as legitimate entities that are embedded within and fit neatly into legal infrastructures and mobilities. These illicit artefacts hide in plain sight. Until they are potentially seized of course.[9]

As with many of the discussions throughout the book this chapter has not set out to overtly valorize (or romanticize) such practices, rather to investigate how they relate to a broader politics of a nascent 'illicit epistemology' through forms of ingenuity, thinking, planning, making, mobilization and ultimately design. In doing so it is hoped that investigating the tactical processes developed by smugglers will foster a keener understanding of illicit practices and their inherent creativity, particularly in relation to the illicit potentiality of artefacts and infrastructures. Whilst these debates may possibly be of benefit to border forces and other security agencies they will of course be operating at a much more sophisticated level. Perhaps the main value of defining an illicit epistemology is to the broader conceptual fields of design and innovation. However, where we saw in the previous chapter that misuse and hacking in particular have led to new forms of technological innovation such a value-system may not be apparent in smuggling. By contrast the actions of traffickers are primarily internalized, with any insights from intercepted consignments of drugs perhaps utilized for later illicit endeavours. However, for Söderberg (2017:129) within the parallel economy of the drug production of illegal highs there is perceivable value to pharmaceutical companies through opened-up drug discovery processes. The ongoing relationship between licit and illicit innovation is also an important facet of the next and final chapter. As is consumption. One of the complex social problems of illicit drug consumption is demand. In very simplistic terms if there weren't a market for such products the commercial opportunities sought out by organized criminal groups would not exist. In Chapter 6 I consider a further facet of consumption, this time focused on the design cultures of counterfeits and fakes. As we will see, this extends many of the discussions up to this point by considering in more depth both the production, distribution and explicitly the consumer demand for fakes goods, but ultimately the complex relationship between intellectual property, imitation and innovation.

6 COUNTERFEIT DESIGN

Introduction

Cabbage: when you see this word you are most likely to think of the brassica. You are less likely to think of the histories of illicit innovation in the garment trade. But in this setting the term 'cabbage' refers to the practice of producing extra garments on a production line and selling these additional ones on the informal market, in bars or street markets for example.[1] Traditionally the fabric cutter played a vital role in the manufacture of clothing items, particularly in the 'schmutter' trade (or rag trade) in post–Second World War London (see Halbert, 2019). The cutter was responsible for the planning and cutting of as many patterns as possible from a bale of cloth. As Granger (2009:179) notes this might be fifty garments as agreed by the manufacturer and the client. However, in 1950s London it was not uncommon for the cutter to manage to cut an extra few garments from the bale of cloth. These extra garments – exactly the same as the legitimate ones – were then sold on the grey market for a fraction of the price. Wily consumers could have an expensive coat for a vastly reduced cost. As with earlier discussions on the intersection of licit and illicit practices, the cabbage trade is a clear case of this: some factory owners were complicit in these activities; whilst at other times it was carried out by cutters and machinists to supplement their meagre wages. The imbrication of the illicit and licit emerges out of the inconsistencies and failures of the purportedly legitimate clothing trade. For the poor working conditions and low pay of 1950s London are emblematic of capitalism's exploitational foundations just as it is in clothing factories today albeit in different geographies. Likewise, as in the rag trade of the post–Second World War period so today we also see the continuing practice of 'cabbaging' in the globalized clothing industries of the Asian markets (Hilton et al., 2000). In both the historical example and contemporary manifestations, there is a corresponding trade where the 'illicit cabbage trade has always run parallel with the legitimate rag trade' (Granger, 2009:180). Indeed today, this idea of parallel enterprises is explicitly evident in what is known as *shanzhai*, the Chinese neologism for fake goods, particularly technological products (Han, 2017:72).[2]

However, there is of course a clear difference between the cabbage trade in 1950s London and the contemporary world of knock-off Chinese mobile phones with brand names such as Nokir or Samsing. With the former the garment is exactly the same as the original – it is the same fabric, cut by the same cutter, made by the same machinist. In the case of the Nokir phone it is a knock-off, a copy that ostensibly looks similar to the original but is not made from the same components or materials. It is marketed as a copycat brand, hence the subtle and almost comedic shift in brand name. By contrast the cabbage garment was sold as the original brand but at markedly reduced prices. What does link both these examples is the informal markets in which they are sold – the 1950s street market in east London and the equivalent street vendor in Shanghai or Shenzhen today. This is the murky milieu of clones, copies, fakes and counterfeits. A world of copyright infringements, but equally of grey markets where the legal definitions of brand identities are difficult to ascertain, where the distinctions between original pieces of hardware or artefacts and their copies are ostensibly impossible to tell. As a recent Organisation for Economic Co-Operation and Development & European Union Intellectual Property Office report highlights, whilst counterfeiting ranges across a vast array of products from leather goods to watches and perfumes, certain categories such as spare parts, toys or pharmaceuticals pose threats to health and safety (OECD and EUIPO, 2017b:384). This brief indication of the range of counterfeit products only skims the surface of the trade in pirated goods. For example, according to the United States International Trade Commission (USITC, 2011:2–1) imports of counterfeit goods from China to the United States alone amounted to USD187.3 million in 2010. Whilst in 2013 the trade in fake goods accounted for 2.5 per cent of world trade, equating to USD461 billion (OECD and EUIPO, 2017a:11).

This chapter takes such data as the backdrop to a much broader discussion of counterfeiting. Following earlier outlines of illicit innovation and the entanglement of the licit with the illicit it does not simply judge counterfeiting as a wholly negative set of illegal practices – although we will see the damaging effects across social, cultural, and economic registers. Rather I attempt to consider the place of counterfeiting within the increasingly far-reaching spectrum of design cultures. So, where the wider economic and social impact of counterfeiting is clearly evident, there is also a range of even more complex discussions to consider. For instance, there is something decisive about the context of *shanzhai* in relation to the broader theme of illicit innovation that pervades this book. For as a growing number of researchers have noted, there is a shift in perception in the seeming lack of innovation with *shanzhai*'s origins as simply copying existing brands (see Lindtner et al., 2015). Instead, with the new *shanzhai* (Li, 2014) we see evidence of original innovation where new product development platforms designed by tech start-ups and shared openly amongst competitors have fostered the development of new products often superior to the ones originally copied (Fernandez et al., 2016). To return to the discussions in Chapter 3: this is truly disruptive innovation in that the practice of illegally copying has led to the development of new, more advanced products.

Where Chapters 4 and 5 dealt with the material aspects of deviant design through the lens of misuse as well as the ingenuity of drug smuggling, the scope of this chapter extends the focus on materiality. It still considers aspects of production through the manufacture of fakes and latterly the value of illicit innovation in this context, but another of its primary orbits is design culture's explicit relationship with consumption. For example, although much of the discussion in Chapter 1 dealt with the expanded field of design this was primarily through the application of design thinking beyond traditional domains. However, design has always been more than the making of material artefacts or problem-scenarios: this chapter builds on the extensive precedents and literature dealing with the sociological and anthropological centrality of manufactured goods to the construction of identity. The socio-cultural dimensions of copycats, counterfeits and fakes reflect the world of consumption we live in today. A culture of consumption where particular brands and designed goods seemingly position individuals, making distinctions within and across social groupings. Where traditionally this was achieved through the use of goods as markers of pecuniary status and taste, today this can be achieved through a diverse ecology of means, be that the taste cultures of social media or the production of (virtual) identities through online gaming platforms. But branded goods still do an awful lot of work in building identity, particularly through the age-old outward signification of luxury brands – original or fake. This is a culture that is indeed premised on the social, cultural and economic status of a person carrying an outwardly authentic Louis Vuitton bag. It's also a culture that is built on the foundations of capitalist society where conspicuous consumption and displays of aesthetic repute were and continue to be at its core (Veblen, 1992). In short, a social world and a design culture premised on the production and consumption of fakes should come as no surprise.

What does this tell us about design today? And more decisively my thesis on deviant design? A tentative proposition: the culture of counterfeits highlights the pervasiveness of designed goods more generally, but also the culture of branding and consumerism that exemplifies common underpinnings of what design is concerned with. For as discussed in the Introduction to the book, although it is incredibly important and valuable to consider more radical interpretations of what design can achieve as a tool for social change (Escobar, 2018), the world of counterfeit goods speaks to a more entrenched notion of the cultures of waste and excess that has often typified the commercial foundations of industrial design. As with the underpinning ideological arguments of the book this chapter does not seek to encourage such practices of wastefulness and rampant desire for cheap and nasty knockoffs. Rather I hope it fosters further understanding of the ever-present desire for brand-derived services and branded products, even more so the increasing demand for fake products.

This latter comment links directly to the inherent deviancy of consumption. Although the anthropological underpinnings of consumption clearly demonstrate the pre-capitalist logic of the fundamental role objects play in social, cultural, economic and religious life, the rapid growth of consumer culture in the eighteenth and nineteenth centuries shows how the origins of mass production and mass consumption were concerned with differentiation, hegemonic expansion through market domination, the production of desire, wasteful excess (Packard, 1961) and ultimately the potential violence of consumption itself (Moxon, 2011; Osterweil, 2020). In the context of design studies the histories of planned obsolescence to the product lifecycles of the American automobile industry are well documented (Hounshell, 1984) as are more recent critiques of the increasingly accelerated speed of fashion cycles.

Building on these discussions of the deviancy of consumer culture itself the chapter proceeds as follows. I begin by addressing the broader debates to emerge from the study of counterfeits and fakes. Given the context of illegality the key sources deal with the place of counterfeiting within organized criminal activity (Large, 2019), and although the primary focus of this chapter will be the design-related areas of fashion and consumer branding, the dangers of counterfeit pharmaceuticals are an increasingly dominant backdrop to the study of counterfeit cultures (Hall and Antonopoulos, 2016). Threaded throughout this gamut of illicit activities are questions concerning intellectual property infringement, and the geographies of production, distribution and consumption. Following this initial scene-setting the next section concerns the emergence of consumer culture and specifically the place of branded goods in the construction of identity. Utilizing a range of small-scale case studies this section considers how counterfeit goods such as fake branded fashion accessories play a fundamental role in perpetuating consumer culture, offering important insights into understanding how counterfeits themselves exemplify the logic of capital, and thus deviance. The second key section of the chapter contemplates the question of innovation, folding back to the concerns of Chapter 3. Much of the literature on counterfeiting highlights how the infringement of intellectual property reduces the profits of businesses and thus disincentivizes companies from investing in research and development, as well as new product or service innovations. However, whilst mindful of this pervasive and persuasive argument, I want to consider this question in light of the earlier outline of illicit innovation and the creativity of misuse in Chapter 4. Doing so, I posit the idea that innovation can indeed emerge from the copying or imitation of original goods, in this case through a brief outline of *shanzhai* design and manufacturing.

Cultures of the counterfeit

On a relatively recent trip to Vancouver, I visited a London Drugs store hoping to find authentic Canadian hardware, some tools or other DIY paraphernalia not usually found back home. Apart from the odd object that felt distinctly Canadian much of the merchandise was broadly familiar. What I didn't expect to see was a Charles and Ray Eames LCW chair (Figure 8). Partly because the rest of the merchandise didn't seem quite so design-led, and also as I'd become accustomed to seeing such products in high-end design stores as opposed to a more general one such as this. The Eames chair sat raised up on a cheap Formica tabletop with a children's teddy bear lying face down underneath it, other bears crammed into a metal cage next to the chair. I then spotted an Isamu Noguchi coffee table pushed up behind the Eames chair.

The price labels said it all: CAD79.99 for the chair; CAD179.99 for the table. Rather than vastly discounted bargains, these weren't licenced versions of the original designs by Charles and Ray Eames, or Noguchi – they were 'copycats'. Tellingly the information labels on these products did not even allude to the original designs or their designers. The chair simply described on the label as 'L D Bamboo Chair', the coffee table as 'L D Glass Top Coffee Table'. Subsequently looking on the London Drugs website it was a similar case: no mention of the origins of either design. In the 'reviews' section only one customer makes note of the fact the table was a Noguchi knock-off. This same reviewer went on to say the quality of the legs wasn't terribly good and they are prone to scuffing. Similar complaints about lack of quality are made by other reviewers, but they are also pragmatic: this is a cheap product so what's to be expected? The legs can be touched-up or repainted. Some of the reviewers also note that the inferior quality is only apparent when one is up

FIGURE 8 'L D Bamboo Chair', London Drugs store, Vancouver. Photo by author.

close to the table, with one amusingly posting, 'Perfect accent piece for those with near-sighted friends' (HotSpringHiker, 2013).

Like many 'global' cities Manhattan feels evermore anodyne, the same familiar brands, the ubiquitous aesthetic of independent coffee shops, the increasing homogeneity and loss of its singularity. Of course, there are pockets of difference. China Town being one, and just below this Canal Street. As you head along Canal Street there are still traces of a more heterogeneous and ultimately interesting Manhattan. Walking from the corner of Bowery and Canal Street hawkers begin to appear. Slowly they build in number. The first you hear are familiar brand names: Louis Vuitton, Rolex, Gucci. People with well-fingered A4 sheets show you what they have. These tattered sales catalogues of sorts primarily feature handbags, purses and wallets. I ask to look at the sales sheets a little more closely, but they're resistant. I'd really like to get hold of one, although this would just raise even more suspicion. Around the Subway entrances people have set up makeshift sales pitches. Some a blanket or tarpaulin with goods laid out. Others just a suitcase with the goods piled up. One 'Gucci' bag is USD43 dollars I'm told. He'll take USD35. This seller has a wide array of copycat goods. The bag with the 'Gucci' logo looks nothing like the original branding. This doesn't seem to deter desperate buyers who are huddled around the products frantically trying to haggle the sellers down. As with the age-old frenzy of the market place the art of haggling creates a sense of desire to buy anything, no matter how removed from the original. For these consumers the word *Gucci* itself is apparently enough to mark this out as something they need to buy. 'Does it matter to you these aren't originals?' I ask one person. 'Nah, not at all' they laugh. Further along Canal Street the Gucci logo on a bag looks relatively recognizable, but you soon realize this means nothing. As with the Gucci logo on the bags these are simply *approximations* of the original, they are not identical to the authentic product. 'Rolly!' I hear from the next seller. It's immediately obvious what he's selling. The names of brands are so familiar we're at ease with their shortening. I ask to look at the 'Rolly' but the seller seems a little reluctant. 'Top quality' is all he says.

Strolling along Canal Street you become privy to the consumer culture of copycats (Barnett, 2005). Only a few blocks from the stores selling the originals here one is confronted with the world of consumption in all its manifestations. Buyers who likely were just walking past the apparent authenticity of the shop windows in Chelsea (see Zukin, 2008) flock to Canal Street. Throngs of tourists, groups of young Americans, every one eager to purchase these approximations. There is an air of heightened desire, people jostling one another to get to the front of the small patches where the goods are piled up. What becomes striking as you head from the junction of Bowery along towards 6th Avenue is the realization that everyone is selling the same items.

These two examples from North America reveal a range of factors pertinent to the study of design cultures, copycats and counterfeits. In particular, they foreground the different cultures of consumption: neither claim to be originals but different approximations of the originals. These are not illegal counterfeits which violate the intellectual property of the authentic brands; rather, they are close enough to resemble the original but distinct enough not to infringe the original. So, whilst as consumers we are perhaps more attuned to the potential of these goods as markers of perceived status, the legal definitions of counterfeit products are more concerned with intellectual property and protecting the rights of designers and manufacturers. In the case of furniture items such as those from London Drugs these are not knock-offs in the way one might understand the term with examples such as fake Louis Vuitton handbags claiming to be originals. Instead, these products are legitimate replicas of the originals made possible through the expiration of copyright protection on the Eames and Noguchi designs. In the UK and European Union there has – until recently – been a burgeoning trade in replica furniture items by the likes of Charles and Ray Eames, Arne Jacobsen and Eileen Gray. As with the London Drugs products they may look almost identical to the originals but the quality of materials and manufacturing process are vastly inferior. Where the examples from the UK and EU differ from those by London Drugs in Canada is in the identification of the original designer. The L D Bamboo Chair makes no reference at all to the work of Charles and Ray Eames, but in the case of the UK furniture market replica Eames products such as the Lounge Chair with Ottoman from 1956 were recently available at a price of approximately £450 (USD591) compared with one produced under licence for £6800 (USD8935). The decisive difference between the two was that the cheap replicas were not made under licence whereas the more expensive products are and with the full agreement of the designers' estates.

A 2017 newspaper advertisement for a UK-based retailer of replica furniture, for instance, hints at apparently subtle distinctions between originals and replicas, whilst implying a level of authenticity even with the latter. For instance, the tagline 'Our inspired version captures every detail of the original' is a telling statement. Although it may attempt to 'capture' every detail it is nonetheless *inspired* by the original rather than identical to the original design and production specifications. Likewise, although adverts like this show images of Charles and Ray Eames as the designers of the original version the underlying tone of the advert is that of an Eames-inspired product. As such, the advertisement is truthful in its positioning of the product as a replica rather than original, but the manipulation of the consumer is also evident with the narrative surrounding the design of the original version.

The advert in question provides a further revealing point in its emphasis on 'LAST EVER SALE'. For the law in the UK changed on 28 January 2017, so that copyright protection on designs has been extended from twenty-five to seventy years after the death of the designer. Whereas the Eames Lounge Chair was previously able to be produced without licence, the copyright protection has now been extended to 2058 following Ray Eames' death in 1988.[3] The change in law in the UK and EU has been implemented to provide 'protection to British designers for a longer period of time' (Smithers, 2016:40), but also to bring the law on furniture copyright into closer alignment with music and literature. However, the complexity of copyright infringement becomes evident when the difference between exact replicas and those 'inspired by' the original is considered. For as a copyright lawyer notes, 'The intent of the change to the legislation is to stop "exact" copies of existing industrially designed artistic works, although this means products that are "inspired by" the works may still be allowed, so long as they do not cross the line' (Woods, cited in Smithers, 2016:40). Indeed, it is clear that the 'L D Bamboo Chair' falls into this latter category of 'inspired by' as opposed to an unlicensed replica. However, although the Wallace Sacks version of the Eames Lounge Chair may claim to have been inspired by the original it is, in fact, too close to the original design and thus affected by the change in consumer law.

The cases of replica productions of iconic mid-century designs provide a beneficial overview of the complex forces at play in the discussion of counterfeits. They also highlight the distinctions between goods that circumvent copyright protection through the timeframe in which the copyright holder died, and those goods which are illegal in their infringement of trademarks. It is the latter which marks out a distinct culture of counterfeits or fakes. By definition, 'counterfeit products are fakes bearing a trademark that is identical to, or indistinguishable from, a trademark registered to another party, infringing the rights of the holder of the trademark' (De Barnier, 2014:341). In the case of the L D Bamboo Chair, it may look similar to the Eames LCW chair, but it does not infringe the copyright by bearing the trademark of the original. Key to understanding the dynamics of counterfeits is the attempt on the part of the producers to pass fakes off as the authentic product.

The illicit copying of trademarks and infringement of intellectual property rights are at the core of counterfeiting, and always have been. For the histories of commercial activity are intertwined with the need to protect these commodities from being copied by unscrupulous traders as well as protecting consumers from inferior copies. This is the case today with goods such as pharmaceuticals, but also with adulterated wine in the Roman period. As Rakoff and Wolff (1982:149) discuss, wine producers in Rome began to distinguish their products from others by stamping or inscribing the bottles with a trademark – the very beginning of copyright (see Paster, 1969). In this historical context, as well as today, the trademark was about trust: consumers could rely on the fact that this particular wine was produced by the same maker as one they'd previously consumed, the trademark guaranteeing authenticity. But of course, even in the Roman period the nature of commerce being imbued with illicit entrepreneurialism was such that

> after the Romans began marking their wine, merchants in Gaul began scratching what looked like Roman lettering on jugs of inferior local wine, impressing the 'trident' trademark on the jugs, and passing them off to purchasers as the famous wines of Campania.
>
> (Rakoff and Wolff, 1982:149)

As with today the increasing proliferation of counterfeit products is a condition of both commercial opportunity (as spotted by the merchants in Gaul), and crucially for my discussion in this chapter, *demand* for fake goods, particularly within fashion and technology sectors. Three aspects are key to understanding the cultures of counterfeiting. Firstly, although counterfeiting is an historical fact, the sheer growth of branding in the twentieth and twenty-first centuries has created a market for and a surge in demand for fake goods, as well as the copycat goods on Canal Street. At the same time the costs of luxury brands in particular are beyond the economic means of many consumers. Secondly, coupled to cultures of branding is the critical importance of global trade and particularly the outsourcing of production, leading to highly complex supply chains which are difficult to fully monitor (European Commission, 2018:2). Thirdly, the recognizability of brands is also critical, for the desire to consume fake goods is based upon visible means of status projection: being seen by one's peers to own particular sought-after artefacts (Higgins and Rubin, 1986). Whilst I discuss the latter point in the next section, here I briefly consider the first two.

Counterfeit products form distinct groupings. Partly according to value, partly to social impact, but also dependent on the complicity of consumers in knowingly purchasing fake goods as opposed to copycats. For example, whilst the social effect of wilfully buying fake fashion accessories may not be dramatic, being duped into purchasing counterfeit pharmaceuticals is another matter. The latter situation, known as the *deceptive* market (Rojek, 2017:28), is an important factor in De Barnier's (2014:343–4) identification of four main groups of counterfeit products. The first grouping consists of well-known brands which have high visibility, but are low cost. Goods such as toothpastes and confectionary are exemplars. Flipping the high visibility/low cost relationship are goods which are high in price and likewise high in technological merit, including computer parts and automotive or aviation parts. Perhaps the most familiar group is that of 'exclusive status-gratifying commodities' (De Barnier, 2014:344) such as fashion accessories, perfumes and particularly clothing (also see Rojek, 2017; Wall and Large, 2010). The final, and growing category is that of pharmaceutical products as well as other goods such as cigarettes, alcohol or children's toys which pose a danger to consumers (Richardson, 2006; Zabyelina, 2017). In contrast to the deceptive market in fake goods, the market in *non-deceptive* counterfeit products is where consumers are *complicit* in creating and perpetuating demand for these goods particularly through items associated with fashion and lifestyle goods, DVDs or technology products, but clearly less so with goods which pose health risks such as pharmaceuticals or spare parts for aviation. It is the non-deceptive market which forms the primary focus of this chapter.

The diversity of products which are now illegally copied is not particularly shocking. This is perhaps due to the sheer abundance of commodities which pervade the global systems of production, distribution and consumption. Indeed, although the historical trajectories of counterfeiting are clear to see, Antonopoulos et al. (2017:248) argue that the growth of the trade in fakes is inherent to the rise of global trade networks in the late twentieth century. They go on to suggest other important drivers for this rise. For instance, outsourcing of production to traditional 'peripheral' economies is identified as one reason for the increase in counterfeit production, partly due to a lack of surveillance and monitoring of manufacturing. China in particular is the main producer of fake products entering the European markets, constituting 66 per cent of the volume of fake items seized at EU borders (Large, 2019:109). The United States also provides a lucrative market for Chinese manufacturers of fake products, with losses of around USD48 billion to US companies in 2009 (USITC, 2011:xiv).[4] The complexity of outsourced production networks in countries where counterfeit manufacture takes place is such that control over this is equally as complex (in some ways akin to the example of cabbage at the start of the chapter). The lack of legal apparatuses to police the production and distribution in these countries also leads to the increase in manufacture due to the lack of risk in being apprehended. Two further factors are critical to Antonopoulos et al.'s identification of the proliferation of counterfeiting, both of which have an important bearing on the next two sections of this chapter. They see 'technological innovation contributing to increased opportunities for production and distribution' (Antonopoulos et al., 2017:248). This is particularly the case with distribution and supply where online markets provide ample opportunity for purveyors of counterfeit goods to sell to willing customers (Wilson and Fenoff, 2014). And as a final point they note that people are indeed willing consumers of fake products, creating an incredibly viable market.

There is then a paradox at the heart of the culture of counterfeits. For whilst the massive demand on the part of consumers for fake or copycat products clearly exists, legitimate brands and anti counterfeiting organizations point to the detrimental effects of this industry. Where the threat to public safety through the deceptive production, distribution and sales of these latter fake products is clear to see, for these organizations the wider socio-economic effects of counterfeiting are manifestly evident. Perhaps the most harmful of these is the associated practices of organized crime including money laundering, prostitution and smuggling activities (UNICRI, 2011:103–18). At the societal level other perceived threats include lost revenues from taxation on the importation and sale of licensed goods, and thus lost capacity for public sector spending. Similarly, the geographical location of certain production facilities can lead to poor working conditions for workers with no oversight from unions and other recognized workers' rights organizations. At the level of companies who produce legitimate products there is a loss in revenue, as well as wasted investment in product development, and overall drivers to innovation (Prebula, 1986:341; USITC, 2011). One notable factor for companies whose products are copied is reputational damage, primarily through the consumer market being perceivably overrun with their products, thus devaluing their exclusivity. These is clearly the case at the luxury end of the market, so much so that fashion and accessories brand Burberry burnt £28.6 million of inventoried stock in 2017 to prevent counterfeiters copying the goods, but also to ward off the goods being sold on the grey market (Burberry, 2018:165; Khomani, 2018).[5] The existence of grey markets also highlights the complexity of the consumer culture of counterfeits and copies. Whilst the black market is exemplified by counterfeit goods which infringe copyright, or stolen goods, the grey market is less clearly illegal. For Hanson, 'gray goods are brand-name products manufactured abroad which bear an authentic trademark authorized by the owner of the trademark in the market for which the goods are intended' (Hanson, 1987:249). However, what marks them out as 'grey' is their subsequently being sold in markets they were not to intended to be, often at markedly reduced prices. In the case of Burberry they clearly felt their goods being sold on the grey market devalued the products and their brand reputation.

The problem of brand reputation and consumer perception is intrinsic to attempts by numerous companies such as Apple or Samsung to prevent the growing rise of fake products. Protecting intellectual property through patents and other mechanisms is foundational to the birth of modern capitalism even though its emergence in the eighteenth century seems relatively recent; later still was the fact that up until 1945 'it [IP] was only important to a tiny group of people – newspaper proprietors, film studios, engineering firms, and toothpaste companies' (Op den Kamp and Hunter, 2019:1; also see Hughes, 2012; and Schwartz, 1996:243–5).[6] Although a more recent phenomenon than one may have assumed it is plain to see that the interlinked laws surrounding IP, trademarks, patents and copyrights frame the contemporary fight against counterfeits. This section has shown the intricacies of licensed and unlicensed copycats which are approximations of the original but simultaneously inspired by them. There is a distance between them – a point I will return to shortly. By contrast, true counterfeits or fakes are as close as possible to the original, a direct copy but without the rigour of production or quality of materials. The early histories of fakery speak to this condition: the trademark, logo or formal characteristics of a product's design are the measure of authenticity. They bestow economic, social and aesthetic value. Hence why they are copied. Just as the rise of transnational supply chains has created new and (perhaps) unforeseen opportunities for illicit trafficking of narcotics, so too has the dynamics of outsourcing. We saw how aspects of deregulation have resulted in new openings for the manufacture of counterfeit goods. But the most important discussion to emerge from this section is the paradoxical relationship between the negative implications of counterfeiting (loss of taxes, reduced commercial revenue for copyright holders, lack of incentive for investment in new innovation, the overarching presence of organized crime groups) and the demand from consumers for such products, particularly in the domains of fashion, accessories and domestic/personal technologies. The presence of the non-deceptive market is much like the earlier outline in Chapter 5 where the smuggling of contraband has long been extolled for the promise of cheap goods, a factor investigated below in more detail. In the following section this line of reasoning will be explored through the importance of fakes to the constitution of consumer culture particularly its increasing complexities and nuances.

'For near-sighted friends': Status, emulation and active deception through counterfeits

There is something uncanny about fake products. To a certain extent these designed goods – for they are 'designed' – speak to Freud's notion of the uncanny as the unheimlich or the unhomely (Freud, 2003). By this I don't refer directly to Freud's classic rendering of the uncanny as that which frightens, rather his argument that the threat of the uncanny is driven by the *unfamiliar*. What makes counterfeit goods uncanny in this sense is that they are immediately familiar in our recognition of them as a particular brand, but simultaneously when we get close to them, hold them in our hands and inspect them, something is not quite right. They become unfamiliar; they jar our sense of acquaintance. This is one of the key points that interests me about counterfeits and fakes – the interplay between the communicative resonance of the surface of goods we identify with, and the apparent lack of quality in the materials and manufacture. The mismatch between the two. In many ways there is something unspeakable about fakes: a challenge to understand what makes them wrong. A gap in our understanding of them as materialized entities of a particular value system, that of consumer culture where our desires are never satiated.

It should come as little surprise then that counterfeit goods satisfy a basic tenet of capitalism: they fulfil the ethos of overconsumption and the genealogy of the throwaway society to an even greater extent due to their lower price points. As part of the ephemerality of populist fashion cultures there is perceivably less concern at throwing away a cheap copy of a high-end or luxury product than it is to discard an item that has been invested in, cherished and bears the marks of use and care (see McCracken, 1988:31–43). Equally, as I argue in this section, counterfeit goods, as well as the approximations of copycat products, adhere to the fundamental premise of consumer culture. That is, they speak to conditions of status projection, conformity and assimilation, all the whilst complexifying them. Rather than consumers valuing the quality of materials, the traceability of sources, or evidence of positive workers' rights, the *sine qua non* of capital is the symbolic prowess of the brand. It is little wonder then that the design culture of counterfeits, knock-offs and copycat products is so extensive as the figures in the last section suggest. Indeed, counterfeits speak directly to the emergent culture of conspicuous consumption developed since the late nineteenth century (Veblen, 1992) and evermore entrenched today. This section specifically addresses the relationship between counterfeits, copies, or knock-offs, and the wider socio-cultural politics of consumption. More specifically, I argue that the proliferation and expansion of counterfeit goods is intertwined directly with the culture of consumption so intrinsic to global capital. Fakes speak to the complexity of consumer culture.

This sense of uncanny slippage between familiarity and unfamiliarity was evident when looking at a 'Louis Vuitton' bag with Sue, a member of cabin crew who has recently started working for a global airline. The relationship between the debossed logo and the surface of the fake leather said it all. The debossing lacked definition. The surety of the stamped logo was limited. From a distance the stamp on the 'leather' fob at the end of the zip looked authentic: '®LOUIS VUITTON PARIS, made in France'. But as with the earlier review posting of the 'L D Coffee Table', on closer scrutiny it became clear it lacked the quality of workmanship one would associate with a bag costing in the region of USD2500. 'For near-sighted friends' indeed. Apart from the lack of definition with the debossing there was also something amiss with the typographic layout of the lettering, including the lowercase 'm' on 'made in France'. The yellow stitching was also wearing away, missing in certain parts even though the bag looked relatively new.

This was a fake Louis Vuitton bag purchased in Hong Kong by Sue. The Louis Vuitton bag was amongst an array of fashion garments and accessories we were looking through whilst discussing her experience of buying fake products in a range of cities throughout East Asia. Another fake bag, this time a 'Longchamp Le Pliage' tote bag, offered a striking example of the fluid nature of the knock-off market (see Figure 9).

Where the Louis Vuitton was fake in that it attempted to pass itself off as the authentic product the Longchamp bag was a different matter. The distanced

FIGURE 9 'Les Pliages Longchamp Type' bag. Photo by author.

authenticity and surface logic of fakes rendered the Longchamp bag initially legible as an original, but like the knockoffs on New York's Canal Street when one inspected the bag it did not even attempt to hide its lack of authenticity. The debossed label read: LES PLIAGES LONGCHAMP TYPE MODELE DEPOSE MADE IN FRANCE. The suffix made it immediately clear this was a copycat: Longchamp *type*. Added to this, the spelling of Le Pliage was incorrect: 'Les Pliages' on the copy rather than 'Le Pliage' on the original. Although commonplace with the emergence of Chinese fakes in the 1990s (Low, 2002:22) there is still something uncanny about the appearance of familiarity with the overall form, shape and appearance of this bag, then the slippage into unfamiliarity with the suffix and misspelling. Here is the gap I speak of. Sue had bought these two bags alongside numerous other fake products during her long-haul trips to a range of Asian cities, including Hong Kong and Singapore.[7] There are a number of striking aspects with Sue's willing consumption of fakes. The desire for cheap versions of expensive luxury items is central to the proliferation of counterfeits, and – as discussed in more depth below – intrinsic to the nature of consumer culture itself. But what marks out the example of counterfeit goods being consumed by cabin crew and other consumers is the link between the geographies of counterfeit manufacturing, global tourism and critically the sharing of knowledge about retail sites in global cities such as Singapore.

What is perhaps most striking about Sue's story is that it mirrors the experiences of so many consumers. On the one hand we purchase fakes in order to communicate our taste in goods and our *apparent* ability to afford particular luxury brands. But equally there is a pragmatic element to many of Sue's purchases. She simply needed a bag to carry things, why not buy one of these whilst in Singapore? Her daughter required a coat, why not a fake Superdry? It fulfils the basic function of providing warmth. This is characteristic of consumer culture. An admixture of utility and social positioning. These goods do things for us; they say things about us. In the case of counterfeits there is perhaps a 'knowingness' about the similarity between the original and the fake, a wiliness that demonstrates the astuteness of the consumer. In many ways there is of course nothing radical about this: ever since Veblen's (1992) treatise on the leisure class was published in 1899 the idea that commodities communicate much more than mere utility has proliferated. Consumer culture is fundamentally predicated on the way in which consumers utilize designed goods as a means of self-expression; identity formation; social belonging; and the propagation of values, beliefs and tastes. These goods are 'charged with cultural meaning' (McCracken, 1988:xi).

The idea of positional projection is evident in social situations where consumers deploy goods as markers of identity and status, particularly through luxury products. For Veblen the burgeoning material culture of the early modern period was a vital means for the bourgeoisie to display their economic as well as cultural capital. His infamous phrase – *conspicuous consumption* – captured this astutely. Although the term has perhaps largely become diluted in contemporary culture

(Campbell, 2001:247) the nuances of the original historical social settings of late nineteenth century Western societies are worth restating. Veblen's discussion of conspicuous consumption must be situated within the context of the emergent 'leisure class' of this period where the ownership of private property and goods was synonymous with displays of wealth, social standing and the 'conventional basis of reputability' (Veblen, 1992:15; 36). That is, the consumption of particular goods and cultural activities, as well as property afforded a reputation to the individual through positioning them within certain social strata. Critically, the rise of consumption is intrinsically linked with one having the time to consume, and in this period it was the leisured classes who possessed both the financial and temporal means of doing so. Although the consumption of leisure activities such as sports, sewing circles and charity events formed an important facet of the display of leisure time it is the consumption and projection of status through household goods and personal products in particular that defines conspicuous consumption. Above all, pecuniary status and strength are confirmed by one's ability to consume goods, and, as Veblen discusses (1992:77–86), clothing is a particularly powerful signifier of social standing, thus why it stood – and still stands – as a key mechanism for the conspicuous display of wealth, taste and identity. Clothing provides one of the most immediate registers of social position and status, be it through the recognizable group allegiances afforded by a particular subcultural form, an awareness of contemporary taste cultures or the ability to consume niche luxury brands. It is also central to the tensions inherent in consumer culture, namely the conflict between assimilation to group affiliation and individual identity. Whilst one might readily associate such conditions with contemporary society, this has been a commonplace for the study of fashion throughout much of the twentieth century and beyond (Simmel, 1904). Central to clothing and its attendant material culture of accessories is the way in which it is deployed for the purpose of communicating social position, taste and status. A culture of consumption dominated by fashion is marked out by the consumer's use of goods to gratify desire (Bauman, 2007:10) and to position their identities as opposed to the traditional means of doing so, be that through their labour, political affiliation or religious belief. Whilst some may lament the rise of identity formation through the mutability of clothing and the everyday material culture of designed goods, work in the field of social anthropology (Douglas and Isherwood, 1996) like that of Veblen and Simmel has long recognized the centrality of goods as positional devices. Although it is not the aim of this section to examine in detail the wide-ranging debates on consumer culture (see Baudrillard, 1998; Featherstone, 2007; Lury, 1996; McCracken, 1988; Sassatelli, 2007; Slater, 1997) the key aspects outlined here are critical in their relation to counterfeit design cultures. For I argue that of significant importance to the consumer cultures of design are the ways in which copycats, knockoffs and fakes further *intensify* the already-complex entanglements between designed goods and consumption.

As shown with Sue's purchase of counterfeit products in Asian cities, people often purchase fake brands – and luxury ones in particular – for the perceived *status* they afford individuals. But Sue also noted the functional qualities of certain fake items: so, whilst one of the likely reasons consumers seek out and wilfully purchase counterfeits is for the signifying potency of luxury products it is more complex than this alone. For instance, there is a touristic aspect where certain cities (such as those visited by Sue, as well as Canal Street in New York or Dubai) have a reputation for selling fakes or copycats. Crucially, however, in the study of consumption, positional status, the display of taste, knowledge and emulation have been critical barometers for understanding how and why consumers utilize commodities beyond their functional attributes (Douglas and Isherwood, 1996; McCracken, 1988). But this alone is not sufficient in determining the myriad of reasons many of us choose to consume certain products over others. In this reading status is concerned above all else with a hierarchy of economic, social, cultural and political value. It is also about assimilation; fitting into socially prescribed roles and allegiances. The hierarchical nature of such social practices has been one of many reasons why these widely held views on consumption have simultaneously been critiqued. For example, processes of emulation have been highly contested. Traditional notions of emulation – and the related idea of envy – subscribe to the idea that lower social groups seek to emulate higher social classes through *imitating* taste in clothing and other such positional goods (Forty, 1986; Hirsch, 1978). However, whilst clearly apparent in certain situations this has been critiqued as 'monological and capable of recognising neither the active discriminatory capacities of consumers, nor the complexity of the processes involved in the reproduction of consumer society' (Shove and Warde, 1998:4). There is also a political dimension to this, whereby 'lower' classes actively challenge the dominant taste of 'higher' social groups, seen most obviously through the sartorial supremacy of subcultural groups. Sassatelli also argues that 'reference to envy, imitation and status symbols has become a default explanation and indeed a straitjacket for all and every act of consumption' (Sassatelli, 2007:68). Her argument is that these positions cannot solely account for the divergent ways in which consumers act. For example, with imitation and emulation the Veblenesque version does not allow for both the idea of imitation as a form of mimesis whilst simultaneously acknowledging the creative ways in which consumers make these choices (Sassatelli, 2007:69). Equally, the classic notion of 'trickle down' theory, whereby innovations in taste and design flow downward from elite social groups to the 'masses', has been largely jettisoned when we consider the means through which advances in street style for example flow upward. Given the myriad debates on contemporary consumer culture from across design cultures, sociology, anthropology and the broader humanities and social sciences any straightforward conceptualization of counterfeits and their relationship with consumption is unworkable. Indeed, it further complexifies the discussion. We have seen how copycat commodities such as the Eames-inspired chairs in London Drugs make no reference to the original design, so in this case it is unlikely consumers would necessarily purchase these for status value alone. Whilst emulation and status projection may be an important facet for why many consumers actively purchase counterfeit products there is also the functional value recognized by the likes of Sue. Anecdotally, one may be familiar with the 'celebratory' nature of counterfeit consumption, whereby consumers openly admit to the fake credentials of a particular commodity. The copycat Rollys on Canal Street being a likely example. In the context of the non-deceptive market in counterfeit goods it is explicitly clear that consumers are *active* participants in determining their own needs and desires through fake items (Bianchi, 1998). This may well be concerned with status projection and emulation, but rather than these consumers simply assenting to dominant taste they might also be actively choosing to do so in often ironic ways.

Although Packard's (1960) seminal book *The Status Seekers* coined the phrase in relation to the burgeoning growth of consumer culture in mid-twentieth-century America, Erving Goffman's (1951) earlier study of status provides an important argument in relation to the active consumption of counterfeit products. Whilst Goffman's position is somewhat guilty of the criticisms levelled by Sassatelli – particularly in his lack of recognition for the fluidity of class – the historical juncture of his arguments may account for this. He notes how the symbolic nature of status displays is necessarily separate to the things they signify – a rudimentary but important point. Crucially he goes onto say: 'it is always possible, therefore, that symbols may come to be employed in a "*fraudulent*" way, i.e. to signify a status which the claimant does not in fact possess' (Goffman, 1951:296 my emphasis). Given there is a gap between the symbol and the thing itself this space is open to 'fraudulent' manipulation. The economic and social status apparently afforded by the display of a luxury item can be co-opted fraudulently by consumers through the purchase of a fake version of the commodity. To signify status which the claimant does not possess, as Goffman put it. But crucially, the consumer who carries this out is actively manipulating the symbolic rather than the material power of fake commodities.

Traditionally one might consider that the status value of a luxury commodity is conferred through a range of attributes, be they cost and the ability to afford these goods, retail environment, relational associations but perhaps above all material quality. This is challenged by the consumption of fakes. For Veblen central to the positional value of luxury clothing in particular was the economic worth of the goods and their material quality. As he put it: 'the requirement of expensiveness is so ingrained into our habits of thought in matters of dress that any other than expensive apparel is instinctively odious to us' (Veblen, 1992:78). Of course, the context of middle-class consumption was central to Veblen's analyses, but it is not simply the fact he wrote this in the late nineteenth century that makes it a rather curious statement. For whilst the quality of goods does still have a bearing for particular social classes today the rise of mass production and mass consumption in the twentieth century jars most obviously with Veblen's assertion. Where Veblen goes onto describe the nature of 'cheap and nasty' (1992:78) goods the dominance of such consumer products in contemporary society proves we do not have quite the same distaste at such seemingly worthless things. Even more starkly for this chapter Veblen singles out the almost causal relationship between cheapness, lack of taste and counterfeits. He states in full:

> With few and inconsequential exceptions, we all find a costly hand-wrought article of apparel much preferable, in point of beauty and of serviceability, to a less expensive imitation of it, however cleverly the spurious article may imitate the costly original; and what offends our sensibilities in the spurious article is not that it falls short in form or color, or, indeed, in visual effect in any way. The offensive object may be so close an imitation as to defy any but the closest scrutiny; and yet so soon as the counterfeit is detected, its aesthetic value, and its commercial value as well, declines precipitately. Not only that, but it may be asserted with but small risk of contradiction that the aesthetic value of a detected counterfeit in dress declines somewhat in the same proportion as the counterfeit is cheaper than its original. It loses caste aesthetically because it falls to a lower pecuniary grade.
>
> (Veblen, 1992:78)

It may still be true that for many consumers such an argument holds, particularly in the context of deceptive markets where buyers are duped into believing a counterfeit item is original. But as the focus of this chapter on willing consumption of copycats and fakes suggests the loss of aesthetic value in fakes is perhaps not as profound an issue as Veblen implies. Data on the conscious consumption of counterfeit goods provides empirical evidence of this, whilst Goffman's notion of the fraudulent space of symbol manipulation affords further conceptual verification. There is not a necessarily *direct* correlative relationship between the material quality of a commodity and its potential status-displaying power. Perceived status can be manufactured through symbolic power of fakes. For Bekir et al. 'fake products allow the holder to free ride on the status benefits tied to original items without incurring the whole cost' (2011:718). Much in the same way that Goffman describes the fraudulent exploitation of status symbols, so too the notion of 'free riding' on status through fakes evokes Sassatelli's point that consumers are actively shrewd – or indeed devious – in their usage of (fake) consumer goods. Van Kempen (2003) uses the cognate idea of 'deception' to describe how some consumers are deceptive in how they attempt to signal their status through the use of counterfeit goods.[8] Both fraudulence and deception constructively articulate the way in which consumers might choose to *mislead* others in communicating a range of purported personal attributes, be that economic status, class affiliation or wider notions of identity. I conflate these various ideas under the term 'active deception'.

When such consumers actively deploy artefacts to deceptively communicate their apparent social status, economic capital or indeed their knowing consumption of fake products they do so through their communicative power. Active deception relies on the communicative mechanisms of counterfeit goods; their recognizability through the design language of the original. Crucially, for this to operate one cannot get too close to fake goods. Their in-authenticity becomes manifest when we realize the poor quality of manufacture or the inconsistencies of branding. The inferior debossing or the misspelt brand name for example. But in opposition to Veblen's criticism of bad workmanship this is not why the majority of people purchase fakes: they do so for the power of the brand itself, the recognition of the logo or the formal qualities of shape or colour that identifies a particular fashion item or accessory. But crucially they may also do so fully cognisant of the counterfeit nature of the product, indeed actively *celebrating* fakes.

This section has worked through a range of different perspectives on the interactions between design culture, brands, consumption and counterfeit products. Specifically addressing the willing consumption of fake goods by individuals points to the logic of consumer culture itself: the manufacture of desire, the drive towards overconsumption, the wastefulness of cheap goods and the accelerated cycles of fashion cultures. But in addition to this one of the core ideas to emerge here has been how fakes exemplify the ever-fraught nature of consumer culture, where some consumers advocate the status projection of counterfeits whilst others knowingly praise the fake qualities of these products. Above all, many consumers actively deploy counterfeits for a range of purposes. They creatively engage with the potential power of fakes. In the following section of the chapter these discussions of creativity, active consumption and the complexity of emulation through imitation are considered in relation to the innovative nature of copying and manufacture.

Imitation as innovation: Lessons from *shanzhai*

An article in the media and marketing magazine *Campaign* offers an interesting tale of counterfeits that resonates with much of the previous section and simultaneously challenges the assumption that counterfeits are wholly negative in terms of their impact on mainstream brands and manufacturers (Ritson, 2007). The article describes the scenario of a chief executive of a leading European luxury brand flying from Paris to New York. On the flight he notices another passenger in first class carrying one of his company's handbags. Given his familiarity with the product he notices immediately this is a fake. He berates his fellow passenger for knowingly purchasing the bag. It is widely acknowledged that the production of counterfeit products is said to harm legitimate manufacturers both in relation to loss of revenues from authentic products and as a result of this reduction in future product investments. The *Campaign* article contests some of these assumptions: firstly, it is argued a consumer who mistakenly purchases a fake would not necessarily have bought the legitimate version; secondly, brand equity is not always harmed by counterfeits; in fact, it is suggested that fakes are a sign of a brand's importance, its cultural kudos (also see Mackinney-Valentin and Teilmann-Lock, 2014:95–6). Such *counterarguments* form the basis of this final section.

It is clear that the infringement of copyright and the subsequent reduction in taxable duties are dominant motivational drivers in attempts to reduce the proliferation of fake goods (Wall and Large, 2010), and have been since the emergence of trademarks in early Rome. Behind these concerns over the economic impact of research and development is also criticism of the lack of innovation in the design, development, manufacture, distribution and sales of counterfeit goods. Central to such a position is that innovation is only possible through *originality*: the creation of a product or service that is original in both its technical, material and aesthetic form as well as the identification and manipulation of new opportunities and markets. Copying is said to stifle innovation (Raustiala and Sprigman, 2006:1688). Although innovation does not always materialize from wholly new designs or ideas the nature of intellectual property, copyright and patents are such that the novelty of Schumpeter's 'gale of creative destruction' bestows originality through eradicating the old. This is where innovation is said to lie. In this context intellectual property is confirmation of innovation, enshrining value. To infringe IP or copyright is to disregard innovation, to devalue originality. However, as with the discussion of hacking and the value of misuse at the end of Chapter 4, in this closing section I explore the possibility that imitation, counterfeiting and fakery may be seen as innovative in their own right. The previous consideration of the impact of counterfeiting on consumer culture has already highlighted how fake goods are utilized in complex ways by consumers. I now consider whether similar questions around innovation might emerge through the value of copying. Concentrating on this I choose not to adhere to the legalistically inclined positions on what defines innovation and originality. Instead my reading of innovation returns to its radical, revolutionary origins of change, but primarily that *innovation can emerge through imitation*.

Central to this assertion are the critiques of copyright law. Whilst this is highly complicated in terms of international law – and beyond the scope of this chapter and the book itself – the key facet of the argument I propose here is that the imposition of copyright is driven by Western agendas of enforcing economic power on 'developing' economies for the purpose of capturing new markets. Indeed, the origins of intellectual property, patenting and copyright stem from the drive to maximize profits through retaining control over material as well as abstract ownership. Given the centrality of copyright to the exploitation of new markets, critiques highlight the (neo)colonialist ideologies of market exploitation whereby control is exercised by both corporations and nation states through a range of commercial and legal instruments such as international economic law treaties (Rahmatian, 2009:41). Schwartz sees it thus:

'Developing' countries have resented the monopoly on information: to enforce foreign copyrights would be to serve as sheriff for 'developing' powers, to perpetuate colonial tyranny, or at a minimum to collude in a scale of prices that mocks the common people.

(Schwartz, 1996:244)

To be sure, attitudes towards copying more generally are framed by Western-centric perceptions from the Global North. What becomes evident from these discussions is that copyright law is not ontologically grounded, it is 'neither natural nor universal' (Schwartz, 1996:243). It is a facet of historical transformation and socio-economic doctrine, as well as cultural specificity. For example, writing of the histories of innovation and the relationship to African forms of technology Clapperton Mavhunga argues that 'until the mid-eighteenth century, imitation was positively viewed as selective borrowing and creative copying that substituted for imported goods and lowered costs of original products' (2017:8). Just as Schwartz identifies the use of pricing as a mechanism to dominate economically deprived groups, so Mavhunga notes that copying provided lower cost goods – a facet that in many ways still pervades today in the context of knowing consumption of fakes. This perhaps provides a key determining factor for the historical transformation of imitation as an inherent part of the process of invention, to its present-day status as highly inscribed by illegality. It marks out a more general shift towards the power of legal instruments for economic control. However, the value of imitation can be seen in other eighteenth-century commercial practices where the aesthetic value of luxury items as well as technological innovations were imitated or 'borrowed', leading to subsequent advances in taste and technology. Whilst the aesthetic influence of Japan is evident in late-nineteenth century *Japonisme* (Tornier, 2017), in engineering Europe 'borrowed from and imitated other cultures, gaining iron suspension bridges, seed drills, porcelain, calicoes, satin, damasks and japan, arabic numerals, and lateen sails' (Berg, 2002:6). Just as we saw earlier with the role of material goods in status *emulation,* so too with *imitation* in the furtherance of technological prowess through innovation. Once more, Godin's research makes this argument in great detail, highlighting the shift from the value of imitation to that of originality (Godin, 2008:13). As with the previous discussion of his work on the radical origins of innovation his approach to the question of imitation is highly perceptive and adds measurably to the rhetoric of originality. Echoing Berg's identification of borrowing as a necessary step in technological improvement, earlier perceptions of imitation were not predicated on the twentieth-century premise that invention is only possible through originality. Rather it was presented in a positive light, indeed it made luxury items more readily available to people through the creation of 'semi-luxuries' in clothing, decorative items and household commodities (Godin, 2008:11). However, one has to be mindful of the context of Godin's argument: his point is that these forms of imitation were not 'slavish or mechanical imitation, but selective borrowing and creative copying' (Godin, 2008:10). There was awareness on the part of the imitator as to how the original might be improved or made more accessible in economic terms. Of course, many of the contemporary counterfeit products discussed in this chapter are indeed slavish copies of the original with seemingly little perceivable innovation.

Nonetheless, I suggest there are cases of 'creative copying' in relation to copycat goods such as the bags discussed earlier. They may not demonstrate technological advancement in the way eighteenth-century technologies were imitated and improved, but in relation to the creativity or *ingenuity* of approach there is evidence of advancements in the use of lean manufacturing techniques and the speed at which copycats or fake goods reach market (Ritson, 2007). Indeed, in terms of industrial development counterfeiting has been an important facet in the maturation of the manufacturing base of countries typically associated with the proliferation of fake goods. For example, where today China has been marked out as one of the most prolific manufacturers of counterfeit goods, in the past this was the case with other Asian economies including Japan in the 1950s and Taiwan in the 1980s (Burns, 1986). To a certain degree it is argued that nations such as Japan and Taiwan in the past, and China more recently, initially developed their technological capacity to manufacture goods through copying existing products before honing the technological and commercial means to create original and technologically advanced products of their own (Prebula, 1986:342). Imitation itself entails levels of skill, imagination, experimentation and resourcefulness (Godin, 2008:12) so the eventual rise of technological and creative capacity is unsurprising.

Many of these points are clearly demonstrated today through the Chinese notion of *shanzhai*. Much in the same way that Jugaad refers to broader sensibilities of Indian culture (Jauregui, 2016), what now embodies the wider cultural and philosophical characteristics of Chinese society (see Han, 2017) began in the context of crude imitations of big-brand technology products, particularly mobile phones (Fernandez et al., 2016). Out of this came the widely held notion of *shanzhai* as the coinage for Chinese fakes and copycats. We saw examples of this in the Introduction to the chapter with the playfulness of deliberate brand name slippages such as Nokir or Samsing (Han, 2017:72). Although there is admittedly something amusing about these names *shanzhai* also demonstrates a more radical tendency in how it brings together criticisms of the hegemonic, neo-colonialist drive of intellectual property and the innovative nature of copying itself. Indeed, *shanzhai*'s literal meaning as mountain stronghold (see Fernandez et al., 2016; Han, 2017:75; Lindtner et al., 2015:np) denotes a tradition of anti-establishment autonomy from mainstream politics and society.[9] Whilst *shanzhai*'s cheap mobile phones and smart watches are clearly capitalist products the implications of how such devices came to market refer to more informal, networked and open forms of design and manufacture that run counter to Western perceptions of originality, copyright and intellectual property. Indeed 'the creativity inherent in *shanzhai* will elude the West if the West sees it only as deception, plagiarism, and the infringement of intellectual property' (Han, 2017:78).

The backdrop to these discussions emanates out of the political upheavals of Mao Zedong's rise to power in 1949 and the subsequent flight of Shanghai-based entrepreneurs to Hong Kong where they set up small-scale, family-run enterprises which manufactured low quality, unauthorized imitations of products. As Lin notes, at this time *shanzhai* referred to the situation where 'three to five workers from the same family [...] composed unauthorized products to sell' (2011:3). These early practices of copying in the 1950s led later on to the cheap fakes of famous fashion accessories by the likes of Gucci (Lindtner et al., 2015). However, the setting of Hong Kong was part of a series of wider geopolitical changes in the 1980s and 1990s with the liberalization of world trade and crucially the growth of outsourced manufacturing. In the context of China, Low (2002) explains how a number of factors led to its rise as a global manufacturing base including the economic reforms of the early 1990s, companies from Hong Kong and Taiwan setting up production facilities on the Chinese mainland as well as greater access to world markets through the lowering of export controls. In the context of manufacturing and counterfeit cultures, these economic and geopolitical shifts are most obviously evident in the Chinese city of Shenzhen. The city has latterly become synonymous with the rise of open source manufacture and maker movements, but prior to these being lauded as new forms of commercial enterprise Shenzhen was known as a hub of 'contract manufacturers' who manufactured outsourced electronic products, in part because of its status as a Special Economic Zone from 1979 onwards (Lindtner et al., 2015). Whilst the outsourcing of production to cities such as Shenzhen typifies neo-colonialist conceptions that design takes place in the West with manufacturing is passively carried out in Asia, the rise of Shenzhen challenges these assumptions. Indeed, as Fernandez et al. (2016) note, Shenzhen's complex manufacturing ecosystem saw the growth of manufacturers' own expertise in parallel to their origins in outsourced manufacturing. By manufacturing electronics hardware practices such as reverse engineering afforded Shenzhen companies with in-depth design knowledge of the devices they were producing. Further to this their agility meant that they were able to identify new market opportunities provided by the gaps left in the market by large-scale Western companies who were only interested in large-scale production runs. Lindtner et al. describe how 'a dense web of manufacturing businesses emerged in Shenzhen, catering towards less well-known or no-name clients with smaller quantities, who were of no interest to the larger players' (2015:np). Whilst *shanzhai* refers to the cheap imitations already noted, it also now describes such examples of less-formalized manufacturing practices that defy Western ideas of competition. Shenzhen's latter status as a maker-hub grew out of this dense web of production coupled with an open-source ethos where small companies collaborated on design, sourcing, assembly, testing, packaging and distribution (Fernandez et al., 2016:31). This ethos also provided a high degree of flexibility, making *shanzhai* manufacturers more adaptable than the long planning and production cycles of companies designing and engineering original products at this time (Han, 2017:72). A pivotal aspect of the move from *shanzhai* simply being a reference to copycat iPhones to its latter innovative status came with the availability of 'turnkey' processors in the early 2000s (Fernandez et al., 2016:31) and more recently the publicly accessible open hardware platforms designed in such a way to 'extend its functionalities and build new creations on top' (Lindtner, 2015:868). Employing these standardized boards enabled electronics manufacturers to transcend copycat production and develop the capabilities and features of electronics design and functionality.

Although just a brief summary of the scholarly research into *shanzhai*, the key points raised here show how *shanzhai* challenges many preconceptions of the design and manufacture of electronic products in particular. This is demonstrated through the use of approaches which embrace short manufacturing cycles able to react much quicker to market demands than large-scale corporations. Equally, the open-source ethos to the manufacturing ecosystem provides opportunities to share and co-develop new approaches. Fundamentally, 'with its roots in and ongoing practices of piracy and open sharing, *shanzhai* challenges any inherent link made between technological innovation and the tools, instruments and value systems of proprietary, corporate research and development' (Lindtner et al., 2015:np). Ultimately it may well be the case that the creativity and innovation inherent in the practices of *shanzhai* are fundamentally at odds not only to the mechanisms of intellectual property but equally the very constitution of Western ideas of originality and authenticity.

Such a statement demonstrates the ontological and moral chasm between Chinese and Western approaches to originality more generally. As Low points out, 'the West sees it [counterfeiting] as taking away a person's proprietorial rights, whilst the Chinese attitude is that to copy is divine' (2002:23). The manufacturing ecosystem of *shanzhai*, with its emphasis on openness and networked allegiances, is also a register of the broader traditions of Chinese culture and philosophy. Where the Western construct of intellectual property effectively *fixes* the material and legislative function of a product Han notes how the idea of the original in Chinese culture is typified by the 'unending process' of continuous *change* (2017:11). Just as Chapter 3 considered innovation's radical origins as a form of change and Chapter 4 outlined the unfinished potentiality of the improvised nature of informal design, so the approach to copying in Chinese culture recognizes the value of change as opposed to the fixity of originality, to the extent that even Chinese masterpieces are continually overwritten (Han, 2017:13). Copying in Chinese culture is also important to learning processes whereby the development of new knowledge and skills is provided through detailed understanding of an artefact, a facet clearly central to the technological prowess of Shenzhen through the use of reverse engineering. Undergirding this ethos is a tradition of Chinese intellectual culture premised on different variants of truth. Western notions of truth are linked to an idea of originality that Han sees as essentially exclusionary and transcendent, whereas Chinese culture 'operates using inclusion and immanence' (Han, 2017:29; also see Schwartz, 1996:243).[10] Considering this in light of copyright law there is an exclusionary characteristic to allowing only certain groups access to products and services, typically from a position of economic ability. By contrast, the histories and geographies of imitation point to the inclusivity of enabling lower-priced products to be accessible to broader spectrums of society.

Stemming from such philosophical foundations the *shanzhai* approach is appreciable in its use of modification, variance, combination and transformation, all agents of change. The inclusivity of open source approaches to tech development in Shenzhen fundamentally demonstrates how innovation has the potential to arise from copying. However, there is an irony at the heart of these debates on the value of open approaches to innovation. As shown in the conclusions to Chapter 4, ethical or 'white hacking' rose out of the illegality of early hacker communities and has now been institutionalized (Chakraborty et al., 2019), so too with the co-opting and legitimization of other purportedly illicit practices that have subsequently become emblematic of capital's contemporary logic. *Shanzhai* demonstrates this. Whilst counterfeiting remains demonized as an illicit practice that fosters a lack of research and development investment through the loss of revenue, at the same time the *shanzhai* ethos of networked collaboration and the sharing of resources, skills and ideas has been lauded as a valuable ecosystem in its own right for other mainstream commercial enterprises through the moniker of 'open innovation' (Chesborough, 2006). The very notion of *shanzhai*-based 'openness' becomes a register of maker-driven tech cultures (Lindtner et al., 2015), cutting-edge alternative design practices (van Abel et al., 2011; Fuad-Luke et al., 2015:30) and increasingly standard business practices. Once more, mainstream innovation is seemingly reliant on the illicit.

Conclusions

The cultures of copycats and counterfeits are complex. Both legally – as much of the intellectual property literature shows – but as this chapter has primarily investigated, in a range of other situations. We saw in the earlier section of the chapter that there are different categories of products, ranging from legally sanctioned copycats 'inspired' by original designs such as mid-twentieth-century furniture, through to highly dangerous fake pharmaceuticals. In between there are grey markets where legitimate commodities are sold in markets they were not originally intended for. Many consumers unwittingly purchase counterfeits in the belief they are buying legitimate artefacts. Others knowingly consume fakes. The focus of the chapter has been the latter, and more specifically the intersection of copycat and fake fashion, accessory and consumer electronics items. These different classifications of fake or copycat goods confront us in different settings: on street corners in downtown Manhattan; in Canadian chain stores; in newspaper advertisements; in the back of shops in Hong Kong; and, of course, online. These goods are also slippery. They slip between the surface logic of all consumer goods and poor-quality production. And whilst the majority of items discussed in this chapter have been closer to 'exclusive status-gratifying commodities' (De Barnier, 2014:344) I suggest that in some respects fake products define the logic of all mass-produced goods: there is a promise in the surface registers of branding but ultimately the promise fades when we use them. They leave us unsatiated.

All of which highlights how the cultures of copycats and counterfeits run parallel to mainstream consumer culture. This point was central to one of the core discussions in this chapter on how such goods play an important role in the production of status for consumers. The deceptive nature of such social practices was highlighted in order to raise the importance of positional consumption through fakes. It is evident that many consumers are complicit in the creation and perpetuation of counterfeit cultures of consumption. There is a desire, a market for such things. Related again to the enmeshing of the licit and the illicit, capitalism is figured around the production, distribution and consumption of goods and services, so the development of a parallel industry facilitating the knowing consumption of evermore branded goods – albeit fake – should come as little surprise. *Fakes are emblematic of consumer culture itself.* They also highlight the sophistication of consumers in their use of 'active deception', be that in attempting to project a particular economic status through the display of counterfeit products or equally the knowing and conspicuous brandishing of obvious copycats. With counterfeits the traditional locus of status becomes ever more fluid as the fake products jettison the perceived surety of knowing that particular brands are part of the social, cultural and economic milieu of class-based groups. Overall, one of the significant points to emerge from the study of counterfeits is the centrality of consumption and consumer culture to the perpetuation of this enterprise. The conflation of design with branding culture is such that the demand for artefacts that fulfil the mantras of status projection and lifestyle is almost a pre-condition of global capital itself.

The design cultures of counterfeits also exemplify the longstanding interrelationships between production and consumption. The consumer-driven demand for cheap goods (be they fakes or not) has a profound effect on the design and manufacture of products. And the inverse. As discussed earlier in the chapter whilst the production of fake goods does clearly reduce profits and potential investment by companies producing the original products some have argued that fakes can provide companies with a level of cultural esteem, notably in fashion (Mackinney-Valentin and Teilmann-Lock, 2014:95–6). But perhaps one of the most significant criticisms of counterfeit or copycat products is that they lack innovation, and thus innovation can only be present through the fixity of the original, its hallowed status afforded by copyright and trademark law. In keeping with the ethos of the book as a whole this chapter has attempted to question such rigid definitions of innovation and argue instead that there are long histories of innovation through imitation. This was made evident through consideration of the aesthetic plundering of Japonisme, as well as the technological importance of initially copying then improving suspension bridge design, lateen sails or porcelain. Rooted in design and technology development is the value of learning from that which has preceded us through imitation. Chinese philosophy argues such, which according to Han (2017) may indeed account for the growth of *shanzhai* manufacturing. Although the closing section of the chapter provided only a short outline of *shanzhai* practices, it is clear that the business model developed by manufacturers in cities such as Shenzhen demonstrates that innovative design, production and commercial processes have emerged through a result of the initial copying of original consumer electronics products. Indeed, we saw how *shanzhai* producers have gained their own expertise and knowledge through an intimate understanding of the products and manufacturing initially outsourced to them, a process of maturation evident in earlier Asian economies. Once again in the context of fashion, Georg Simmel famously stated that imitation 'affords the pregnant possibility of continually extending the greatest creations of the human spirit, without the aid of the forces which were originally the very condition of their birth. Imitation, furthermore, gives to the individual the satisfaction of not standing alone in his actions' (Simmel, 1904:132).

Imitation can indeed give rise to innovation. It also challenges certain presumptions of innovation itself.

CONCLUSION: THE ETHICS OF CHANGE?

Deviant Design has shown that design matters. It puts people, things, ideas and worlds into being. Design is imbued with prefigurative power, with the envisioning and creation of new social forces. What Arturo Escobar has termed 'futural praxis' (Escobar, 2021). In examining the conditions of design in its manifold formations, I have attempted to demonstrate how it profoundly determines so many of our socio-material relations. From the design of artefacts, products, buildings, services, environments, systems, infrastructures to behaviours, all of which have the potential to serve the public good. More and more people realize this. Policymakers exploring new democratic formations (Design Commission, 2015) or scientists seeking out new biological futures (Myers, 2018). Design suffuses everything.

Yet, the book's wilful act of looking askew at design has attempted to redress widely held assertions of how such power is manifested through benevolence. I have argued above all that one must fully comprehend design's central position in the malevolency of social forms, in perpetuating inequalities through failings in the structural design of services; or through profoundly masculinist and racialized hierarchies of how products, buildings, cities and infrastructural systems have been designed. But rather than endorse these deleterious effects of design, the book has also set out to consider what must be learnt from this exponential power – not simply presuming the social value of design and its perceived ability to instantiate positive change. Instead, I have examined the multifaceted dimensions of where designerly forms of knowledge and practice take place outwith those normative spaces one might traditionally associate with design, not least in the three substantive case studies: acts of creative misuse, illicit forms of material and logistical design associated with drug trafficking, the technological and entrepreneurial acumen of fakery. By reflecting upon these heterodox configurations of design as socio-material practices formed of practical intelligence, wiliness, planning know-how and wider contextual knowledge, we can redouble efforts to prefigure design's ontological potential beyond traditional disciplinary constraints. Consciously expanding the repertoire of design to encompass these and so many other diffuse acts of worldmaking, Latour's argument that design now has no limits urgently requires us to reflect upon the implications of this for how everyone practices, studies and engages design. Indeed, as Fry and Nocek argue, design has been constrained under the logic of Eurocentrism and the Enlightenment: 'It follows that design disciplines obstruct an adequate thinking of design, which then renders taking responsibility for designing inoperable' (2021b:159).

This is where the nomadic ethics of *Deviant Design* resides. By examining heterodox forms of designerly intelligence and practice through the lens of deviancy, my hope is that we can deconstruct these and so many other examples in order to reflect upon and fundamentally undermine the established practices of design to embrace the complexity of social forces (Fry and Nocek, 2021b:159). The origins of innovation as transgressive and revolutionary might be key to this, not least its roots as a radical form of becoming, of change itself. As noted at the outset, whilst not about the ethics of design per se, the book argues for a profound understanding of *responsibility*. That is, taking seriously the need to design in ways that contribute to the complexities of worldmaking, but equally who is responsible for this. Everyone, as we saw with Ezio Manzini's work on diffuse design. Fry's (2004:151) discussion of 'the sustainment' clearly situates this task as an ethical endeavour, where design must 'contribute to creating the means by which "we" can become otherwise'. By recognizing the complicity of design in devising the very conditions that have caused so many of the multiple but clearly entangled crises that engulf us today, we might better create the skills and practices to change this. In part what I have attempted to achieve in this book is to stress how the prefigurative power of design can be recognized through its extremities, in the practices of design not recognized as such, and through this to redirect design itself, to make it sustaining. Given my own belief in the potency of heterodox design formations, the following brief discussion attempts to determine the importance of responsibility and the ethics of how change in the face of crisis can be prefigured through the heterodoxies of design.

These concluding thoughts are written under ever-changeable conditions of crisis. In the case of Covid-19 through both the emergence of new variants and the intensely unequal distribution of vaccinations. The vaccination programme in particular accentuates the structural inequalities which permeate the social fabric discussed at length throughout the book. The huge disparities in vaccination programmes highlight the devastating imbalances in the global order, where 85 per cent of vaccine doses administered up to May 2021 have been to those in upper-middle and high-income countries (Cohen and Kupferschmidt, 2021). The World Health Organization's 'Coronavirus (COVID-19) Dashboard' starkly illustrates the differences in numbers of vaccinations administered between those countries in the Global North and those in the Global South, notably across much of the African continent.

An ever-growing body of literature argues for radically new political paradigms for post-pandemic futures based on new rationalities and sensibilities (see for example Bratton, 2021). Critically, the structural conditions that led to the global Covid-19 pandemic also demonstrate the need for substantive change. A deeper understanding of how things, humans, nonhumans and viruses circulate; the impact of limited welfare and social care support in so many countries; the ever-clearer need for state-based provision to care for the vulnerable in our societies. The list will inevitably expand. The global pandemic also demonstrates the nature of complexity, a core conceptual thread throughout the entire book. Societies are far from stable, linear, causal or predictable. Covid-19 has shown us this in a deeply disconcerting manner. There is a deeper existential crisis at work that exposes conditions of weak governance, deep-seated, class-based and racialized restrictions in access to health and social care, as well as neoliberalism's reliance on private capital. Rather than an exception to norms of social life, the emergencies we encounter reveal the 'pre-existing conditions' (Bratton, 2021:8). Such pre-existing conditions of negligence and poor governance are symptomatic of the intertwined crises of the Covid-19 pandemic, climate emergency, eco-social collapse, political populism, racial injustice, etc.

This point is put perhaps most usefully for the issue of design by Fry and Nocek (2021c:218), who argue that the very condition of being human is a form of perpetual crisis, in the Heideggerian sense of 'being-toward-death'. As a perpetual condition, crises have defined epochs but none more so than now where we are living through and towards an amplification in scale and 'still growing severity' (Fry and Nocek, 2021c:219). Whilst the planetary-level actions of governments, nation states, corporations, social classes, of capital, above all, have led us to the moment of emergency across so many different registers, for Fry and Nocek design is also complicit, echoing many of my arguments in the book. As I outlined in Chapter 1, although we should be mindful and appreciative of the origins of design in the construction of flint tools (Colomina and Wigley, 2016:32), we must also be acutely conscious – as George Nelson's 1960 film *How to Kill People: A Problem of Design* demonstrated – that from such needs comes the desire for and technologies of destruction. Apropos Fry and Nocek, the question emerges of how design can attune to the severity of these entangled crises, in order to potentially redirect these crises, and design itself. Unfortunately, 'currently the action being taken is negligible, insufficiently cognisant of what is occurring, and so completely failing to fully identify and arrest causal processes and related forces of destruction' (Fry and Nocek, 2021c:225).

Mindful of the limitations of a 'solutionist' approach to such complex planetary challenges, as well as the ontological condition of crisis, Fry and Nocek (2021c), amongst others (Escobar, 2018), attempt to outline the potential for prefigurative, redirective design practices that acknowledge the complicity of design in creating the very conditions of crisis. 'Design after design' (Fry and Nocek, 2021c:225) must deal with its own crisis through moving beyond the confines of its histories, embracing its heterodoxies. Acutely aware of the colonialist, patriarchal and militaristic foundations of design Escobar attempts to redefine it; to effectively redesign design in an ontological manner so that through design 'we are creating ways of being' (Escobar, 2018:4; also see Willis, 2006). The potential of design to be an ethical practice of making worlds is clearly distinct from short-term approaches to the immediate crisis of Covid-19 – it is a question of the new directions in which design should set out. Escobar rightly favours the matristic, convivial, relational and horizontal as opposed to the – wonderfully termed – 'techno-alchemies' (Escobar, 2018:17) of a posthuman future founded on the conceit of technology-driven solutions such as the biological futures set out earlier in Chapter 1 (Cf. Bratton, 2021). Echoing my arguments in Chapter 4 on the value of the informal designer, a convivial approach in the manner of Ivan Illich (1975) recognizes the resourcefulness of everyone as opposed to the singularity of the expert. Claiming back a space where everybody is implicated in constructing their life-worlds, Escobar goes on to state that we must abandon 'designer man' so 'humans can again play a more constructive role in the praxis of being alive' (2018:52). In both Illich's reading of conviviality and Escobar's notion of pluriversal design there is humility: an understanding of what is achievable, what is not and who is responsible for the creation of collective worlds. So, whilst designers have a vitally important part to play in the current crisis and beyond there must be a multivalent understanding of *what* is needed, but equally *who* enacts change. With so much potential comes an ethical and existential burden: the challenge to understand, conceptualize and plan how 'design after design' can be part of the pluriversal, producing multiple ways of conceiving worlds. But to understand such potential we must fully comprehend the power design has to undo this, to undo itself and continue with its entrenched cultures of promoting over-consumption, wastefulness, excess, social and environmental crisis. To create social forces that do not provide convivial futures.

Echoing Papanek's infamous claim that 'there are professions more harmful than industrial design, but only a very few of them' (1973:14) there is an arrogance in assuming that designers alone can radically alter the social fabric in order to produce spaces, objects, systems or services that are agile and more responsive to future pandemics, the climate crisis and ultimately a transition towards the sustainable, pluriversal practices described by Escobar and increasingly many others. E.F. Schumacher spoke of such arrogance in relation to technology and the assumption that 'there are no insoluble problems' (1973:130). Everything is seemingly solvable through design. As a reminder of discussions in Chapter 1, Lucy Suchman, in her critique of Bruce Mau's book *Massive Change*, argued we must be careful not to simply return to the mantras of the nineteenth-century conquest of nature, for this might lead to the situation: 'Now that we can do anything what will we do?' (Suchman, 2011:5). The danger is to believe that the prefigurative power of design – its enveloping totality in all that pertains to social, political, cultural and environmental change – can simply be transfigured for solely positive ends, its deviant histories simply ignored or wilfully rewritten. This has been the backbone of *Deviant Design*.

NOTES

Introduction

1 The critique of the expert suggested here and by the authors cited is not intended to feed into the political populism in recent years where the expert has been used as a 'straw man' figure by dominant power groups as a means to bolster their own popularity and political dominance (for a critique of this see O'Neill, 2018). Similarly, writing of post-pandemic politics, Bratton (2021) argues for the need for much greater *competency* by those governing societies.

Chapter 1

1 For the purpose of clarity, I use design thinking here without inverted commas to refer to the practices and methodologies of design more generally. However, later in the chapter I discuss 'design thinking' with inverted commas in reference to the application of designerly intelligence to business practices and other spheres.

2 The pervasiveness of 'design thinking' has rightly been critiqued for its domination of design and resultant diminution of the systematic nature of the design process (Fiell and Fiell, 2019). It has also led to a now ubiquitous and clichéd process of how design takes place via 'Post-it Note' workshop formats (see Manzini, 2015:66). For perhaps the most systemic critique, see Ansari (2016).

Chapter 2

1 To a certain degree the idea of weird juxtapositions between human and nonhumans speaks to Object-Oriented Ontology, notably Ian Bogost's *Alien Phenomenology* (Bogost, 2012).

2 In a telling indicator of this relatively new field of enquiry, there are differing accounts regarding the scale at which social design operates. In contrast to Amstrong et al.'s assertion that it can affect change at a national or international scale, other authors insist that the more appropriate space for social design is community-based, small-scale engagement (see Chen et al., 2016:3; Markussen, 2017:161).

3 I thank Garnet Hertz, Canada Research Chair at Emily Carr University of Art and Design, for identifying these two areas of critical social design.

4   Even in literature that purportedly investigates design and social complexity (Thackara, 2005), the underlying premise is how to *deal* with complexity; that is, how to simplify it. For an alternative reading, see Fry and Nocek (2021c).

Chapter 3

1   Downes and Rock (2011:260) suggest that the work of Becker and labelling theory is simply a way of understanding the complexity of deviancy, rather than a paradigm for examining it in its totality. One of the criticisms levelled at this type of work is that it simply transposed one model of understanding deviance for another: that is, it argued control defines deviance rather than the inverse.

2   Farberman describes how the monolithic automobile manufacturers imposed unfair pricing policies on automobile dealerships leading to a range of illegal practices on the part of the dealers. These included fraudulent service operations, and short-selling.

Chapter 4

1   This project was funded by the UK Economic and Social Research Council, as part of the research grant reference ES/P005047/1 (2016–18). The data used in this chapter was generated collaboratively by the University of Edinburgh and Practical Action. The overall project team consisted of Jamie Cross (Principal Investigator), Craig Martin, Arno Verhoeven, Charlotte Ray, Megan Douglas (University of Edinburgh); Sarah Rosenberg-Jansen, Anna Okello, Elizabeth Njoki, Achille Lebongo, Adolph Yemtim (Practical Action).

2   For a full breakdown of the various examples of repurposed humanitarian goods, see Cross et al. (2019).

3   Marx offers a fuller outline of the relationship between use value and exchange value through considering use value as labour. He makes the point that use value and exchange value are predicated on the alienated relationship between capital and labour, each standing on opposite sides to each other. Each alienated from one another. For the labourer a product they produce does not have direct use value, that is it does not provide 'a direct means of subsistence' (Marx, 1993:266) as it may for a consumer using the same product. If this was the case then the labourer would only produce products directly of use to them and them alone. Rather, as Marx argues, the worker themselves are the use value – they offer the capitalist their potential to produce, this being the worker's 'capacity' (Marx, 1993:267). Labour itself is use value.

4   Given the interdisciplinary approach of this book it is intriguing to survey so many different discourses around the themes of use and function, and to see how many of these distinct sub-disciplines from engineering design studies, philosophy of mind, design history, cultural theory and anthropology could learn so much from one another. It brings to mind a thought: if only those working in 'artifact function' had read Baudrillard; or Baudrillard had read some engineering literature.

5   In Parsons' outline of 'proper function' he alludes to the realist notion of the autonomy of objects out-with of human perception by noting that the third characteristic of proper function is where function is 'belonging to the thing itself'

(2016:87). However, he veers away from any potential autonomy of function with the thing itself by describing this as metaphorical. But also see Preston (2009:220) for discussion of how intention is completely dependent on the actions of users.

6   Illich's influence on anarchist critiques of the professional domination of design and architecture is clearly evident, particularly in the work of Colin Ward (see Ward, 2011:129–34).

7   Some of the key definitions of adhocism in this section have been adapted from earlier material on adhocism including Martin (2014; 2016a).

8   I would like to thank Prof. Lorraine Gamman for her insights into this project and the specific discussion of 'perpetrator techniques', as well as the wider contexts of prisoner creativity (see for example Gamman and Thorpe, 2018).

9   There are, of course, a number of precedents to my outline of 'informal design'. Most famously, Bernard Rudolfsky (1964) identified architectural construction without the need for professional architects, or what he termed 'architecture without architects'; Papanek (1973:70–1) described the place of anonymous design in the context of communities fulfilling their own needs; Brandes et al. (2009) provide a rich theoretical and visual lexicon of non-intentional design; and more recently, Anna Lowenhaupt Tsing's uses the term 'unintentional design' in her book *The Mushroom at the End of the World*. Although just briefly described, she outlines unintentional design as the prerogative of 'many agents, human and not human' (Lowenhaupt Tsing, 2015:152; also see Stender, 2018).

10   Where my focus here is on the practicalities of adhocism, Jencks and Silver do go on to discuss the ways in which ad hoc approaches can be integrated into the design process itself, thus scaling-up the improvised nature of ad hoc design. In a different context the exhibition *Disobedient Objects* at the Victoria and Albert Museum in London (26 July 2014–1 February 2015) included downloadable 'How-to-Guides' for a range of 'disobedient' objects including a 'makeshift tear-gas mask'. The point being that the ad hoc principles of the makeshift are scaled up in the sense that they are capable of being repeated in different contexts. Indeed, the archived website states that since their inception in Istanbul in 2013 'the idea spread and handmade gas masks have appeared on protestors as far away as Caracas, Venezuela' (Victoria and Albert Museum, 2015).

11   Jauregui describes the polysemous nature of *jugaad* in India, and whilst it still refers to resourcefulness and recombination in the way adhocism does, *jugaad* has wider implications beyond physical objects. For example, it is a social practice where resourcefulness is used as a form of wiliness. In this context it is seen as both positive in relation to bending rules to survive, but also negatively in terms of corruption.

12   I thank the Brazilian artist Daniel Lie for this reference.

13   Whilst I suggest there are commonalities of practice among these diverse forms of ad hoc design, the term *jua kali* also denotes the geographical specificity of the Kenyan context. For the term itself means 'very hot sun' in direct reference to the activities taking place in outdoor settings (Kinyanjui, 2011).

14   In the context of humanitarian provision and specifically 'design for disaster', Davis (1978:40) outlines the important relationships between local, ad hoc solutions to the construction of emergency shelters and the role of improvisation (also see Martin et al., 2020).

15   The 'lazy narratives' surrounding indigenous philosophies, epistemologies and technologies becomes more complex when we consider how practices associated with *jugaad* or *jua kali* have become touchstones for new formalized business practices and entrepreneurial innovation. Indeed the co-option and scaling-up of

such local knowledges is evident in the ever-growing literature within the business community (see Radjou et al., 2012).

16 There is also an interesting relationship between adhocism's practice of repurposing material artefacts and the combinatory relations of innovation. Salter and Alexy outline Schumpeter's ideas on the importance of combination to innovation: 'His idea was that most innovations are not novel in themselves; they are novel combinations of elements that already exist' (2014:30). An almost perfect definition of adhocism.

17 Thanks to Hadi Mehrpouya, who first informed me of the Microsoft Kinect story.

Chapter 5

1 Elements of the discussions on the distinct relationship between smuggling and material practices as a form of 'illicit design' have been explored in other settings including Martin (forthcoming).

2 Meyer and Parssinen note that "Many reputable European pharmaceutical companies produced morphine and heroin in massive quantities: Hoffman La Roche, Mercjk, and Bayer" (1998:2).

3 Caulkins et al. (2009:67) also cite an earlier study from Desroches (2005), where 'of 70 high-level, Canadian traffickers [...] 33% of the interviewees had originally been in legitimate importing and exporting businesses before getting involved in the drug trade'.

4 Whilst narcosubs are primarily used in waters off Central America, a recent incident in the Atlantic off the coast of Spain involved a 20-metre narcosub which was intercepted carrying three tonnes of cocaine (Jones, 2019).

5 I use scare quotes for 'potential' as I am fully mindful of the clear harm done to the camels through this smuggling operation. However, the fate of the camels was equally foreboding as they were being imported into Egypt for slaughter.

6 The article notes specialists at this time estimated that camels could 'travel for days or even weeks without showing signs of inconvenience or falling off in condition' (Russell, 1940:302).

7 An inverse example provides evidence of how important 'fit' or lack of fit is. In January 2018, UK Border Force officials searched a private jet at Farnborough airport after arriving from Bogota where they discovered five passengers carrying fifteen suitcases filled with 500 kilos of cocaine (Border Force, 2019). It is claimed that suspicions were raised after the five passengers were said to have paid USD300,000 for flight even though they were identified as construction workers, a hairdresser, an assistant chef and one as unemployed (Clavel, 2018). The assumption being that such individuals did not fit the profiles of regular private aircraft passengers.

8 Whilst the visual realm is one of the most powerful security strategies utilized by border forces olfactory surveillance is also well documented, particularly the use of drug detection dogs (Marks, 2007) and emergent technologies of detection through smell (Bonfanti, 2014). As with visual forms of misdirection used by traffickers, parallel methods of tactically disguising the smell of drugs have been deployed. These include the use of coffee paste in suitcases to hide the smell of drugs (Dean et al., 2015:5); and as outlined previously, in the case of the six pairs of jeans impregnated with liquid cocaine moth balls were employed to similar disguise the smell (McDermott and Power, 2005); whilst in the 1930s rubber sheeting wrapped around containers was used to hide the smell of opium and hashish stored again in suitcases (Russell, 1939:350).

9 There is something ironical about the attempt to fix the perception of disguised illicit drugs. Conceptually the smugglers are utilizing the 'openness' of artefacts in redefining their materiality and thus meaning. But by inserting disguised drugs into legal supply chains such as container flows, they are also employing the fixity of perception.

Chapter 6

1 I thank Gordon Hamme for first telling me of the origins of the 'cabbage' trade in east London.

2 Thanks to Garnet Hertz for originally introducing me to the concept of *shanzhai*.

3 Wallace Sacks, the company responsible for producing this Eames-inspired version of the Lounge Chair with Ottoman, went into administration in February 2017, leaving many orders unfulfilled (Smithers, 2017). Likewise, many other companies trading in replica furniture have also gone into receivership signalling an interesting change in the retail landscape for such goods.

4 Although China constitutes the main manufacturer and distributor of fake products, other 'priority' countries form second- and third-tier producers of counterfeits. Priority group 2 includes Argentina, India, Indonesia, Russia, Turkey and Ukraine; Priority group 3, Brazil, Ecuador, Malaysia, Mexico, the Philippines, Thailand and the United States (European Commission, 2018:6).

5 A noticeable backlash against Burberry's actions emerged soon after media reports of the burning of stock, principally in relation to the environmentally unsound practice of burning the goods rather than recycling them. Burberry subsequently reacted by guaranteeing that in future it will reuse or recycle such items (Kollewe, 2018).

6 For discussion of intellectual property rights in relation to post–Second World War fashion and design, see Pouillard and Kuldova (2017).

7 Hilton et al. (2000:70) provide an intriguing footnote describing an article from British Airway's *High Life* in-flight magazine that outlines the touristic value of shopping for counterfeits products in Dubai's souk.

8 Citing Cooper (2001:85–96), van Kempen outlines a fascinating example of status deception where police in Santiago pulled over drivers for using mobile phones only to discover many were using toy ones. Likewise, other motorists in Chile are said to overheat when driving with their windows closed to signify they can afford air conditioning (van Kempen, 2003:157).

9 In a different geographical setting, James C. Scott (1985) describes class-based traditions of evasion and resistance in Malaysian mountain villages.

10 For discussion of the divergences between Chinese and Western thought and the potential for a reinvigorated relationship, see François Julien's *Vital Nourishment* (2007).

REFERENCES

3rd Istanbul Design Biennale (2016). 'Curatorial Statement: Are We Human? The Design of Species: 2 Seconds, 2 Days, 2 Years, 200 Years, 200,000 Years'. http://tasarimbienali.iksv.org/en/archive/newsarchive/p/1/1230 (last accessed 16/2/2018).

Abraham, I., and van Schendel, W. (2005). 'Introduction: The Making of Illicitness'. In: van Schendel, W. and Abraham, I. (Eds.). *Illicit Flows and Criminal Things: States, Borders, and the Other Side of Globalization*. pp.1–37. Bloomington, IN: Indiana University Press.

Adler, P.A., and Adler, P. (1983). 'Shifts and Oscillations in Deviant Careers: The Case of Upper-Level Drug Dealers and Smugglers'. In: *Social Problems*. Vol.31(2). pp.195–207.

Agence France-Presse (2021). 'Interpol warns Fake Vaccines Seized in China and South Africa Are 'tip of iceberg'. https://www.theguardian.com/world/2021/mar/04/interpol-warns-fake-vaccines-seized-in-china-and-south-africa-are-tip-of-iceberg?CMP=Share_iOSApp_Other (last accessed 4/3/2021).

Agre, P.E. (1997). 'Toward a Critical Technical Practice: Lessons Learned in Trying to Reform AI'. In: Bowker, G.C., Leigh Star, S., Turner, W., and Gasser, L. (Eds.). *Social Science, Technical Systems and Cooperative Work: Beyond the Great Divide*. pp.131–58. New York: Psychology Press.

Aitken, J., and Shackleton, D. (2014). *Co-creation and Co-design: Applied Research Methods in Healthcare Service Design*. London: SAGE.

Akrich, M. (1992). 'The De-Scription of Technical Objects'. In: Bijker, W.E., and Law, J. (Eds.). *Shaping Technology/Building Society: Studies in Sociotechnical Change*. pp.205–24. Cambridge, MA: MIT Press.

Allison, E., and Hattenstone, S. (2018). 'Drug Fears Prompt Ban on Glittery Christmas Cards in Jails'. In:*The Guardian*. 24 December. p.16.

Ameripol (2013). *Situational Analysis of Drug Trafficking – A Police Point of View: Bolivia, Brazil, Colombia, Ecuador Panama and Peru*. Bogotá: Ameripol Executive Secretariat.

Anderson, B. (2018). 'Cultural Geography II: The Force of Representations'. In:*Progress in Human Geography*. Vol.43(6). pp.1120–32.

Andreas, P. (2013). *Smuggler Nation: How Illicit Trade Made America*. Oxford: Oxford University Press.

Ansari, A. (2016). 'Politics & Method: Design Thinking Arrives in Pakistan'. https://aansari86.medium.com/politics-method-cd4cc2c8f5e6 (last accessed 7/5/2019).

Antonelli, P. (2018). 'Vital Design'. In: Myers, W. (Ed.). *Biodesign: Nature, Science, Creativity* [revised and expanded edition]. pp.6–7. London: Thames & Hudson.

Antonelli, P., and Hunt, J. (2015). *Design and Violence*. New York: Museum of Modern Art.

Antonopoulos, G.A., Hobbs, D., and Hornsby, R. (2011). 'A Soundtrack to (Illegal) Entrepreneurship: Pirated CD/DVD Selling in a Greek Provincial City'. In: *British Journal of Criminology*. Vol.51. pp.804–22.

Antonopoulos, G.A., Hall, A., Large, J., and Shen, A. (2017). 'An Introduction to the Special Issue on "Counterfeiting"'. In: *Trends in Organized Crime*. Vol.20. pp.247–51.

Archer, B. (1979). 'Design as a Discipline'. In: *Design Studies*. Vol.1(1). pp.17–20.

Arendt, H. (1998). *The Human Condition*. Chicago: The University of Chicago Press.

Arkhipov, V. (2006). *Home-Made: Contemporary Russian Folk Art*. London: FUEL.

Armstrong, L., Bailey, J., Julier, G., and Kimbell, L. (2014). *Social Design Futures: HEI Research and the AHRC*. Brighton: University of Brighton.

Associated Press (2016). 'US Agents Find Major Mexico Drug Tunnel Covered by Bin in California'. In: *The Guardian*. 21 April. https://www.theguardian.com/world/2016/apr/21/us-agents-find-major-mexico-drug-tunnel-covered-by-bin-in-california (last accessed 21/4/2016).

Associated Press (2018). 'Mother of 5 Held in $1M Drug Smuggling Scheme'. https://nypost.com/2018/04/11/mother-of-5-held-in-1m-drug-smuggling-scheme/ (last accessed 11/4/2018).

Baer, S. (1968). *Dome Cookbook*. Corrale, NM: Lama Foundation.

Barmaki, R. (2016). 'On the Origins of the Concept of "Deviant Subculture" in Criminology: W.I. Thomas and the Chicago School of Sociology'. In: *Deviant Behavior*. Vol.37(7). pp.795–810.

Barnett, J.M. (2005) 'Shopping for Gucci on Canal Street: Reflections on Status Consumption, Intellectual Property and the Incentive Thesis'. In: *Virginia Law Review*. Vol.91(6). pp.1381–423.

Baudrillard, J. (1981). *For a Critique of the Political Economy of the Sign*. Candor, NY: Telos Press.

Baudrillard, J. (1998). *The Consumer Society*. London: SAGE.

Baudrillard, J. (2005) [1968]. *The System of Objects*. London: Verso.

Bauman, Z. (2007). *Consuming Life*. Cambridge: Polity Press.

Bayazit, N. (2004). 'Investigating Design: A Review of Forty Years of Design Research'. In: *Design Issues*. Vol.20. pp.16–29.

BBC (2017). 'Ten Sentenced for Smuggling Drugs into Prisons by Drones'. http://www.bbc.co.uk/news/uk-42341416 (last accessed 2/1/2018).

BBC (2018). 'Spice Found Soaked into HMP Lincoln Letter'. https://www.bbc.co.uk/news/uk-england-lincolnshire-45251143 (last accessed 20/8/2018).

Becker, H.S. (1991)[1963]. *Outsiders: Studies in the Sociology of Deviance*. New York: The Free Press.

Beegan, G., and Atkinson, P. (2008). 'Professionalism, Amateurism and the Boundaries of Design'. In: *Journal of Design History*. Vol.21(4). pp.305–13.

Bekir, I., El Harbi, S., and Grolleau, G. (2011). '(Deceptive) Status Seeking Strategies in France and Tunisia'. In: *Journal of Economic Issues*. Vol.XLV(3). pp.717–32.

Bennett, J. (2004). 'The Force of Things: Steps Toward an Ecology of Matter'. In: *Political Theory*. Vol.32(3). pp.347–72.

Berg, M. (2002). 'From Imitation to Invention: Creating Commodities in Eighteenth-century Britain'. In: *Economic History Review*. Vol.LV(1). pp.1–30.

Betts, A., and Bloom, L. (2014). *Humanitarian Innovation: The State of the Art*. OCHA Policy and Studies Series, November, 009. United Nations Office for the Coordination of Humanitarian Affairs.

Bhattacharyya, G. (2005). *Traffick: The Illicit Movement of People and Things*. London: Pluto Press.

Bianchi, M. (Ed.) (1998). *The Active Consumer: Novelty and Surprise in Consumer Choice*. London: Routledge.

Bjögvinsson, E., Ehn, P., and Hillgren, P-A. (2012). 'Design Things and Design Thinking: Contemporary Participatory Design Challenges'. In: *Design Issues*. Vol.28(3). pp.101–16.

Blackman, S. (2014). 'Subculture Theory: An Historical and Contemporary Understanding of the Concept for Understanding Deviancy'. In: *Deviant Behavior*. Vol.35. pp.496–512.

Bogost, I. (2012). *Alien Phenomenology: Or What It's Like to Be a Thing*. Minneapolis: University of Minnesota Press.

Boguslaw, R. (1965). *The New Utopians: A Study of System Design and Social Change*. Englewood Cliffs, NJ: Prentice-Hall.

Bonfanti, M.E. (2014). 'From Sniffer Dogs to Emerging Sniffer Devices for Airport Security: An Opportunity to Rethink Privacy Implications?'. In: *Science and Engineering Ethics*. Vol.20. pp.791–807.

Border Force (2019). 'Border Force Stop Farnborough Smuggling Attempt'. https://www.gov.uk/government/news/border-force-stop-farnborough-smuggling-attempt (last accessed 1/2/2019).

Bottos, L.C. (2015). 'Assemblages of Sovereignty and Anti-Sovereign Effects on the Irish Border'. In: *Focaal–Journal of Global and Historical Anthropology*. Vol.71(71). pp.86–99.

Bouchard, M., and Amirault, J. (2013). 'Advances in Research on Illicit Networks'. In: *Global Crime*. Vol.14(2–3). pp.119–22.

Braidotti, R. (2013). 'Nomadic Ethics'. In: *Deleuze Studies*. Vol.7(3). pp.342–59.

Braidotti, R., and Pisters, P. (2012). 'Introduction'. In: Braidotti, R., and Pisters, P. (Eds.). *Revisiting Normativity with Deleuze*. pp.1–8. London: Bloomsbury Academic.

Brandes, U., Stich, S., and Wender, M. (2009). *Design by Use: The Everyday Metamorphosis of Things*. Basel: Birkhäuser.

Bratton, B. (2021). *The Revenge of the Real: Politics for a Post-Pandemic World*. London: Verso.

Brown, T. (2008). 'Design Thinking'. In: *Harvard Business Review*. June. pp.84–92.

Brown, T. (2009). *Change by Design*. New York: Harper Business.

Bridges, T.C. (1906). 'The Romance of Modern Smuggling'. In: *Macmillan's Magazine*. 1 November. pp.751–8.

Buch-Hansen, H. (2018). 'The Prerequisites for a Degrowth Paradigm Shift: Insights from Critical Political Economy'. In: *Ecological Economics*. Vol.146. pp.157–63.

Buchanan, R. (1992). 'Wicked Problems in Design Thinking'. In: *Design Issues*. Vol.8. pp.5–21.

Buchanan, R. (1995). 'Rhetoric, Humanism and Design'. In: Buchanan, R., and Margolin, V. (Eds.). *Discovering Design: Explorations in Design Studies*. pp.23–66. Chicago, IL: University of Chicago Press.

Buchanan, R. (2001). 'Design Research and the New Learning'. In: *Design Issues*. Vol.17(4). Pp.3–23.

Burberry (2018). *Annual Report 2017/18*. London: Burberry.

Burns, J.F. (1986). 'Taiwan Curbs Its Counterfeiters'. In: *The New York Times*. 30 March. https://www.nytimes.com/1986/03/30/business/taiwan-curbs-its-counterfeiters.html (last accessed, 14/4/2018).

Byrne, D.S. (1998). *Complexity Theory and the Social Sciences: An Introduction*. London: Routledge.

Cabin, R.J. (2011). *Intelligent Tinkering: Bridging the Gap between Science and Practice*. Washington: Island Press.

Caldwell, T. (2011). 'Ethical Hackers: Putting on the White Hat'. In: *Network Security*. Vol.7(7). pp.10–13.

Campbell, C. (2001). 'The Desire for the New: Its Nature and Social Location as Presented in Theories of Fashion and Modern Consumerism'. In: Miller, D. (Ed.). *Consumption: Critical Concepts in the Social Sciences (Vol. 1: Theory and Issues in the Study of Consumption)*. pp.246–60. London: Routledge.

Campbell, T.D., and Ross, I.S. (1981). 'The Utilitarianism of Adam Smith's Policy Advice'. In: *Journal of the History of Ideas*. Vol.42(1). pp.73–92.

Castells, M. (2010). *The Information Age: Economy, Society and Culture, Vol.III: End of Millennium* [2nd edition with new preface]. Chichester: Wiley-Blackwell.

Caulkins, J.P., Burnett, H., and Leslie, E. (2009). 'How Illegal Drugs Enter an Island Country: Insights from Interviews with Incarcerated Smugglers'. In: *Global Crime*. Vol.10(1-2). pp.66–93.

Chakraborty, M., Chakrabarti, S., and Balas, V.E. (Eds.) (2019). *Proceedings of International Ethical Hacking Conference 2019: eHaCON, Kolkata, India*. Singapore: Springer.

Chen, D.-S., Cheng, L.-L., Hummels, C., and Koskinen, I. (2016). 'Social Design: An Introduction'. In: *International Journal of Design*. Vol.10(1). pp.1–5.

Chesborough, H. (2006). *Open Innovation: The New Imperative for Creating and Profiting from Technology*. Harvard, MA: Harvard Business Review Press.

Chouvy, P-A. (2016). 'The Myth of the Narco-State'. In: *Space and Polity*. Vol.20(1). pp.26–38.

Christensen, C.M., Raynor, M.E., and McDonald, R. (2015). 'What Is Disruptive Innovation?' In: *Harvard Business Review*. December. https://hbr.org/2015/12/what-is-disruptive-innovation (last accessed 20/12/2015).

Churchman, C.W. (1967). 'Guest Editorial: Wicked Problems'. In: *Management Science*. Vol.14(4). pp.B-141-B-142.

Clavel, T. (2018). 'Huge UK Cocaine Seizure on Private Jet Signals Traffickers' Growing Boldness'. https://www.insightcrime.org/news/brief/private-jet-smuggled-cocaine-uk/ (last accessed 7/2/2018).

Claver Fine, P. (2021). *The Design of Race: How Visual Culture Shapes America*. New York: Bloomsbury Academic.

Cohen, E., Cohen, S.A., and Li, X. (2017). 'Subversive Mobilities'. In: *Applied Mobilities*. Vol.2(2). pp.115–33.

Cohen, J., and Kupferschmidt, K. (2021). '"Rich Countries Cornered COVID-19 Vaccine Doses". Four Strategies to Right a "scandalous Inequity"'. https://www.sciencemag.org/news/2021/05/rich-countries-cornered-covid-19-vaccine-doses-four-strategies-right-scandalous (last accessed 27/5/2021).

Cohen, S. (2011). *Folk Devils and Moral Panics: The Creation of the Mods and Rockers*. Abingdon: Routledge.

Collier, S.J., Cross, J., Redfield, P., and Street, A. (2017). 'Little Development Devices/ Humanitarian Goods'. In: *Limn* (9). https://limn.it/issue/09/.

Colomina, B., and Wigley, M. (2016). *Are We Human? Notes on an Archaeology of Design*. Zürich: Lars Müller.

Connolly, W.E. (2011). *A World of Becoming*. Durham: Duke University Press.

Connor, M. (1984). *Sneak It Through: Smuggling Made Easier*. Boulder, CO: Paladin Press.

Conti, G. (2006). 'Hacking and Innovation'. In: *Communications of the ACM*. Vol.49(6). pp.33–6.

Cooper-Hewitt (2013). *Design and Social Impact*. New York: Cooper-Hewitt, National Design Museum.

Corbyn, D., and Vianello, M., for Practical Action. (2018). *Prices, Products and Priorities: Meeting Refugees' Energy Needs in Burkina Faso And Kenya*. London: Chatham House.

Costanza-Chock, S. (2020). *Design Justice: Community-Led Practices to Build the Worlds We Need*. Cambridge, MA: MIT Press.

Criado Perez, C. (2019). 'One-Size-Fits-Men'. In: *Invisible Women: Exposing Data Bias in a World Designed for Men*. pp.157–68. London: Chatto & Windus.

Crilly, N. (2010). 'The Roles That Artefacts Play: Technical, Social and Aesthetic Functions'. In: *Design Studies.* Vol.31. pp.311–44.

Cropley, A.J. (2010). 'The Dark Side of Creativity: What Is It?' In: Cropley, D.H., Cropley, A.J., Kaufman, J.C., and Runco, M.A. (Eds.). *The Dark Side of Creativity.* pp.1–14. Cambridge: Cambridge University Press.

Cropley, D.H. (2010). 'Malevolent Innovation: Opposing the Dark Side of Creativity'. In: Cropley, D.H., Cropley, A.J., Kaufman, J.C., and Runco, M.A. (Eds.). *The Dark Side of Creativity.* pp.339–59. Cambridge: Cambridge University Press.

Cropley, D.H., Cropley, A.J., Kaufman, J.C., and Runco, M.A. (Eds.) (2010). *The Dark Side of Creativity.* Cambridge: Cambridge University Press.

Cross, J., Douglas, M., Grafham, O., Martin, C., Ray, C., and Verhoeven, A. (2019). *Energy and Displacement in Eight Objects: Stories from Sub-Saharan Africa.* London: Chatham House.

Cross, N. (1982). 'Designerly Ways of Knowing'. In: *Design Studies.* Vol.3(4). pp.221–7.

Cross, N. (2001). 'Designerly Ways of Knowing: Design Discipline versus Design Science'. In: *Design Issues.* Vol.17(3). pp.49–55.

Cross, N. (2011). *Design Thinking*: London: Bloomsbury Academic.

Crowley, D., and Pavitt, J. (Eds.) (2008). *Cold War Modern: Design 1945–1970.* London: V&A Publishing.

Davies, W. (2020). 'The Last Global Crisis Didn't Change the World. But This One Could'. In: *The Guardian.* https://www.theguardian.com/commentisfree/2020/mar/24/coronavirus-crisis-change-world-financial-global-capitalism (last accessed 24/3/20).

Davis, I. (1978). *Shelter after Disaster.* Oxford: Oxford Polytechnic Press.

De Barnier, V. (2014). 'Counterfeiting: The Challenges for Governments, Companies and Consumers'. In: Gill, M. (Ed.). *The Handbook of Security* [2nd edition]. pp.340–58. London: Palgrave.

De Cock, C., Rehn A., and Berry, D. (2013). 'For a Critical Creativity: The Radical Imagination of Cornelius Castoriadis'. In: Chan, J., and Thomas, K. (Eds.). *Handbook of Research on Creativity.* pp.150–61. Cheltenham: Edward Elgar.

Dean, G., Fahsing, I., and Gottschalk, P. (2010). 'Entrepreneurialism of Organized Crime'. In: Dean, G., Fahsing, I., and Gottschalk, P. (Eds.). *Organized Crime: Policing Illegal Business Entrepreneurialism.* pp.4–19. Oxford: Oxford University Press.

Decker, S.H. and Townsend Chapman, M. (2008). *Drug Smugglers on Drug Smuggling: Lessons from the Inside.* Philadelphia: Temple University Press.

Deflem, M. and Henry-Turner, K. (2001). 'Smuggling'. In: Luckenbill, D., and Peck, D.L. (Eds.). *Encyclopedia of Criminology and Deviant Behaviour: Volume 2, Crime and Juvenile Delinquency.* pp.473–5. Philadelphia: Brunner-Routledge.

Department of Justice (2019). 'Joaquin "El Chapo" Guzman, Sinaloa Cartel Leader, Convicted of Running a Continuing Criminal Enterprise and Other Drug-Related Charges' [press release] https://www.justice.gov/opa/pr/joaquin-el-chapo-guzman-sinaloa-cartel-leader-convicted-running-continuing-criminal (last accessed 14/2/2019).

Design Against Crime Research Centre & BA Product Design, Central Saint Martins (2019). *Cell Furniture: Designs for Safety, Wellbeing, and Sustainability.* London: Central Saint Martins, University of the Arts London; Design Against Crime Research Centre; Ministry of Justice.

Design Commission (2015). *Designing Democracy: How Designers Are Changing Democratic Spaces and Processes.* London: Policy Connect.

Design Council (2013). *Design for Public Good.* London: Design Council

Design Studio for Social Intervention (2020). *Ideas, Arrangements, Effects: Systems Design and Social Justice.* Brooklyn, NY: Minor Compositions.

Dillon, M. (2000). 'Poststructuralism, Complexity and Poetics'. In: *Theory, Culture & Society*. Vol.17(5). pp.1–26.

Dilnot, C. (2019). 'Foreword'. In: Fisher, T., and Gamman, L. (Eds.). *Tricky Design: The Ethics of Things*. pp.xi–xvi. London: Bloomsbury Academic.

DiSalvo, C. (2012). *Adversarial Design*. Cambridge, MA: MIT Press.

DiSalvo, C. (2016). 'Design and Prefigurative Politics'. In: *The Journal of Design Strategies: (New) Public Goods*. Vol.8(1). Fall. pp.29–35.

Dominguez, J.I. (1975). 'Smuggling'. In: *Foreign Policy*. (20). pp.87–96 and 161–4

Dorst, K. (2003). *Understanding Design*. Amsterdam: BIS.

Dorst, K. (2011). 'The Core of "Design Thinking" and Its Application'. In: *Design Studies*. Vol.32. pp.521–32.

Douglas, M., and Isherwood, B. (1996). *The World of Goods: Towards an Anthropology of Consumption*. London: Routledge.

Downes, D., and Rock, P. (2011). *Understanding Deviance* [6th edition]. Oxford: Oxford University Press.

Drucker, J. (2020). 'Foreword: Assumptions of Ethics and Agency in Design'. In: Scherling, L., and DeRosa, A. (Eds.). *Ethics and Design and Communication: Critical Perspectives*. pp.xiii–xv. London: Bloomsbury.

Drucker, P.F. (1985). 'The Discipline of Innovation'. In: *Harvard Business Review*. May–June. pp.67–72.

Drucker, P.F. (2015). *Innovation and Entrepreneurship*. Abingdon: Routledge.

Dunne, A., and Raby, F. (2001). *Design Noir: The Secret Life of Electronic Objects*. London: August/Birkhäuser.

Durkheim, E. (2014) [1895]. *The Rules of Sociological Method*. New York: Free Press.

Eisenman, R. (2008). 'Malevolent Creativity in Criminals'. In: *Creativity Research Journal*. Vol.20(2). pp.116–19.

Escobar, A. (2018). *Designs for the Pluriverse: Radical Interdependence, Autonomy, and the Making of Worlds*. Durham: Duke University Press.

Escobar, A. (2021). 'Designing as a Futural Praxis for the Healing of the Web of Life'. In: Fry, T., and Nocek, A. (Eds.). *Design in Crisis: New Worlds, Philosophies and Practices*. pp.25–42. Abingdon: Routledge.

European Commission (2018). *Report on the Protection and Enforcement of Intellectual Property in Third Countries*. Brussels: European Commission.

Evans, I. (2015). 'Pet Relocation Smuggler Gets Seven Years in the UK'. In: *Saturday Star*. 20 June. p.4.

Fallan, K. (2015). 'Nordic Noir: Deadly Design from the Peacemongering Periphery'. In: *Design and Culture*. Vol.7(3). pp.377–402.

Farberman, H.A. (1975). 'A Criminogenic Market Structure: The Automobile Industry'. In: *The Sociological Quarterly*. Vol.16(4). pp.438–57.

Featherstone, M. (2007). *Consumer Culture and Postmodernism* [2nd edition]. London: SAGE.

Fernandez, V., Puel, G., and Renaud, C. (2016). 'The Open Innovation Paradigm: From Outsourcing to Open-sourcing in Shenzhen, China'. In: *International Review for Spatial Planning and Sustainable Development*. Vol.4(4). pp.27–41.

Fiell, C., and Fiell, P. (2019). 'We Have Lost Sight of What Design Thinking Actually Is'. https://www.dezeen.com/2019/05/10/design-thinking-opinion-charlotte-fiell-peter-fiell/ (last accessed 11/5/2019).

Fisher, T., and Gamman, L. (Eds.) (2019). *Tricky Design: The Ethics of Things*. London: Bloomsbury Academic.

Fleetwood, J. (2014). *Drug Mules: Women in the International Cocaine Trade*. Basingstoke: Palgrave Macmillan.

Flood, A. (2018). 'Spanish Publisher Subverts Court Gag by Using Don Quixote to Recreate Banned Book'. https://www.theguardian.com/books/2018/mar/21/don-quixote-cervantes-spain-farina (last accessed 21/3/2018).

Flood, C., and Grindon, G. (2014). *Disobedient Objects*. London: Victoria & Albert Museum.

Flowers, S. (2008). 'Harnessing the Hackers: The Emergence and Exploitation of Outlaw Innovation'. In: *Research Policy*. Vol.37(2). pp.177–93.

Flusser, V. (1999). *The Shape of Things: A Philosophy of Design*. London: Reaktion Books

Forsyth, I. (2013). 'Subversive Patterning: The Surficial Qualities of Camouflage'. In: *Environment and Planning A*. Vol.45(5). pp.1037–52.

Forty, A. (1986). *Objects of Desire: Design and Society since 1750*. London: Thames & Hudson.

Freud, S. (2003) [1919]. 'The Uncanny'. In: *The Uncanny*. pp.121–62. London: Penguin.

Freudenberg, W.R., and Alario, M. (2007). 'Weapons of Mass Distraction: Magicianship, Misdirection, and the Dark Side of Legitimation'. In:*Sociological Forum*. Vol.22(2). pp.146–73.

Fry, T. (1999). *A New Design Philosophy: An Introduction to Defuturing*. Sydney: University of New South Wales Press.

Fry, T. (2004). 'The Voice of Sustainment: Design Ethics as Futuring'. In: *Design Philosophy Papers*. Vol.2(2). pp.145–56.

Fry, T. (2005). 'The Scenario of Design'. In: *Design Philosophy Papers*. Vol.3(1). pp.19–27.

Fry, T., and Nocek, A. (2021a). 'Design in Crisis, Introducing a Problematic'. In: Fry, T., and Nocek, A. (Eds.). *Design in Crisis: New Worlds, Philosophies and Practices*. pp.1–15. Abingdon: Routledge.

Fry, T., and Nocek, A. (2021b). 'Part III Introduction: Farewell to the Discipline'. In: Fry, T., and Nocek, A. (Eds.). *Design in Crisis: New Worlds, Philosophies and Practices*. pp.159–62. Abingdon: Routledge.

Fry, T., and Nocek, A. (2021c). 'Afterword: Closing in on the Crisis, Opening out of Design'. In: Fry, T., and Nocek, A. (Eds.). *Design in Crisis: New Worlds, Philosophies and Practices*. pp.218–26. Abingdon: Routledge.

Fuad-Luke, A., Hirscher, A-L., and Moebus, K. (Eds.) (2015). *Agents of Alternatives: Re-designing Our Realities*. Berlin: Agents of Alternatives.

Fuller, R.B. (1972). *Utopia or Oblivion: The Prospects for Humanity*. Harmondsworth: Penguin.

Gamman, L., and Thorpe, A. (2018). 'Makeright—Bags of Connection: Teaching Design Thinking and Making in Prison to Help Build Empathic and Resilient Communities'. In: *She Ji: The Journal of Design, Economics, and Innovation*. Vol.4(1). pp.91–110.

Gamman, L., and Fisher, T. (2019). 'Conclusion: Design's Tricky Future'. In: Fisher, T., and Gamman, L. (Eds.). *Tricky Design: The Ethics of Things*. pp.207–18. London: Bloomsbury Academic.

Garriot, W. (2011). *Policing Methamphetamine: Narcopolitics in Rural America*. New York: New York University Press.

Giles, J. (2010). 'Inside the Race to Hack the Kinect'. https://www.newscientist.com/article/dn19762-inside-the-race-to-hack-the-kinect/ (last accessed 23/11/2016).

Gill, J.R., and Graham, S.M. (2002). 'Ten Years of "Body Packers" in New York City: 50 Deaths'. In: *Journal of Forensic Science*. Vol.47(4). pp.843–6.

Ginsberg, A.D. (2014). 'Design as the Machines Come to Life'. In: Ginsberg, A.D., Calvert, J., Schyfter, P., Elfick, A., and Endy, D. (Eds.). *Synthetic Aesthetics: Investigating Synthetic Biology's Designs on Nature*. pp.41–70. Cambridge, MA: MIT Press.

Ginsberg, A.D., Calvert, J., Schyfter, P., Elfick, A., and Endy, D. (Eds.) (2014). *Synthetic Aesthetics: Investigating Synthetic Biology's Designs on Nature*. Cambridge, MA: MIT Press.

Global Initiative Against Transnational Organized Crime (2020). *Crime and Contagion: The Impact of a Pandemic on Organized Crime*. Geneva: Global Initiative Against Transnational Organized Crime.

Godin, B. (2008). *Innovation: The History of a Category*. Project on the Intellectual History of Innovation, Working Paper No.1.

Godin, B. (2012). '"Innovation Studies": The Invention of a Speciality'. In: *Minerva*. Vol.50(4). pp.397–421.

Godin, B. (2015). *A Conceptual History of an Anonymous Concept*. Project on the Intellectual History of Innovation, Working Paper No.21.

Goffman, E. (1951). 'Symbols of Class Status'. In: *The British Journal of Sociology*. Vol.2(4). pp.294–304.

Gottschalk, P. (2010). 'Entrepreneurship in Organised Crime'. In: *Int. J. Entrepreneurship and Small Business*. Vol. 9(3). pp.295–307.

Goudreau, G. (2019a). 'Record 1.6 Tonnes of Methamphetamine Discovered in Music Speakers by Australian Border Officers'. https://www.illicit-trade.com/2019/06/record-1-6-tonnes-of-methamphetamine-discovered-in-music-speakers-by-australian-border-officers/ (last accessed 8/6/2019).

Goudreau, G. (2019b). 'Australian Police Smash Gang That Smuggled Methamphetamine from US to Queensland in Comic Books'. https://www.illicit-trade.com/2019/06/australian-police-smash-gang-that-smuggled-methamphetamine-from-us-to-queensland-in-comic-books/ (last accessed 14/6/2019).

Granger, P. (2009). *Up West: Voices from the Streets of Post-War London*. London: Corgi

Grattet, R. (2011). 'Societal Reactions to Deviance'. In: *Annual Review of Sociology*. Vol.37. pp.185–204.

Greenfield, A. (2017). *Radical Technologies: The Design of Everyday Life*. London: Verso.

Gregson, N., and Crang, M. (2017). 'Illicit Economies: Customary Illegality, Moral Economies and Circulation'. In: *Transactions of the Institute of British Geographers*. Vol.42. pp.206–19.

Guerrero, C. J. (2020). *Narcosubmarines: Outlaw Innovation and Maritime Interdiction in the War on Drugs*. Singapore: Palgrave Macmillan.

Guilbault, S. (1985). *How New York Stole the Idea of Modern Art: Abstract Expressionism, Freedom and the Cold War*. Chicago: University of Chicago Press.

Gunn W., Otto, T., and Smith, R.C. (Eds.) (2013). *Design Anthropology: Theory and Practice*. London: Bloomsbury.

Gutiérrez, K.D., and Jurow, A.S. (2016). 'Social Design Experiments: Toward Equity by Design'. In: *Journal of the Learning Sciences*. Vol.25. pp.565–98.

Halbert, J. (2019). 'Cabbage, Tradition and Bunce: Marion Donaldson and the Black Economy of the British Rag Trade in the 1970s'. In: *Textile History*. Vol.50(2). pp.187–205.

Hall, T. (2012). 'The Geography of Transnational Organized Crime: Spaces, Networks and Flows'. In: Allum, F., and Gilmour, S. (Eds.). *Routledge Handbook of Transnational Organized Crime*. pp.173–85. Abingdon: Routledge.

Hall, A., and Antonopoulos, G.A. (2016). *Fake Meds Online: The Internet and the Transnational Market in Illicit Pharmaceuticals*. Basingstoke: Palgrave Macmillan.

Hall, T., and Scalia, V. (Eds.) (2019). *A Research Agenda for Global Crime*. Cheltenham: Edward Elgar.

Han, B-C. (2017). *Shanzhai: Deconstruction in Chinese*. [Trans. Philippa Hurd]. Boston, MA: MIT Press.

Hanson, H.C. (1987). 'Gray Market Goods: A Lighter Shade of Black'. In: *Brooklyn Journal of International Law*. Vol.XIII(2). pp.249–65.

Haraway, D., Hardt, M., and Hight, C. (2006). 'Designing Commonspaces: Riffing with Michael Hardt on the Multitude and Collective Intelligence'. In: *Architectural Design*. Vol.76(5). September/October. pp.70–3.

Harley, N., and Hedgecoe, G. (2015). 'Six Britons Arrested after Police Find £240m Cocaine Disguised as Wooden Pallets at Spanish Port'. http://www.telegraph.co.uk/news/uknews/crime/12047146/Cocaine-disguised-as-wooden-pallets-seized-in-Spanish-port.html (last accessed 10/10/2017).

Harvey, S. (2016). *Smuggling: Seven Centuries of Contraband*. London: Reaktion.

Harwood, J. (2008). 'The Wound Man: George Nelson and the "End of Architecture"'. In: *Grey Room*. Vol.31. Spring. pp.90–115.

Hasso Plattner Institute of Design (2010). *An Introduction to Design Thinking: PROCESS GUIDE*. Stanford, CA: Stanford University.

Hebdige, D. (1979). *Subculture: The Meaning of Style*. London: Routledge.

Hennessy, R. (1994/95). 'Queer Visibility in Commodity Culture'. In: *Cultural Critique*. Vol.29(29). Winter. pp.31–76.

Henry, S., and Mars, G. (1978). 'Crime at Work: The Social Construction of Amateur Property Theft'. In: *Sociology*. Vol.12(2). pp.245–63.

Hertz, G. (2016). *Disobedient Electronics: Protest*. No publisher.

Heskett, J. (2016). 'What Is Design?' In: Dilnot, C. (Ed.). *A John Heskett Reader: Design, History, Economics*. pp.19–23. London: Bloomsbury Academic.

Higgins, R.S., and Rubin, P.H. (1986). 'Counterfeit Goods'. In: *Journal of Law & Economics*. Vol.XXIX. October. pp.211–30.

Hilton, B., Choi, C.J., and Millar, C. (2000). 'Quality, Counterfeits and Strategy in the Fashion Industry'. In: *Security Journal*. Vol.13(4). pp.53–70.

Hirsch, F. (1978). *Social Limits to Growth*. London: Routledge.

Holert, T. (2011). *Distributed Agency, Design's Potentiality* [Civic City Cahier 3]. London: Bedford Press.

HotSpringHiker (2013). 'Good Accent Table'. https://www.londondrugs.com/london-drugs-glass-top-coffee-table—120-x-69-x-41cm/L3483807.html (last accessed 15/5/2018).

Hounshell, D.A. (1984). *From the American System to Mass Production, 1800–1932: The Development of Manufacturing Technology in the United States*. Baltimore: Johns Hopkins University Press.

Hudson, R. (2019). 'Economic Geographies of the (Il)legal and the (Il)licit'. In: Hall, T., and Scalia, V. (Eds.). *A Research Agenda for Global Crime*. pp. 11–27. Cheltenham: Edward Elgar Publishing.

Hughes, J. (2012). 'A short history of "intellectual property" in relation to copyright'. In: *Cardozo Law Review*. Vol.33(4). pp.1293–340.

Illich, I. (1975). *Tools for Conviviality*. New York: Fontana/Collins.

Illich, I. (1980). 'Vernacular Values'. In: *Philosophica*. Vol.26(2). pp.47–102.

The Index Project (2020). 'Designers Tackle COVID19'. https://theindexproject.org/stories/designers-tackle-covid19 (last accessed 6/4/2020).

Ingold, T. (2011). *Being Alive: Essays on Movement, Knowledge and Description*. London: Routledge.

Interpol (2020). 'Global Operation Sees a Rise in Fake Medical Products Related to COVID-19'. https://www.interpol.int/en/News-and-Events/News/2020/Global-operation-sees-a-rise-in-fake-medical-products-related-to-COVID-19 (last accessed 21/3/2020).

Jacob, F. (1977). 'Evolution and Tinkering'. In: *Science*. Vol.196(4295). 10 June. pp.1161–6.

Jacobs, J. (1962). *The Death and Life of Great American Cities*. London: Jonathan Cape.

Janzer, C.L., and Weinstein, L.S. (2014). 'Social Design and Neocolonialism'. In: *Design and Culture*. Vol.6(3). pp.327–44.

Jaque, A/ Office for Political Innovation (2018). 'IKEA Disobedients Madrid Manifesto'. https://officeforpoliticalinnovation.com/work/ikea-disobedients/ (last accessed 2/2/2019).

Jauregui, B. (2016). *Provisional Authority: Police, Order, and Security in India*. Chicago: University of Chicago Press.

Jencks, C., and Silver, N. (2013). *Adhocism: The Case for Improvisation* [expanded and updated edition]. Cambridge, MA: MIT Press.

Jones, J.C. (1984). *Essays in Design*. Chichester: John Wiley & Sons.

Jones, S. (2019). 'Cocaine Seized off Spanish Coast "Was Probably Headed for UK"', Agency Says'. In: *The Guardian*. Vol.28. November. p.44.

Julien, F. (2007). *Vital Nourishment: Departing from Happiness*. Cambridge, MA: MIT Press.

Jungknickel, K. (2018). 'Tinkering with Technology: Examining Past Practices and Imagined Futures'. https://acola.org.au/wp/new-technologies-contributing-reports/ (last accessed 1/10/2018).

Kamali Dehghan, S. (2018). 'Nearly Half of US Arms Exports Goes to the Middle East'. https://www.theguardian.com/world/2018/mar/12/nearly-half-of-us-arms-exports-go-to-the-middle-east (last accessed 12/3/2018).

Karras, A.L. (2010). *Smuggling: Contraband and Corruption in World History*. Lanham: Rowman & Littlefield.

Kassam, A. (2020). 'We are naked against this': Tales of despair from Spain's frontline'. In: *The Observer*. 29 March. pp.24–5.

Kaufmann Singer, J. (2010). 'Creativity in Confinement'. In: Cropley, D.H., Cropley, A.J., Kaufman, J.C., and Runco, M.A. (Eds.). *The Dark Side of Creativity*. pp.177–203. Cambridge: Cambridge University Press.

Kenney, M. (2007). 'The Architecture of Drug Trafficking: Network Forms of Organisation in the Colombian Cocaine Trade'. In: *Global Crime*. Vol.8(3). pp.233–59.

Kernfeld, B. (2011). *Pop Song Piracy: Disobedient Music Distribution Since 1929*. Chicago: University of Chicago Press.

Keshavarz, M. (2018). *The Design Politics of the Passport: Materiality, Immobility, and Dissent*. London: Bloomsbury Academic.

Khomani, N. (2018). 'Burberry Destroys £28m of Stock to Guard against Counterfeits'. https://www.theguardian.com/fashion/2018/jul/19/burberry-destroys-28m-stock-guard-against-counterfeits (last accessed 19/7/2018).

Khosla, I. (2017). 'Unconscious Design'. https://www.linkedin.com/pulse/unconscious-design-ishan-khosla/?lipi=urn%3Ali%3Apage%3Ad_flagship3_profile_view_base_post_details%3ByEmHgzhnSi%2BB1T%2BnCu6jiw%3D%3D (accessed 13/5/2018).

Kimbell, L. (2011). 'Rethinking Design Thinking: Part 1'. In: *Design and Culture*. Vol.3(3). pp.285–306.

Kimbell, L. (2012). 'Rethinking Design Thinking: Part 2'. In: *Design and Culture*. Vol.4(2). pp.129–48.

King, K. (1996). *Jua Kali Kenya: Change and Development in an Informal Economy, 1970–1995*. London: James Currey.

Kinross, R. (1988). 'Herbert Read's *Art and Industry*: A History'. In: *Journal of Design History*. Vol.1(1). pp.35–50.

Kinyanjui, M.N. (2011). '*Jua Kali* Strategies for Socio-Economic Change in Nairobi'. In: *Hemispheres* (26). pp.29–46.

Kollewe, J. (2018). 'Burberry to Stop Burning Unsold Items after Green Criticism'. https://www.theguardian.com/business/2018/sep/06/burberry-to-stop-burning-unsold-items-fur-after-green-criticism (last accessed 6/9/2018).

Lacan, J. (1972). 'Seminar on "The Purloined Letter"'. In: *Yale French Studies*. Vol.0(48). pp.39–72.

Lambert, L. (Ed.) (2013). *Cruel Designs* [The Funambulist Pamphlets, Volume 7]. Brooklyn, NY: Punctum Books.

Lanchester, J. (2017). 'Short Cuts'. In: *London Review of Books*. 2 February. pp.22–3.

The Lancaster Care Charter (2019). 'The Lancaster Care Charter'. In: *Design Issues*. Vol.35(1). pp.73–7.

Large, J. (2019). 'The Demand for Counterfeiting on the Criminological Research Agenda'. In Hall, T., and Scalia, V. (Eds.). *A Research Agenda for Global Crime*. pp. 107–21. Cheltenham: Edward Elgar Publishing.

Latour, B. (2005). *Reassembling the Social: An Introduction to Actor-Network-Theory*. Oxford: Oxford University Press.

Latour, B. (2011). 'A Cautious Prometheus? A Few Steps Toward a Philosophy of Design with Special Attention to Peter Sloterdijk'. In: Schinkel, W., and Noordegraff-Eelens, L. (Eds.). *In Media Res: Peter Sloterdijk's Spherological Poetics of Being*. pp.151–64. Amsterdam: University of Amsterdam Press.

Latour, B. (2018). *Down to Earth: Politics in the New Climatic Regime*. London: Polity Press.

Latour, B., and Woolgar, S. (1986). *Laboratory Life: The Construction of Scientific Facts*. Princeton: Princeton University Press.

Law, J. (Ed.) (1991). *Sociology of Monsters: Essays on Power, Technology and Domination*. London: Routledge.

Law, J. (2004). *After Method: Mess in Social Science Research*. London: Routledge.

Law, J., and Urry, J. (2004). 'Enacting the Social'. In: *Economy and Society*. Vol.33(3). pp.390–410.

Lawson, B. (1980). *How Designers Think*. London: Architectural Press.

Lawson, B., and Dorst, K. (2009). *Design Expertise*. Abingdon: Architectural Press.

Ledeneva, A. (2018). 'Introduction: the Informal View of the World – Key Challenges and Main Findings of the Global Informality Project'. In: Ledeneva, A. with Bailey, A., Barron, S., Curro, C., and Teague, E. (Eds.). *The Global Encyclopaedia of Informality: Understanding Social and Cultural Complexity*. pp.1–27. London: UCL Press.

Lerup, L. (1977). *Building the Unfinished: Architecture and Human Action*. Beverly Hills, CA: Sage.

Lévi-Strauss, C. (1966). 'The Science of the Concrete'. In: *The Savage Mind*. pp.1–33. London: George Weidenfeld and Nicholson Ltd.

Li, D. (2014). 'The New *Shanzhai*: Democratizing Innovation in China'. In: *Paris Innovation Review*. http://parisinnovationreview.com/articles-en/the-new-shanzhai-democratizing-innovation-in-china (last accessed 3/5/2017).

Lin, X. (2011). *Fake Stuff, China and the Rise of Counterfeit Goods*. London: Routledge

Lindtner, S. (2015). 'Hacking with Chinese Characteristics: The Promises of the Maker Movement against China's Manufacturing Culture'. In: *Science, Technology, & Human Values*. Vol.40(5). pp.854–79.

Lindtner, S., Greenspan, A., and Li, D. (2015). 'Designed in Shenzhen: *Shanzhai* Manufacturing and Maker Entrepreneurs'. In: *5th Decennial Aarhus Conference on Critical Alternatives*. DOI: http://dx.doi.org/10.7146/aahcc.v1i1.21265 (last accessed 5/1/2019).

Lockwood, T., and Papke, E. (2018). *Innovation by Design: How any Organization can Leverage Design Thinking to Produce Change, Drive New Ideas, and Deliver Meaningful Solutions*. Wayne, NJ: The Career Press.

Loo, S. (2012). 'Design-*ing* Ethics: The Good, the Bad and the Performative'. In: Felton, E., Zelenko, O., and Vaughan, S. (Eds.). *Design and Ethics: Reflections on Practice*. pp.10–19. London: Routledge.

Loudis, J. (2019). 'Border Traffic'. In: *London Review of Books*. Vol.41(3). 7 February. p.8.

Low, A. (2002). 'To Counterfeit in China Is Divine: Or Is It?' In: *Deakin Law Review*. Vol.7(1). pp.21–59.

Lowenhaupt Tsing, A. (2015). *The Mushroom at the End of the World: On the Possibility of Life in Capitalist Ruins*. Princeton: Princeton University Press.

Lupton, E. (2018). 'Towards Design Sociology'. In: *Sociology Compass*. Vol.12(2). pp.1–11

Lury, C. (1996). *Consumer Culture*. Cambridge: Polity Press.

Mackinney-Valentin, M. and Teilmann-Lock, S. (2014). 'Copy Chic: Status Representation and Intellectual Property Rights in Contemporary Luxury Fashion'. In *Luxury*. Vol.1(1). pp.93–112.

Mahadevan, P. (2020). *Cybercrime: Threats During the COVID-19 Pandemic*. Geneva: Global Initiative Against Transnational Organized Crime.

Malpass, M. (2017). *Critical Design in Context: History, Theory and Practices*. London: Bloomsbury Academic.

Manaugh, G. (2016). *A Burglar's Guide to the City*. New York: Farrar, Straus and Giroux.

Manzini, E. (2015). *Design, When Everybody Designs*. Cambridge, MA: MIT Press.

Margolin, V. (1997). 'Getting to Know the User'. In: *Design Studies*. Vol.18. pp227–36.

Margolin, V. (2002). 'The Two Herberts'. In: *The Politics of the Artificial: Essays on Design and Design Studies*. pp.234–43. Chicago: University of Chicago Press.

Marks, A. (2007). 'Drug Detection Dogs and the Growth of Olfactory Surveillance: Beyond the Rule of Law?'. In: *Surveillance & Society*. Vol.4(3). pp.257–71.

Markussen, T. (2017). 'Disentangling "the Social" in Social Design's Engagement with the Public Realm'. In: *CoDesign: International Journal of CoCreation in Design and the Arts*. Vol.13(3). pp.160–74.

Marres, N., Guggenheim, M., and Wilkie, A. (Eds.) (2018). *Inventing the Social*. Manchester: Mattering Press.

Mars, G. (1983). *Cheats at Work: An Anthropology of Workplace Crime*. London: Unwin.

Martin, C. (2009). 'Methodology of Mailmen: On the Delivery of Theory in the Work of Michel Serres'. In: Whiteley, G., and Tormey, J. (Eds.). *Telling Stories: Countering Narrative in Art, Theory, and Film*. pp.65–74. Newcastle: Cambridge Scholars Publishing.

Martin, C. (2014). 'Adhocism: Open Materiality and Localised Solutions'. https://www. theoryculturesociety.org/craig-martin-on-adhocism/.

Martin, C. (2015). 'Smuggling Mobilities: Parasitic Relations and the Aporetic Openness of the Shipping Container'. In: Birtchnell, T., Savitzky, S., and Urry, J. (Eds.). *Cargomobilities. Moving Materials in a Global Age*. pp.65–83. New York: Routledge.

Martin, C. (2016a). 'Everything Can Always be Something Else': Adhocism and J.G. Ballard's *Concrete Island*. In: *Literary Geographies*. Vol.2(1). pp.79–95.

Martin, C. (2016b). *Shipping Container*. New York: Bloomsbury Academic.

Martin, C. (Forthcoming). 'Illicit Design Sensibilities: The Material and Infrastructural Potentialities of Drug Smuggling'. In: Khosravi, S., and Keshavarz, M. (Eds.). *Seeing Like a Smuggler*. London: Pluto Press.

Martin, C., Cross, J., and Verhoeven, A. (2020). 'Shelter as Cladding: Resourcefulness, Improvisation and Refugee-Led Innovation in Goudoubo Camp'. In: Scott-Smith, T., and Breeze, M.E. (Eds.). *Structures of Protection? Rethinking Refugee Shelter*. pp.223–33. Oxford: Berghahn Books.

Martin, J. (2014). 'Lost on the Silk Road: Online Drug Distribution and the "cryptomarket"'. In: *Criminology & Criminal Justice*. Vol.14(3). pp.351–67.

Marx, K. (1993). *Grundrisse*. London: Penguin.

Marx, L. (2010). 'Technology: The Emergence of a Hazardous Concept'. In: *Technology and Culture*. Vol.51(3). pp.561–77.

Mau, B. with Leonard, J. and the Institute Without Boundaries (2004). *Massive Change*. London: Phaidon.

Mavhunga, C. (2017). 'Introduction: What Do Science, Technology, and Innovation Mean from Africa?' In: Mavhunga, C. (Ed.). *What Do Science, Technology, and Innovation Mean from Africa?* pp.1–27. Cambridge, MA: MIT Press.

Mayall, W.H. (1979). *Principles in Design*. London: Design Council.

McCracken, G. (1988). *Culture & Consumption: New Approaches to the Symbolic Character of Consumer Goods and Activities*. Bloomington, IN: Indiana University Press.

McDermott, S.D., and Power, J.D. (2005). 'Drug Smuggling Using Clothing Impregnated with Cocaine'. In: *Journal of Forensic Science*. Vol.50(6). pp.1–3.

McLaren, R.B. (1993). 'The Dark Side of Creativity'. In: *Creativity Research Journal*. Vol.6. pp.137–44.

Merrifield, A. (2017). *The Amateur: The Pleasures of Doing What you Love*. London: Verso.

Meyer, K., and Parssinen, T. (1998). *Webs of Smoke: Smugglers, Warlords, Spies, and the History of the International Drug Trade*. Lanham, MD: Rowman and Littlefield.

Michael, M. (2012). '"What Are We Busy Doing?" Engaging the Idiot'. In: *Science, Technology & Human Values*. Vol.37(5). pp.528–54.

Michael, M. (2016). *Actor-Network Theory: Trials, Trails and Translations*. London: SAGE.

Micklethwaite, P. (2009). 'Malevolent Design'. In: *Kiosk*. Vol.3. pp.14–18.

Milestone, J. (2007). 'Design as Power: Paul Virilio and the Governmentality of Design Expertise'. In: *Culture, Theory and Critique*. Vol.48(2). pp.175–98.

Miller, D. (1987). *Material Culture and Mass Consumption*. Oxford: Blackwell.

Moody, K. (2020). 'How "Just-in-Time" Capitalism Spread COVID-19: Trade Routes, Transmission, and International Solidarity'. https://spectrejournal.com/how-just-in-time-capitalism-spread-covid-19/ (last accessed 16/3/2021).

Morselli, C., and Petit, K. (2007). 'Law-Enforcement Disruption of a Drug Importation Network'. In: *Global Crime*. Vol.8(2). pp.109–30.

Morton, T. (2013). *Hyperobjects: Philosophy and Ecology after the End of the World*. Minneapolis: University of Minnesota Press.

Mould, O. (2018). *Against Creativity*. London: Verso.

Moxon, D. (2011). 'Consumer Culture and the 2011 "Riots"'. In: *Sociological Research Online*. http://www.socresonline.org.uk/16/4/19.html (last accessed 3/4/2012).

Muldoon, P. (2015). 'Rita Duffy: Watchtower II'. In: *One Thousand Things Worth Knowing*. pp.30–1. London: Faber & Faber.

Murphy, K. (2016). 'Design and Anthropology'. In: *Annual Review of Anthropology*. Vol.45. pp.433–49.

Myers, W. (2018). *Biodesign: Nature, Science, Creativity* [revised and expanded edition]. London: Thames & Hudson.

Nango, J. (no date). 'Sámi Self-Sufficiency'. https://worksthatwork.com/4/sami-self-sufficiency (last accessed 3/6/2019).

Natarajan, M. (2000). 'Understanding the Structure of a Drug Trafficking Organization: A Conversational Analysis'. In: *Crime Prevention Studies*. Vol.11. pp.273–98.

Navarette, M.A. (2020). 'From Face Masks to Avocados, the Boundless Creativity of Drug Traffickers'. https://www.insightcrime.org/news/brief/drug-traffickers-creative-ways/ (last accessed 4/4/2020).

Naylor, R.T. (1997). 'Mafias, Myths, and Markets: On the Theory and Practice of Enterprise Crime'. In: *Transnational Organized Crime*. Vol.3(3). pp.1–45.

Nelson, G. (1960). 'How to Kill People: A Problem of Design'. CBS *Camera Three*.

Nelson, G. (1961). 'How to Kill People: A Problem of Design'. In: *Industrial Design*. Vol.8(1). pp.45–53.

Nelson, G. (1965). 'The Designer in the Modern World'. In: *Problems of Design*. pp.75–7 New York: Whitney Library of Design.

Nelson, G. (1973). 'The Human Element in Design'. In: *Industrial Design*. Vol.20(5). pp.49–60.

Nelson, H.G., and Stolterman, E. (2003). *The Design Way: Intentional Change in an Unpredictable World*. Englewood Cliffs, NJ: Educational Technology Publications.

New Museum (2013). 'Adhocracy'. https://www.newmuseum.org/exhibitions/view/adhocracy (last accessed 20/1/2020).

Neuman, W. (2012). 'Cocaine's Flow Is Unchecked in Venezuela'. http://www.nytimes.com/2012/07/27/world/americas/venezuela-is-cocaine-hub-despite-its-claims.html?_r=0 (last accessed 9/3/2017).

Niedderer, K., Clune, S., and Ludden, G. (Eds.) (2018). *Design for Behaviour Change: Theories and Practices of Designing for Change*. London: Routledge.

No Author (1846). 'Smuggling and Smugglers: From the Note-Book of a Traveller'. In: *The Albion: A Journal of News, Politics and Literature*. 19 December. p.603.

No Author (1898). 'Modern Smuggling Methods'.In: *The Washington Post*. 27 February. p.5.

No Author (1924). 'Smuggling as One of the World's Great Industries: Traffic in Slaves, silks, Rum and Drugs Since Colonial America'. In: *The New York Times Book Review*. 18 May. p.7.

No Author (1974). 'A Case of Air Smuggling'. In: *Drug Enforcement*. February-March. pp.17–18.

Nordstrom, C. (2007). *Global Outlaws: Crime, Money and Power in the Contemporary World*. Berkeley: University of California Press.

Nordstrom, C. (2011). 'Extra-Legality in the Middle'. In: *Middle East Reportx*. February–March. pp.17–18.

Nutch, F. (1996). 'Gadgets, Gizmos, and Instruments: Science for the Tinkering'. *Science, Technology, & Human Values*. Vol.21(2). Spring. pp.214–28.

OECD & EUIPO (2017a). 'Trade in Counterfeit and Pirated Goods: Mapping the Economic Impact' [Excerpt]. In: *Trends in Organized Crime*. Vol.20. pp.383–194

OECD & EUIPO (2017b). *Trade in Counterfeit and Pirated Goods: Mapping the Economic Impact*. Paris: OECD Publishing.

Ogino, M. (2007). *Scams and Sweeteners: A Sociology of Fraud*. Melbourne: Trans Pacific Press.

Oliver, J., Savičić, G., and Vasiliev, D. (2011). 'The Critical Engineering Manifesto'. https://criticalengineering.org/ (last accessed 21/1/2018).

O'Niell, O. (2018). 'Linking Trust to Trustworthiness'. In: *International Journal of Philosophical Studies*. Vol.26(2). pp.293–300.

Op den Kamp, C., and Hunter, D. (2019). 'Introduction: Of People, Places, and Parlance. In: Op den Kamp, C., and Hunter, D. (Eds.). *A History of Intellectual Property in 50 Objects*. pp.1–7. Cambridge: Cambridge University Press.

Osterweil, V. (2020). *In Defence of Looting: A Riotous History of Uncivil Action*. New York: Bold Type Books.

Packard, V. (1960). *Status Seekers: An Exploration of Class Behaviour in America*. London: Longmans.

Packard, V. (1961). *The Waste Makers*. London: Longmans.

Papanek, V. (1973). *Design for the Real World: Human Ecology and Social Change*. New York: Bantam Books.

Papanek, V. and Hennessey, J. (1977). *When Things Don't Work*. New York: Pantheon Books.

Parker, M. (2008). 'Heroic Villains: The Badlands of Economy and Organization'. In: Kostera, M. (Ed.). *Organizational Epics and Sagas: Tales of Organizations*. pp.105–17. London: Palgrave.

Parker, M. (2009). 'Pirates, Merchants and Anarchists: Representations of International Business'. In: *Management & Organizational History*. Vol.4(2). pp.167–85.

Parker, M., Cheney, G., Fournier, V., and Land, C. (Eds.) (2014). *The Routledge Companion to Alternative Organization*. London: Routledge.

Parsons, G. (2016). *The Philosophy of Design*. Cambridge: Polity Press.

Parsons, T. (1951). *The Social System*. London: Routledge.

Parsons & Charlesworth (2011). 'Adhocism: We Are Here (Exhibitions)'. https://www.parsonscharlesworth.com/adhocism-we-are-here-art-design-out-of-context/ (last accessed 20/2/2018).

Paster, B.G. (1969). 'Trademarks – Their Early History'. In: *The Trademark Reporter* (59). pp.551–72.

Perrow, C. (1984). *Normal Accidents: Living with High-Risk Technologies*. New York: Basic Books.

Peters, G. (2013). *The Philosophy of Improvisation*. Chicago: University of Chicago Press.

Petroski, H. (2006). *Success through Failure: The Paradox of Design*. Princeton: Princeton Architectural Press.

Poe, E.A. (2012). 'The Purloined Letter'. In: *Murders in the Rue Morgue and Other Tales*. pp. 130–138. London: Penguin Classics.

Polese, A., Russo, A., and Strazzari, F. (2019). 'Introduction: "The Good, the Bad and the Ugly": Transnational Perspectives on the Extralegal Field'. In: Polese, A., Russo, A., and Strazzari, F. (Eds.). *Governance beyond the Law: The Immoral, the Illegal, the Criminal*. pp.1–26. Basingstoke: Palgrave Macmillan.

Potter, N. (2002). *What Is a Designer: Things. Places. Messages*. [4th edition] London: Hyphen Press.

Pouillard, V., and Kuldova, T. (2017). 'Interrogating Intellectual Property Rights in Post-war Fashion and Design'. In: *Journal of Design History*. Vol.30(4). pp.343–55.

Prebula, D.E. (1986). 'Countering International Trade in Counterfeit Goods'. In: *Brooklyn Journal of International Law*. Vol.XII(2). pp.339–67.

Preston, B. (2009). 'Philosophical Theories of Artifact Function'. In: Meijers, A. (Ed.). *Handbook of the Philosophy of Science. Volume 9: Philosophy of Technology and Engineering Sciences*. pp.213–33. Amsterdam: Elsevier BV.

Preston, B. (2013). *A Philosophy of Material Culture: Action, Function and Mind*. New York: Routledge.

Press, C. (2020). 'Coronavirus: The NHS Workers Wearing Bin Bags as Protection'. https://www.bbc.co.uk/news/health-52145140 (last accessed 5/4/2020).

Prigogine, I., and Stengers, I. (1984). *Order out of Chaos: Man's New Dialogue with Nature*. London: Heinemann.

Pye, D. (1969). *The Nature of Design*. London: Studio Vista.

Rabinow, P., and Marcus, G.E. (2008). *Designs for an Anthropology of the Contemporary*. Durham, NC: Duke University Press.

Radjou, N., Prabhu, J., and Ahuja, S. (2012). *Jugaad Innovation: Think Frugal, Be Flexible, Generate Breakthrough Growth*. San Francisco: Jossey-Bass.

Rahmatian, A. (2009). 'Neo-Colonial Aspects of Global Intellectual Property Protection'. In: *The Journal of World Intellectual Property*. Vol.12(1). pp.40–74.

Rakoff, J.S., and Wolff, I.B. (1982). 'Commercial Counterfeiting and the Proposed Trademark Counterfeiting Act'. In: *American Criminal Law Review*. Vol.20. pp.145–225.

Ramirez, B., and Bunker, R.J. (2015). *Narco-Submarines: Specially Fabricated Vessels used for Drug Smuggling Purposes*. U.S. Army Foreign Military Studies Office.

Ramsay, G.D. (1952). 'The Smugglers' Trade: A Neglected Aspect of English Commercial Development'. In: *Transactions of the Royal Historical Society*. Vol.2. January. pp.131–57.

Rastello, L. (2011). *I am the Market: How to Smuggle Cocaine by the Ton, in Five Easy Lessons*. New York: Faber and Faber.

Ratto, M. (2011). 'Critical Making: Conceptual and Material Studies in Technology and Social Life'. In: *The Information Society*. Vol.27(4). pp.252–60.

Raustiala, K., and Sprigman, C. (2006) 'The Piracy Paradox: Innovation and Intellectual Property in Fashion Design'. In: *Virginia Law Review*. Vol.92(8). pp.1687–777.

Raviv, S. (2020). 'Design for Distance: How Will We Design Public Space Post Duct-Tape Markings?' https://www.whatdesigncando.com/stories/design-for-distance/ (last accessed 6/4/2020).

Read, H. (1966). *Art & Industry: The Principles of Industrial Design*. London: Faber and Faber.

Redström, J. (2008). 'RE:Definitions of Use'. In: *Design Studies*. Vol.29. pp.410–23.

Richardson, M. (2016). 'Pre-Hacked: Open Design and the Democratisation of Product Development'. In: *New Media & Society*. Vol.18(4). pp.653–66.

Richardson, W. (2006). 'Limiting Counterfeit Goods and Parallel Imports: An Effective Approach'. In: *The In-House Perspective*. Vol.2(2). pp.5–11.

Ritson, M. (2007). 'Fakes Can Genuinely Aid Luxury Brands'. https://www.campaignlive.co.uk/article/fakes-genuinely-aid-luxury-brands/673098?src_site=marketingmagazine (last accessed 4/10/2017).

Rittel, H. and Webber, M. (1973). 'Dilemmas in a General Theory of Planning'. In: *Policy Sciences*. Vol.4. pp.155–69.

Rojek, C. (2017). 'Counterfeit Commerce: Relations of Production, Distribution and Exchange'. In: *Cultural Sociology*. Vol.11(1). pp.28–43.

Rosenberger, R. (2017). *Callous Objects: Designs against the Homeless*. Minneapolis, MN: University of Minnesota Press.

Rosenberger, R. (2020). 'On Hostile Design: Theoretical and Empirical Prospects'. In: *Urban Studies*. Vol.57(4). pp.883–93.

Rowe, P. (1986). *Design Thinking*. Cambridge, MA: MIT Press.

Rudolfsky, B. (1964). *Architecture without Architects: A Short Introduction to Non-Pedigreed Architecture*. New York: Museum of Modern Art.

Russell, T. (1939). 'The Pseudo Priests and Nuns'. In: *The Police Journal*. Vol.12(3). pp.345–51.

Russell, T. (1940). 'Smuggling in the Interior'. In: *The Police Journal*. Vol.13(3). pp.300–2

Sabawi, F. (2018). 'Border Patrol: More than $1.5 Million in Heroin Found in Tomato Shipment'. https://www.mysanantonio.com/news/local/crime/article/More-than-1-5-million-in-heroin-found-in-tomato-12799993.php#photo-15328409 (last accessed 4/4/2018).

Salter, M. (2012). 'Theory of the/: The Suture and Critical Border Studies'. In: *Geopolitics*. Vol.17(4). pp.734–55.

Salter, A., and Alexy, O. (2014). 'The Nature of Innovation'. In: Dodgson, M., Gann, D.M., and Phillips, N. (Eds.). *The Oxford Handbook of Innovation Management*. pp.27–45. Oxford: Oxford University Press.

Sassatelli, R. (2007). *Consumer Culture: History, Theory, and Politics*. London: SAGE.

Sassen, S. (1998). *Globalization and Its Discontents: Essays on the New Mobility of People and Money*. New York: The New Press.

Scheele, M. (2005). *The Proper Use of Artefacts: A Philosophical Theory of the Social Constitution of Artefact Functions*. Delft: TU Delft.

Schön, D. (2008). *The Reflective Practitioner: How Professionals Think in Action*. New York: Basic Books/HarperCollins.

Schumpeter, J. (2003) [1943]. *Capitalism, Socialism and Democracy*. London: Routledge.

Schwartz, H. (1996). *The Culture of the Copy: Striking Likenesses, Unreasonable Facsimiles*. New York: Zone Books.

Scott, J.C. (1985). *Weapons of the Weak: Everyday Forms of Peasant Resistance*. New Haven, CT: Yale University Press.

Scott, J.C. (1990). *Domination and the Arts of Resistance: Hidden Transcripts*. New Haven, CT: Yale University Press.

Segran, E. (2019). 'Ikea is Sharing People's Best Ikea Hacks, and They're Brilliant'. https://www.fastcompany.com/90395305/ikea-is-sharing-peoples-best-ikea-hacks-and-theyre-brilliant?utm_campaign=eem524%3A524%3As00%3A20190827_fc&utm_medium=Compass&utm_source=newsletter (last accessed 28/8/2019).

Serres, M. (1982). *The Parasite*. Baltimore: Johns Hopkins University Press.

Serres, M. (1983). *Hermes: Literature, Science, Philosophy*. Baltimore: Johns Hopkins University Press.

Serres, M. (1995). *Genesis*. Ann Arbor: University of Michigan Press.

Serres, M. (1997). *The Troubadour of Knowledge*. Ann Arbor: University of Michigan Press.

Shell, H.R. (2012). *Hide and Seek: Camouflage, Photography, and the Media of Reconnaissance*. New York: Zone Books.

Shove, E., and Warde, A. (1998). 'Inconspicuous Consumption: The Sociology of Consumption and the Environment'. Lancaster: Department of Sociology, Lancaster University. http://www.comp.lancs.ac.uk/sociology/papers/Shove-Warde-Inconspicuous-Consumption.pdf.

Shove, E., Watson, M., Hand, M., and Ingram, J. (2007). *The Design of Everyday Life*. Oxford: Berg.

Simon, H. (1996). *The Sciences of the Artificial* [3rd edition]. Cambridge, MA: MIT Press.

Slater, D. (1997). *Consumer Culture and Modernity*. Cambridge: Polity Press.

Smith, R., and McElwee, G. (2013). 'The Embeddedness of Illegal Entrepreneurship in a Closed Ethnic Community'. In: *International Journal of Business and Globalisation*. Vol.11(1). pp.45–62.

Smith, W., Higgins, M., Kokkinidis, G., and Parker, M. (2018). 'Becoming Invisible: The Ethics and Politics of Invisibility'. In: *Culture and Organization*. Vol.24(1). pp.54–73.

Smithers, R. (2016). 'Buy Now as Cut-price Replicas of Classic Designs Face EU Ban'. In: *The Guardian*. Saturday 30 July. p.40.

Smithers, R. (2017). 'Furniture Shop Has Gone Bust without Delivering My Eames-Style Chair'. https://www.theguardian.com/money/2017/may/07/furniture-shop-gone-bust-eames-style-chair-eu-copyright-law (last accessed 7/5/2017).

Simmel, G. (1904). 'Fashion'. In: *International Quarterly*. Vol.10. pp.130–55.

Söderberg, J. (2010). 'Misuser Inventions and the Invention of the Misuser: Hackers, Crackers and Filesharers'. In: *Science as Culture*. Vol.19(2). pp.151–79.

Söderberg, J. (2017). 'Comparing Two Cases of Outlaw Innovation: File Sharing and Legal Highs'. In: Godin, B., and Vinck, D. (Eds.). *Critical Studies of Innovation: Alternative Approaches to Pro-Innovation Bias*. pp.115–36. Cheltenham: Edward Elgar.

SOCA (Serious Organised Crime Agency) (2009/10). *The United Kingdom Threat Assessment Of Organised Crime*. London: Serious Organised Crime Agency.

Starkey, D.J. (2001). 'Piracy and Markets'. In: Pennell, C.R. (Ed.). *Bandits at Sea: A Pirates Reader*. pp.107–24. New York: New York University Press.

Staszowski, E., and Tassinari, V. (Eds.) (2021). *Designing in Dark Times: An Arendtian Lexicon*. London: Bloomsbury.

Stearns, P.N. (2001). 'The Darker Side of Western Consumption'. In: *Consumerism in World History: The Global Transformation of Desire*. pp.61–71. London: Routledge.

Stender, M. (2018). 'Mad-Made Mountains and Other Traces of a Fluctuating Market. An Anthropological View on Unintended Design'. In: *Ardeth*. #02. Spring. pp.77–95.

Stengers, I. (2005). 'The Cosmopolitical Proposal'. In: Latour, B., and Weibel, P. (Eds.). *Making Things Public*. pp.994–1003. Cambridge, MA: MIT Press.

Studio d-o-t-s (2019). 'Design without Designers'. Broken Nature: XXII Triennale Milano 2019. http://www.brokennature.org/design-without-designers/ (last accessed 3/4/2019).

Suchman, L. (2011). 'Anthropological Relocations and the Limits of Design'. In: *Annual Review of Anthropology*. Vol.40. pp.1–18.

Suchman, L. (2012). 'Configuration'. In: Lury, C., and Wakeford, N. (Eds.). *Inventive Methods: The Happening of the Social*. pp.48–60. London: Routledge.

Suchman, L. (2018). 'Design' [Theorizing the Contemporary]. *Cultural Anthropology*. https://culanth.org/fieldsights/1355-design (last accessed 1/2/2019).

Swaminathan, N. (2011). '3-D Scanning on the Cheap'. In: *Archaeology*. Vol.64(6). p.14

Swedberg, R. (2003). 'Introduction'. In: Schumpeter, J. (Ed.). *Capitalism, Socialism and Democracy*. pp.ix–xxi. London: Routledge.

Swigert-Gacheru, M. (2011). 'Globalizing East African Culture: From Junk to *Jua Kali* Art'. In: *Perspectives on Global Development and Technology*. Vol.10. pp.127–42.

Taylor, E. (2016). 'Supermarket Self-Checkouts and Retail Theft: The Curious Case of the SWIPERS'. In: *Criminology & Criminal Justice*. Vol.16(5). pp.552–67.

Temporary Services and Angelo (2003). *Prisoners' Inventions*. Chicago: White Walls

Thackara, J. (2005). *Inside the Bubble: Designing in a Complex World*. Cambridge, MA: MIT Press.

Toffler, A. (1970). *Future Shock*. London: Bodley Head.

Tonkinwise, C. (2011). 'A Taste for Practices: Unrepressing Style in Design Thinking'. In: *Design Studies*. Vol.32. pp.533–45.

Tornier, E. (2017). 'Ture or False: Japonisme and the Historiography of Modern Design'. In: *Journal of Japonisme*. Vol.2(2). pp.117–32.

Troup Buchanan, R. (2015). 'Pigeon Stuffed with Cocaine Caught by Guards as It Tries to Fly into Prison'. https://www.independent.co.uk/news/world/americas/guards-capture-drugs-dove-as-it-delivers-cocaine-to-inmates-in-costa-rican-prison-10456007.html (last accessed 6/1/2016).

Tschumi, B. (1981). *The Manhattan Transcripts*. New York: St. Martin's Press.

Turnbull, D. (1993). 'The Ad Hoc Collective Work of Building Gothic Cathedrals with Templates, String, and Geometry'. In: *Science, Technology & Human Values*. Vol.18(3). pp.315–40.

UNICRI (2011). *Counterfeiting: A Global Spread, a Global Threat*. Turin: UNICRI.

UNODC (United Nations Office on Drugs and Crime) (2016). *World Drug Report 2016*. New York: United Nations Office on Drugs and Crime.

US Customs and Border Protection (2019). 'Federal Authorities, Local Partners Seize 333 Pounds of Cocaine in Shipping Container'. https://www.cbp.gov/newsroom/local-media-release/federal-authorities-local-partners-seize-333-pounds-cocaine-shipping (last accessed 27/6/2019).

USITC (2011). *China: Effects of Intellectual Property Infringement and Indigenous Innovation Policies on the U.S. Economy*. Washington, DC: United States International Trade Commission.

Urry, J. (2003). *Global Complexity*. Cambridge: Polity.

Urry, J. (2004). 'The System of Automobility'. In: *Theory, Culture & Society*. Vol.21(4–5). pp.25–40.

van Abel, B., Evers, L., Klaassen, R., and Troxler, P. (2011). *Open Design Now: Why Design Cannot Remain Exclusive*. Amsterdam: BIS Publishers.

van Kempen, L. (2003). 'Fooling the Eye of the Beholder: Deceptive Status Signalling among the Poor in Developing Countries'. In: *Journal of International Development*. Vol.15. pp.157–77.

Vardouli, T. (2015). 'Making Use: Attitudes to Human-Artifact Engagements'. In: *Design Studies*. Vol.41. pp.137–61.

Veblen, T. (1992) [1899]. *The Theory of the Leisure Class*. New Brunswick: Transaction Publishers.

Venturini, T. (2010). 'Diving in Magma: How to Explore Controversies with Actor-Network-Theory'. In: *Public Understanding of Science*. Vol.19(3). pp.258–73.

Victoria & Albert Museum (2015). 'Disobedient Objects: How-To Guides'. http://www.vam.ac.uk/content/exhibitions/disobedient-objects/how-to-guides/ (last accessed 5/10/2017).

Walker, J.A. (1989). *Design History and the History of Design*. London: Pluto.

Wall, D.S., and Large, J. (2010). 'Jailhouse Frocks: Locating the Public Interest in Policing Counterfeit Luxury Fashion Goods'. In: *British Journal of Criminology*. Vol.50. pp.1094–116.

Walther, G. (2015). 'Printing Insecurity? The Security Implications of 3D-Printing of Weapons'. In: *Science and Engineering Ethics*. Vol.21. pp.1435–45.

Ward, C. (2011). 'The Future of Design Professions'. In: Wilbert, C., and White, D.F. (Eds.). *Autonomy, Solidarity, Possibility: The Colin Ward Reader*. pp.129–32. Edinburgh: AK Press.

Wezeman, P.D., Fleurant, A., Kuimova, A., Tian, N., and Wezeman, S.T. (2018). *Trends in International Arms Transfers, 2017* [SIPRI Fact Sheet]. Solna: SIPRI.

White, D. (2021). 'The Institutional Gap in Critical Design Studies'. In: Fry, T., and Nocek, A. (Eds.). *Design in Crisis: New Worlds, Philosophies and Practices*. pp.199–217. Abingdon: Routledge.

Whiteley, N. (1993). *Design for Society*. London: Reaktion.

Wilbert, C., and White, D.F. (Eds.) (2011). *Autonomy, Solidarity, Possibility: The Colin Ward Reader*. Edinburgh: AK Press.

Williams, L. (2019). 'The Co-Constitutive Nature of Neoliberalism, Design and Racism'. In: *Design and Culture*. Vol.11(3). pp.301–21.

Williams, P. (1998). 'The Nature of Drug-Trafficking Networks'. In: *Current History*. April. pp.154–9.

Willis, A-M. (2004). 'Design Ethics'. In: *Design Philosophy Papers*. Vol.2(2). pp.89–94.

Willis, A-M. (2006). 'Ontological Designing'. In: *Design Philosophy Papers*. Vol.4(2). pp.69–92.

Willis, A-M. (2015). 'Transition Design: The Need to Refuse Discipline and Transcend Instrumentalism'. In: *Design Philosophy Papers*. Vol.13(1). pp.69–74.

Willis, A-M. (2019). 'Introduction: What Is Design Fundamentally, What Is Its Essence?' In: Willis, A-M. (Ed.). *The Design Philosophy Reader*. pp.11–12. London: Bloomsbury Academic.

Wilson, J.M., and Fenoff, R. (2014). 'Distinguishing Counterfeit from Authentic Product Retailers in the Virtual Marketplace'. In: *International Criminal Justice Review*. Vol.24(1). pp.39–58.

Winant, H. (2014). 'The Dark Matter: Race and Racism in the 21st Century'. In: *Critical Sociology*. Vol.41(2). pp. 313–24.

World Design Summit (2017). *The Montréal Design Declaration*. Montréal: World Design Summit Organization Inc.

Yaneva, A., and Heaphy, L. (2012). 'Urban Controversies and the Making of the Social'. In: *Arq*. Vol.16(1). pp.29–36.

Young, J. (2009). 'Moral Panic: Its Origins in Resistance, Ressentiment and the Translation of Fantasy into Reality'. In: *British Journal of Criminology*. Vol.49. pp.4–16.

Zabyelina, Y.G. (2017). 'Can Criminals Create Opportunities for Crime? Malvertising and Illegal Online Medicine Trade'. In: *Global Crime*. Vol.18(1). pp.31–48.

Zelenko, O., and Felton, E. (2012). 'Framing Design and Ethics'. In: Felton, E., Zelenko, O., and Vaughan, S. (Eds.). *Design and Ethics: Reflections on Practice*. pp.3–9. London: Routledge.

Zerubavel, E. (2015). *Hidden in Plain Sight: The Social Structure of Irrelevance*. Oxford: Oxford University Press.

Zuberi, M.M., and Levin, R. (2016). 'Schumpeter's Revenge: The Gale of Creative Destruction'. In: *Banking & Financial Services Policy Report*. Vol.35(5). pp.1–8.

Zukin, S. (2008). 'Consuming Authenticity: From Outposts of Difference to Means of Exclusion'. In: *Cultural Studies*. Vol.22(5). pp.724–48.

INDEX

exchange value 80, 81, 163 n.3
extraneous movement 93

fake products 131, 138–42, 146, 147, 154, 166 n.4
Fallan, K. 47, 50
familiarity 121, 122, 141, 142, 147
Farberman, H. A. 163 n.2
Fariña (Carretero) 122
Felton, E. 8
Fernandez, V. 151
flexibility 109, 152
Fry, T. 5, 7, 8, 158–60
Fuller, R. B. 40, 41
functionality 48, 56, 77–9, 81–2, 152
Future Shock (Toffler) 1

Galliano Island 88
gambiarra 95
Gamman, L. 164 n.8
gas mask 87–8, 90, 92, 94
Global Encyclopaedia of Informality, The 91
Godin, B. 9, 62–5, 70, 149
Goffman, E. 145, 146
Granger, P. 129
grey market 129, 130, 139, 153
'Gucci' bag 134
Guzmán, J. 102, 112

hacking 78, 97–100, 128, 148, 153
Han, B. -C. 152, 153, 155
Hanson, H. C. 139
hashish 115–17, 165 n.8
heroin 102, 115, 118, 123, 165 n.2
Heskett, J. 32, 41, 44, 45, 47, 48
heterodox design
    alternative innovation 9–10
    diffusing design 1–3
    ethics of design 7–9
    malevolency and the deviant 3–7
Hilton, B. 166 n.7
Hooker, R. 123
'How to Kill People: A Problem of Design' (Nelson) 45, 46, 52, 69, 159
Hudson, R. 60
Human Condition, The (Arendt) 37

ideation 27
idiot, the 53, 54, 70
IKEA 100

illegality 6, 11, 60, 70, 104, 106, 110, 132, 149, 153
Illich, I. 85, 160, 164 n.6
illicit design 11–12, 49, 101–5, 115, 126, 165 n.1
    construction of 59
    enmeshing 59–61
    epistemology 128
    ingenuity 110–11, 115, 118, 119
    innovation 54, 61–70, 74, 128–32
    and licit 106
    trafficking 115, 117, 139
illicit designerly intelligence 119–26
implementation 27
improvisation 84, 86, 90, 95–9, 103
India 94
informal design 2, 4, 11, 53, 76–8, 86–99, 103, 110, 152, 164 n.9
ingenuity 4, 6, 7, 9, 12, 66, 67, 69, 76, 77, 86, 89, 91, 99, 101, 103–5, 108, 110, 112, 115–19, 122, 123, 127, 128, 131, 150
innovation 9–10
    change and 62–3
    commercial 62
    Drucker and 62
    entrepreneurial 67
    Godin and 62–5
    hacking 98–100
    illicit 54, 61–70, 74, 128–32
    imitation as 147–53
    and ingenuity 110
    outlaw 63
    social 1, 4, 42
    technological 62, 63, 114, 128, 138, 149, 152
innovator 64, 65
inspiration 26
intellectual property 12, 128, 130, 132, 135, 136, 139, 148, 150–3
intentional function 82–6
interdisciplinary approach 27, 163 n.4
intoxication 66, 71

Jacob, F. 98
Jacobs, J. 91
Janzer, C. L. 43
Jauregui, B. 164 n.11
Jencks, C. 1, 11, 22, 77, 90–2, 94, 96, 98, 164 n.10
Jones, J. C. 28

use value 77, 80, 81, 84, 163 n.3
US-Mexico border 102–3, 112, 118

Van Kempen, L. 146, 166 n.8
van Schendel, W. 59, 67
Veblen, T. 142–3, 145–7

Wallace Sacks 136, 166 n.3
'war on drugs' 102, 105, 108, 110
Webber, M. 19–21, 49, 91
Weinstein, L. S. 43

Whiteley, N. 40
wicked problems 5, 19–22, 39, 49, 50, 65, 91
Williams, P. 109–10
Willis, A. -M. 3, 16
Wolff, I. B. 136
Woolgar, S. 82
World Design Summit 40, 41, 45
World Drug Report 2016 126

Zelenko, O. 8
Zerubavel, E. 125